THE RELIGIOUS EXPERIENCE
OF THE PRIMITIVE CHURCH

THE
RELIGIOUS EXPERIENCE
OF THE
PRIMITIVE CHURCH

The Period prior to the Influence of Paul

BY

P. G. S. HOPWOOD
B.D.(Lond.), B.Litt.(Oxon.), Ph.D.(Glas.)

109108

NEW YORK
CHARLES SCRIBNER'S SONS
1937

FOREWORD

BY

Professor G. H. C. MACGREGOR, D.Litt., D.D.
University of Glasgow

A T the present time the most vital books being written
on the New Testament are those which seek to
penetrate into the " twilight period " before the earliest
Christian traditions had taken literary form. Thus
even the most recent German criticism of the Gospels,
seemingly destructive though it be, has this at least to
its credit, that it has awakened fresh interest in the life
and experience of the primitive Christian community,
by placing the earliest Gospel traditions in their true
setting in the life of that community, and by demonstrat-
ing that the beginnings of Christian literature have taken
their form in accordance with the religious needs of
a missionary Church. Similarly in our own country,
scholars have been seeking to trace back the beginnings
of Christian doctrine to the " preaching " which had its
birth in the experience of the pre-Pauline Church.

The present volume is to be welcomed as another
venture upon this same quest. Dr. Hopwood deals with
the religious experience of the " primitive " Church,
which he defines as " the Church prior to the influence
of Paul," during " the twilight years when no historical
records were forthcoming, when there was little or nothing
in the way of organization, and when the participants
in what was taking place had not perceived as yet the

force of what was being enacted." This attempt to reconstruct the evolution of Christian doctrine along the approach of the religious experience of the pre-Pauline Church has not, so far as I am aware, been attempted previously on so large a scale ; and in a field where direct evidence is necessarily scanty or unsatisfactory, and much depends on intelligent inference, it will be agreed that in general the author displays notable acuteness and sane judgment.

Dr. Hopwood rightly claims that this is the only sound way of approach to the study of Christian origins. The purely literary and the purely historical approach are both alike inadequate, for " it is the religious experience which inspired the history and the literature with which we are concerned," and " it is in religious experience alone that the ultimate data are to be found for the appraisal of Church origins." He not unfairly protests concerning certain recent historical studies, which have employed an abstract and analytical method of approach, that " no one would suspect from these thorough researches that there had been any vital phenomenon such as religious experience in the formation of the Church." By such methods " the Christian religion is emptied of the very distinctiveness which caused its actual emergence, namely, the power of religious experience inspired by the creative contacts made with the personality of Jesus."

The most important of Dr. Hopwood's conclusions would seem to be these :

Firstly, the emergence of the Christian Church is not a process which can be separated, as is so often done, from the first believers' experience of the historical Jesus. " The disciples carried forward into the Church the religious experience created by Jesus in his personal contacts with them."

Secondly, the Christian Church was neither in its beginnings a mere " minor Jewish movement," nor in its fuller development did it become a conglomeration of Hellenistic influences at work on a bare minimum supplied by Jesus. " The cardinal elements of the Christian experience were either already to the forefront in the primitive Church, or were implied in the logic of its experienced Gospel."

Thirdly, there is thus no such gap as is sometimes supposed between Jesus and Paul. What has sometimes been thought to be Pauline innovation is seen in fact to have its roots in the experience of the community which preceded him. The " new " attitude to Jesus, whereby he was transformed from Teacher into Lord, was creatively operative among the very first believers. " Thus out of its Christ consciousness the primitive Church transferred to the Church of the ages the essential groundwork of the evangelic tradition."

The reader will find specially helpful Dr. Hopwood's treatment of the evolution of the speeches in the Fourth Gospel, the transmutation of Apocalyptic into its spiritual equivalent, the growth of the doctrine of salvation and of the redemptive efficacy of Christ's death. A striking feature of the book is its frequent reference to recent developments in psychology, and interesting personal illustrations are given of vision and other abnormal psychical experiences. In criticism the author is well-informed and cautious, and in interpretation he is often original without being extravagant. Though his conclusions can hardly be expected always to command universal assent, they are almost always worth serious consideration, and his book may be sincerely commended to all students of early Christianity.

PREFACE

WE hear much to-day about the need for the Christian Church to go back to its earliest years, and recover, if possible, some of the spiritual vitality which animated the first believers. The effort has been made in the present volume to reach behind the gospel tradition to the experiential roots of the Christian Church and to the personal impact made by Jesus upon those who experienced at first-hand His creative influence, and who were thus led to bring into being the primitive Church.

Indebtedness to many writers is indicated here and there in the footnotes, but in most instances the references are simply confirmatory of points of view advanced in the investigation. In the last resort, however, the pages of the Bible, together with the Apocrypha and the Pseudepigrapha, furnish the most authoritative material for any attempt to understand the religious experience which gave rise to the Church.

The author's grateful thanks are accorded to the Rev. Professor G. H. C. Macgregor, D.Litt., D.D., for much kindly encouragement and counsel, to the Rev. A. T. Cadoux, B.A., D.D., for helpful comment so readily given in discussing problems as these emerged, to Miss A. E. F. Allardice, M.A., whose friendship proved a valuable incentive, and to the Rev. F. Kenworthy, M.A., B.D., for careful assistance in reading the proofs and in compiling the indexes.

P. G. S. HOPWOOD.

ACCRINGTON, *October* 1936

CONTENTS

PART ONE

PRELIMINARY INVESTIGATIONS

PART TWO

THE EXPERIENCE OF THE EYE-WITNESSES

CONTENTS

b

PART THREE

THE EMERGENCE OF THE CHURCH

APPENDICES

INDEXES

ABBREVIATIONS

THE following symbols are used to designate certain authorities quoted in the text :

A. and P.	*Apocrypha and Pseudepigrapha of the Old Testament*, ed. R. H. Charles.
BC. FJ. and L.	*The Beginnings of Christianity*, ed. F. J. Foakes Jackson and Kirsopp Lake.
Cam.B.	Cambridge Bible.
CB.	Century Bible.
ed.	edited by.
edn.	edition.
EL.	Everyman Library.
Enc. Bi.	*Encyclopædia Biblica*, ed. T. K. Cheyne.
Eng. Tr.	English Translation.
ERE.	*Encyclopædia of Religion and Ethics*, ed. J. Hastings.
Expos. Ti.	*Expository Times.*
H-CZNT.	*Hand-Commentar zum Neuen Testament.*
HDB.	Hastings' *Dictionary of the Bible*, 5 vols.
Harv. Theol. Rev.	*Harvard Theological Review.*
HZNT.	*Handbuch zum Neuen Testament.*
ICC.	*International Critical Commentary.*
JR.	*Journal of Religion.*
PC.	*Peake's Commentary*
TS. und K.	*Theologische Studien und Kritiken.*
WC.	*Westminster Commentaries.*
WNT.	*Westminster New Testament.*
Z. für K.	*Zeitschrift für Kirchengeschichte.*
ZNW.	*Zeitschrift Neutestamentliche Wissenschaft.*

PART ONE

PRELIMINARY INVESTIGATIONS

CHAPTER I

THE PROBLEM

THE formative years of a man's life are those of his earliest childhood, the most impressionable and plastic stage of human development. The growing personality receives a continual stream of impressions and experiences, the import of which the young child is unable to perceive at the time. Yet it is in this twilight period that the tone and direction of the character are being integrally set. When the child grows into manhood and looks back on the incidents and impressions he may be able to recollect, he discerns the significance of much that took place within him during his earliest years. A man indeed grows up in the dark, and the characteristics which make him the man he comes to be are being influenced at the very time when their force is not apprehended. While the character may be afterwards modified, its essential determinants are laid down in the earliest years.

How true is this of the Christian Church! It came into being in the dark and grew up in the dark. The period between the ministry of Jesus and the emergence of the Church as a going concern in Palestine and Syria is one of almost complete obscurity. The childhood of the Church was momentous, for the formative determinants were shaping the essential character of the Church for all time. Through the later modifications due to developments of thought and organization, the specific shape and character of the Church has been essentially preserved. As a man grows up in the dark,

3

when the life processes are defining his personality unknown to himself, so the Church grew up in the dark, its character was laid down, its direction determined, and the first believers were unable to perceive the force and significance of what was unfolding in their midst.

Our problem is to investigate the nature and character of the infancy of the Church, the period when it emerged and in which it began to grow up. We are to study the years prior to the influence of Paul, for when he came upon the scene in any direct way the Church had already come into being and was extending its borders beyond Palestine. The period we have in mind is prior to the apostle's activity as a formative influence in the growth of the Church. Later developments cannot be understood unless some attempt is made to appraise the rise and character of the Church from the very first. While this principle is duly recognized in theory, in actual practice there has been a general neglect of the earliest years which are regarded as negligible inasmuch as they have left so scanty an impression on the records. The period has usually been taken as the anteroom leading to the stately halls beyond. The achievements of Paul were so remarkable that it is little wonder that what took place prior to him is slurred over with a view to enhancing his influence, or regarded as no more than a short prelude to the great symphony that followed.

It is historically more correct to view the earliest years as revealing the new " something " without which there would have been no material for Paul to use. The fact that they have left such scanty impression is no evidence that they are in themselves of scanty importance. If the Church was born and grew up in the dark, the darkness should not be allowed to obscure the fact that something was born and was growing up in the dark, and that the essential religious determinants of the Church's character were creatively operative by the time Paul was exercising his influence on Church developments.

It is not easy, however, to discover a term which adequately describes the period we have in mind. To designate it as " pre-Pauline " is to assume that Paul is the architect of the ecclesiastical structure, that what came before him is " pre-Pauline " just as what followed him is " post-Pauline." The great apostle's influence was so vitally creative that the period subsequent to him may fittingly be referred to as " post-Pauline," and this not merely by way of chronological sequence, but as indicative of his epoch-making activity. But to speak of the earliest period as " pre-Pauline " implies his influence in a retrospective manner, and may minimize unjustifiably what took place in the earlier years. It is sometimes said that the original disciples did not appraise the real drift of Jesus' teaching, nor perceive the significance of His personality. While they accepted Him as Messiah, in other essentials they were typical Jews. But for Paul, the new faith would have dwindled down into a tiny Jewish sect. Paul is thus said to be the creator of the Church. It is therefore better to avoid prejudging the issues involved, and this means that we cannot speak of the earliest period of the Church as " pre-Pauline."

Again, titles such as " Church Origins " or " Church Beginnings " are inadequate, since they provide no incentive for keeping the earliest years clear in idea. The designation " Christian Beginnings " is still less satisfactory, inasmuch as the term " Christian " was not applied to believers nor to the Church until many years of expansion had taken place, and even then it was not applied to the members of the Judæo-Christian community.

The word " Primitive " should be strictly used of the period, and all through our discussion we shall speak of the Primitive Church as the Church prior to the influence of Paul. Unfortunately, even this term has been rendered ambiguous in meaning by the looser reference which includes the second and third, as well as the whole of the first centuries within the purview of what is considered the Primitive Church.[1] The result is that the study of the initial period very quickly shades off into the Church of Paul, and into the subapostolic and the ante-Nicene developments. It would be better to reserve the designation " Ancient Church " or " Ancient Catholic Church," for this wider reference. This would confine the term " Primitive " to the twilight years when no historical records were forthcoming, when there was little or nothing in the way of organization, and when even the participants in what was taking place had not perceived as yet the force of what was being enacted. Throughout our discussion we shall refer to the Church of the earliest years as " The Primitive Church."

What is the ultimate basis on which the Christian Church rests ? What are the basic facts, the final data, upon which its life and witness are founded ? We may approach our answer from the standpoint of dogmatic theology and look for the ultimate data in the great creeds of antiquity, the considered statements of what Church belief embodied. Or there are the statements of Holy Scripture which afford ultimate facts when

---

[1] Examples of this ambiguity are to be seen in B. H. Streeter's *The Primitive Church*, 1929, and A. B. Macdonald's *Christian Worship in the Primitive Church*, 1934.

expounded by competent scholarship, giving us a system of faith and practice expressed in the Church. The drawback to such an approach is that the ultimate data of the dogmatic method are anything but ultimate, whether based on creed or Scripture or on both. How were the data arrived at ? What in the first place gave rise to belief in Jesus Christ, and why should these data have expressed themselves in the birth of the Church at all ? The dogmatic approach to Church origins has to be rejected in the interests of scientific examination of the dynamic facts as these are seen in the experience of the human spirit.

Similar considerations apply to the purely ecclesiastical approach to Church origins. This takes its start from some form of Church theory or another, Catholic, Episcopal, Lutheran, Presbyterian, etc., and tends to read Church origins in terms of such theory. The view of the Church coming down out of heaven all complete with orders, sacraments, appointments, and paraphernalia, restricts at the outset any possibility of studying the rise of the Church from its human, experiential origins. The real difficulty is to forget the Church as we know it to-day with its various ecclesiastical forms, or at least to approach Church origins with an entire absence of partiality to any particular Church theory or expression of the Church as we know it in our time.

More recently, the interest in Church origins has been chiefly historical. The literature presenting the history to be investigated has been intensively and critically analysed, the result being that invaluable data have been afforded for the study of Church beginnings. Even so, we are only the more confronted with what made the literature inevitable and produced the history embodied in it.

It is the religious experience which inspired the history and the literature with which we are concerned. Our investigation seeks to approach the study of the Primitive Church by observing the religious phenomena which gave birth to the Church. It is on religious experience alone that the ultimate data are to be found for the appraisal of Church origins. There was the religious environment in which Jesus and the Primitive Church believers were nurtured. There was the experience which those had who came into personal, religious contact with Jesus. What are the experiential data which made the eye-witnesses conclude that Jesus was risen from the dead ? What took place when these people began to relate to others what they had seen and heard ? What experiential processes set up the religious ferment in the childhood of the Church ? We have to observe what William James describes as " the feelings, acts, and experiences of individual men," [1] when these are creatively influenced by Jesus the Christ, and by the growing power of the new community which had emerged round His name. The new group itself becomes a momentous fact of religious experience ; we have a " group " experience at least as significant for our purpose as the data of individual experience.

The facts to be discerned in our investigation are both historical and experiential in character. We have to observe the historical impressions which Jesus produced on His contemporaries, and further, the historical operation of the experiential forces and processes as these influenced the emergence of a new religious community, together with the actual course of events which led the Church from step to step until Paul's creative activity came to bear upon its development. But the record of this period is scanty ; as for the one document

---

[1] *The Varieties of Religious Experience*, 1920, p. 31.

which purports to set forth the " Acts of the Apostles,"
the greater part of this, curiously enough, is assigned
to the activity of Paul, about whom we know so much
already from his own epistles. We possess hardly
any personal notices or letters of the original apostles
which come from the initial period of the Church's life.
The First Epistle of Peter, even if written by the
apostle, is a document which reflects the later period
of the apostolic age. But this state of affairs is what
we expect with the Church in its infancy, growing up in
the dark, with little clear understanding of what was
taking place, with no incentive to co-ordinate in a history
the events that unfolded with bewildering rapidity as
the new experience carried onward its recipients. They
were too near the origins of the Church to be at all clear
about it,[1] and what traditions they had naturally
gathered around Jesus as He had lived and taught.
And when records began to be set down in writing, it
was the life and activities of Jesus with which these
had to do.

The experiential or psychological facts, the religious
experience concerned, are bound up with the religious
inheritance and environment into which Jesus and His
disciples came. We have to study this background
influence to appraise its place in the formation of the
religious experience from which emerged the Church.
The experienced facts were received within a mental
framework characteristic of the recipients, who interpreted the facts accordingly. Edwyn Bevan finds it
impossible to distinguish between the experiential
content and the mental categories that contain it.[2]

[1] It is said that we are still too near the Great War for any
trustworthy history of it to be forthcoming. Apparently we have to
wait fifty years before this will be possible.

[2] *Sibyls and Seers*, 1928, p. 64.

While it is true that when we analyse religious experience, our explanations and analysis themselves belong to experience, and that in this way both the facts and their interpretation become blended into an empirical unit, yet the attempt must be made during our investigation, since it is not unknown for Church historians to mistake the interpretation for the actual facts of the experience interpreted. At Pentecost the believers received an experience which had abnormal psychological accompaniments (Acts ii. 1–3). They found themselves speaking with " other tongues " (ver. 4). The abnormal facts were interpreted by reference to the Holy Spirit. Luke misinterprets the speech by supposing that it is a case of speaking in foreign languages. Some effort must therefore be made to distinguish what is experienced and the explanation of what is being experienced. Thus we shall be able to sort out fact and its explanation, fact and its interpretation, within the circle of the experience concerned. This enables us to check to some extent the reference back of later interpretations into more primitive facts, and to detect erroneous deductions made by the compilers of the New Testament documents, or by the tradition of which they make use.

CHAPTER II

THE LITERARY SOURCES

THE New Testament is a collection of documents the writing of which was inspired by religious experience. As the process of compiling the evangelic tradition went on, the new Christian experience was shaping its character, while many traces of a more developed standpoint are to be discerned. "Incidents were described from the point of view of actual conditions; sayings were adapted so as to bear more immediately on present difficulties and needs; later reflection on the gospel story was thrown back on the historical picture." [1] Inner meanings were more and more discovered in what Jesus said and did, and such later discoveries were attached to the gospel nucleus.

The Synoptic Gospels in their present form are much later than the events they chronicle. Literary criticism has firmly established the fact that Mark is the basis of Matthew and Luke, who also made use of a corpus of sayings usually designated by the symbol Q. The attempt to reconstruct Q from Matthew and Luke is a delicate and hazardous task, but it seems to have been a collection of some sayings of Jesus, the product of reminiscence and thoughtful recollection on the part of those who had heard Jesus speaking. Arising from the necessities of the case a process began of gathering together the words of Jesus as these came back to the memory, and such a collection came to be used by the authors of the First and Third Gospel.

[1] E. F. Scott, *The Beginnings of the Church*, 1914, p. 8.

The searching analysis of J. Weiss,[1] and the more recent explorations of the *Formgeschichte* school, have not materially affected the probability that in Mark's Gospel we have a copy of the original autograph, based on notes of Peter's preaching.[2] This Gospel, with its naïve style, the non-literary character of the language, its series of anecdotes, its lack of systematic teaching, its " electric " atmosphere, and its freedom from the influence of later interpretations, is cast in a primitive mould. But Mark gives a prominence to the Cross and to the events leading up to it which has inspired the theory that Paul has brought his thought to bear upon the Gospel tradition on this point.[3] Yet even so we are forced back upon the ultimate question as to where Paul received his doctrine of the Cross, and the answer lies finally in the personal contact of the eye-witnesses with Jesus. They did not know what to make of the forthcoming death of Jesus ; their failure to understand Him made them at latent cross-purposes with their Master. They could not bring together the ideas of Messiahship and suffering in the Jesus whom they had designated as Messiah. The very intensity of the latent opposition, however, could not fail to impress the eye-witnesses with what was taking place as Jesus went deliberately to His death. The deeper the impression, the more profound the misunderstanding. We are therefore justified, on grounds of empirical probability, in accounting for the Marcan emphasis on the Cross less by the retrospective influence of Paul upon the original data of the gospel tradition, and more by the likelihood that Mark preserves important elements which Paul

---

[1] *Das älteste Evangelium*, 1903. For a recent attempt to resolve Mark into its sources, cf. A. T. Cadoux, *Sources of the Second Gospel*, 1935.

[2] Cf. Eus. *H.E.* iii. 39.

[3] B. W. Bacon, *The Beginnings of Gospel Story*, 1909, pp. xxvii. f.

also received from the same source, namely, the impressions and experiences of those who saw and heard. Paul may have interpreted the facts more freely in the light of his own experience, but they were already there within the orbit of the primitive Church itself.

The two-document hypothesis being firmly established, these sources were examined in detail. Earlier revisions and combinations had been traced within the Gospels, but the newer efforts have been directed towards distinguishing and characterizing the elements that made up the narratives according to their " form " or " pre-literary " type, and *Formgeschichte* has become " the history of certain pre-literary forms not consciously created by individuals but developed by the force of constant oral repetition."[1] Such types are the moral or religious illustration, tale, legend, myth, apothegm, sententious saying, comparison, parable, the connecting links between these elements in the gospel story being regarded as artificial.[2] The interest of such analysis for our investigation lies in the attempts made to account for the origin and character of these several types. By tracing back their history we may find ourselves within the activity of the primitive Church experience, or at least light would be shed on the religious ferment which gave rise to these types or units of tradition. There is, however, much to be done before such a possibility comes within our purview ; the determination of the " form " is too much a matter of subjective judgment, as is also the standard whereby to test the historical validity of the " form " concerned.[3]   H. J. Cadbury

[1] B. S. Easton, *The Gospel before the Gospels*, 1928, p. 31.
[2] K. L. Schmidt, *Der Rahmen der Geschichte Jesu*, 1919, illustrates this standpoint.
[3] M. Dibelius, *Die Formgeschichte des Evangeliums*, 1919, and R. Bultmann, *Die Geschichte der synoptischen Tradition*, 1931, are the best authorities for this method of approach.

illustrates the danger of overstating the possible results of this method when he says, " as surely as the excavator's spade yields to the trained archæologist reliable information on extinct civilizations, so does the analysis of the written record disclose the forces at work in its transmission."[1]   Alas! would that we had a reconstruction of primitive Church conditions such as Flinders Petrie has given of ancient Egyptian civilization!

Matthew's Gospel reflects later explanation and interpretation at work on the new experience.   Jesus is commended to the Jewish religious consciousness ; His genealogy is traced to the Davidic dynasty (i. 1–17), and His birth takes place according to prophecy (i. 22–25).   The self-consciousness of the Church is revealed as being at a fairly mature stage (xvi. 16–19, xviii. 17 f.), and the later awareness of the universal mission of the Church is traced back to a command of Jesus (xxviii. 19). The threefold reference to the Father, the Son, and the Holy Spirit, in a defined baptismal formula, suggests a time when theological definition was at work on the religious experience.   Luke reveals the presence of later interpretations in the gospel experience ; the failure of the disciples to understand the coming death of Jesus is explained on the view that its significance was purposely withheld from their understanding (ix. 45, xviii. 34).   Luke is also instructive as to the way in which the universal scope of the Gospel has become interwoven with the original experience and the apprehension of it by the first believers (ii. 10, 31 f., iii. 6).

While Matthew had grouped his Q material to a great extent, Luke has scattered the sayings up and down his Gospel, and these are frequently found in a context different from that in which they appear in the First

[1] *The Making of Luke–Acts*, 1927, p. 33.

Gospel.[1] But the value of a saying is not lessened for religious experience if two versions of it appear in diverse contexts. The experiential content of the evangelic tradition is not necessarily affected by such changes.

In view of these principles we may see all the more clearly how the true starting-point for understanding the significance of the religious experience of the primitive Church, as the motive force behind the gospel tradition, is the preface to Luke's Gospel (i. 1–4). First, we have the recipients of the original impressions due to the personal impact of Jesus on the experience of those who saw and heard, *i.e.* "those who from the very beginning were eye-witnesses " (i. 2). As far as we know, Jesus never left any word in writing, at least on papyrus or parchment, but He wrote deeply on the hearts of those around Him. Thus they wondered at what they saw, they gave God the praise, they took courage, and rejoiced at what they heard. Later on, they remembered and related it. They recalled how their hearts burned within them. They recognized that Peter and John had been with Jesus. They never failed to remind one another of the words of the Lord Jesus. Second, these personal impressions and experiences were shared with the new converts to the primitive Church. A body of tradition began to grow, motived in the first place by all this personal experience of Jesus. The tradition was " about the matters which have been fully established amongst us, just as those who from the very beginning were eye-witnesses . . . handed down to us " (i. 1 f.). The growing awareness of all that Jesus was, would tend to exercise a selective control of the impressions and experiences accumulated, and some of these would be rejected as unworthy. Third, the pre-literary or oral

[1] Cf. Luke vi. 40 with Matt. x. 24 f.

stages, and their expression in anecdote, story, parable, apothegm, proverb, and the like, reached out to the literary stage when the growing tradition was written down and compiled into gospels, and " many have taken it in hand to draw up a narrative . . . " (i. 1).

The Synoptic Gospels are therefore motived by a religious experience derived from the personal contact of many eye-witnesses with Jesus of Nazareth. Allowing for the influence of later interpretation, we have here the record of what these eye-witnesses made of Him who stood in their midst for a brief while. These Gospels are therefore basic authorities for the knowledge of the religious experience which created the primitive Church.

The real problem of the Fourth Gospel is, How far does it go back to the religious experience of the primitive Church ? How far does it rest upon the personal impressions which were received from Jesus and recalled in the growing life and light of the Church's progress ? Any supposed dependence of this Gospel on the Synoptics [1] may be due to the fact that the Synoptic tradition was known also to the compilers of the Johannine narrative, and the specific Johannine material may be present because preference was deliberately given to it over against Synoptic attestation.

What, for example, are we to make of the classic discourse in the Upper Room (xiii.–xvii.) ? Is it modelled after the manner of Thucydides who used to make his orators speak what he supposed to be the appropriate words for the particular occasion (*Hist.* i. 22) ? Were the words of Nicodemus, again, no more than the writer's idea of what Jesus would say under the circumstances ? What we really have to consider in the

[1] Cf. E. F. Scott, *The Fourth Gospel*, 2nd edn. 1920, pp.32–45.

Fourth Gospel is the growth of Christian experience, living, and insight into the meaning of what Jesus said and did. The words of Jesus given in the later Gospel, and absent from the Synoptics, start from the fact that when they were spoken the hearers were not sufficiently developed in their experience to be paying attention to them. The simpler Synoptic data would be first apprehended, the later tradition taking much longer to make its way.

Among the disciples in the Upper Room there may have been one who was more responsive than the others, and upon his more receptive mind the discourse of Jesus made a deeper impression than he at the time realized. Either his receptivity was mainly subconscious, or at the moment the strength of his religious insight was not sufficiently developed for him to grasp consciously the import of what Jesus was saying. In any case there was no time to ponder the words, for the disciples went out into the dark night of a tragedy issuing in the crucifixion of their Master. The shock which this gave to their Messianic hopes in Jesus took away the effect of any impressions for the time being. Then came the unexpected reunion with Jesus in the resurrection experience, and with it, the memory processes were vitally quickened to recall what Jesus had said and done, interpreted in the light of the new contacts made with His risen presence.

In the mind of the more receptive disciple the process of recall took a more individual turn. As time went on the words of Jesus which had subconsciously rested in his mind took root and gradually emerged into his conscious thought. They were then brooded over, developed, and expanded in terms of the effect they were producing on his mind, influenced at the same time by the contemporary religious experience which was

2

fashioning the primitive Church. Further, as these sayings returned and found their place in the forefront of the disciple's conscious meditation, they were being worked up with other ideas already present in his mind, being subject to the psychological influences therein. As a saying was recalled it mixed with and grew within the texture of the receptive self, and was therefore modified accordingly by the ideas, emotions, dispositions, and experiences already there. The exact words would not always be forthcoming ; his active intelligence meditated on what he was remembering, and so gradually and insensibly his reflection modified his reminiscences. We have to reckon with the vital influence of intelligent meditation on recollection where the two processes are at work within one and the same thoughtful mind. Indeed, on occasions when this more thoughtful disciple expounded what he conceived to be the words of Jesus in the Upper Room, he may not always have been able to distinguish original germs of reminiscence from the subsequent development in meditation. Gaps would also have to be bridged, and in this way explanations and interpretations, prompted by the eye-witness's own thinking, came into the Johannine tradition. The whole process of recall was profoundly influenced by the environment of the growing church with its increasing perception of the significance of the exalted Jesus, and may be likened to the activity of germs which contain the potency of life within themselves, yet draw on the environment within which they grow. As the words of Jesus came back to the mind, they were intertwined with many other ideas inspired by the earliest tradition and the growing insight of the Church into the meaning of what Jesus said and did.

This process must be viewed as going on during a number of years. The reflective disciple would most likely compare notes with other eye-witnesses, yet his creative intuitions would inspire the particular channel of tradition which was to culminate at long last in the Fourth Gospel when the later streams of influence were incorporated.[1]

If we take the discourse with Nicodemus (iii. 3 ff.) there is a fitness of words which suggests a germinal historical reality, but it has undergone development under a growing mystical experience working on the germs, such experience itself being stimulated by them. It does not follow that Jesus was entirely alone with Nicodemus, and our witness may have been there along with other disciples. Into his mind there entered the germs of the conversation, later to be recalled, meditated upon, and interwoven with other words and ideas derived from further contacts with Jesus, and influenced by later religious experience viewed through the death, the resurrection, and the ascension of Jesus.

The discourses on the bread of life (vi. 26 ff., 41 ff.) take what many feel to be a sacramentarian turn, but here again, the words of Jesus have been reinterpreted as they were recalled, in the light of later mystical experience. Moreover, the sayings may have been grouped by the later interpretations, or possibly by the disciple himself as he recalled them. He would not always be sure of the occasion on which they were spoken, and would remember only isolated portions. Jesus must have spoken on many occasions about the bread of life and cognate themes, and as His words were recalled they were combined with other remembered sayings, were meditated upon and brooded upon, and

[1] Such as those of Alexandrian philosophy, Pauline ideas, or aims which the redactor of the Gospel may have had in view. Cf. W. F. Howard, *The Fourth Gospel in Recent Criticism and Interpretation*, 1931, pp. 158 ff., and E. F. Scott, *op. cit.* pp. 46 ff.

finally emerged into a discourse containing words which
Jesus may well have uttered on diverse occasions.

The discourses to the Jews (vii. 15 ff., 28 ff., viii. 31 ff.,
etc.) derive their tone from the later Jewish attacks on
the Christian Church towards the end of the first century.
Jesus had undoubtedly to make many stern utterances
to the Jews, and some of them have found a place in
the recollections of our eye-witness, being worked up
into discourses which reveal later ideas of polemic.

In the discourse in the Upper Room we meet with a
series of ideas derived from the common experience of
the *Kiddûsh* meal held to hallow the Sabbath or any
approaching feast. Jesus and His friends met to
observe the *Kiddûsh* for the Passover (pp. 293 f.), and
the conversation turned on the deep things of the
religious life, especially in view of the imminent death
of Jesus. Dr. Oesterley comments on such points as the
Vine (xv. 1 ff.), a natural topic in view of the *Kiddûsh*
cup ; the completion of the work of Jesus (xvii. 4 f.)
recalls the finishing of the work of Creation and the
Sabbath rest that followed ; we have the election of
Israel alongside Jesus choosing His friends (xiii. 18,
xv. 16), and the experience of joy which was a marked
feature of the *Kiddûsh* (xv. 11, xvi. 22, xvii. 13). Such
Kiddûsh echoes in the Last Supper reveal the religious
ideas in the mind both of Jesus and of His friends, who
included the more receptive disciple with his mind
quick to observe the inner connection of the *Kiddûsh*
ideas with the words and significance of Jesus. There is
indeed a larger nucleus of genuine utterances of Jesus
in this farewell discourse than is sometimes supposed,
for the *Kiddûsh* ideas would facilitate much useful
recollection.[1]

[1] Cf. W. O. E. Oesterley, *The Jewish Background of the Christian
Liturgy*, 1925, pp. 170 ff.

There is some reason, therefore, for discerning behind the Fourth Gospel a genuine experiential nucleus made up of the impressions and experiences of a disciple who was more spiritually receptive than his friends. It is tempting to see in this beloved disciple the personality of John, son of Zebedee, and to feel that at its heart the Fourth Gospel has the religious experience of the apostle. The evidence, however, is against any such identification. The divergence of the Johannine tradition from the accepted Synoptic cycle based on apostolic warrant (Mark is based on Peter's preaching) makes it unlikely that another apostle was the authority for another, somewhat inconsistent, tradition. The beloved disciple is on a higher spiritual level than the son of Zebedee with his ambitious disputations (Mark x. 35, 41), his vindictive spirit (Luke ix. 54), his narrow jealousy which would hinder any one from doing good on the ground that he did not belong to the inner circle of authority (Luke ix. 49), and whom Mark sums up as a " son of thunder " (iii. 17). Whoever the disciple was, his spiritual responsiveness set in motion a semi-independent corpus of gospel tradition which took its own way and grew alongside the more authoritative Synoptic account. If he was not of the actual Twelve, his tradition would lack apostolic approval, and possibly found little place within the primitive Church. It seems, however, to have centred around some particular circle of believers who preserved the germinal nucleus which ultimately was to result in the Fourth Gospel.

The opening chapters of the Acts of the Apostles are significant for understanding the religious experience of the primitive Church, but their precise historical value is not easy to determine. This fact is in itself no proof that we are dealing with no more than an imaginative portrayal of the primitive Church by a later generation. Events and experiences must have occurred which in the first place afforded the incentive to write about the doings of the apostolic leaders. What produced in the first instance the beliefs we see operative in these early chapters ? Thus we are carried back to the personal contacts of the eye-witnesses with Jesus. There are, however, one or two reasons why Acts may be regarded as being more trustworthy than some critics are inclined to admit.

In the first place, there is little doubt that the Third Gospel and the Acts are by the same author. " Their unity is a fundamental and illuminating axiom. Among all the problems of New Testament authorship no answer is so universally agreed upon as is the common authorship of these two volumes," declares Professor Cadbury.[1] J. de Zwaan suggests that Acts was edited by a post-Pauline Christian, whose work was based " on the unfinished writings of Luke, the author of the Gospel, who had collected and partially arranged a variety of material drawn from various sources, including a diary of his own experiences, but had never finished his work." [2] This theory breaks down in view of the linguistic consistency and continuity of both Gospel and Acts, for if anything can be tested successfully by linguistic data, this fact is. Now the historian who in one writing works on definite principles to present his data as accurately as he can, is likely to execute a second work under the inspiration of similar ideals, especially when this is a sequel to the first work (Acts i. 1). The historical value of the Third Gospel receives various estimates, but there are good grounds for regarding it as trust-

[1] *Op. cit.* p. 8.
[2] " Was the Book of Acts a Posthumous Edition ? " in *Harv. Theol. Rev.*, vol. xvii.

worthy. Its preface (i. 1–4) indicates the author's intention to go back to the original eye-witnesses; everything is to be undertaken in a spirit of thoroughness as he inquires into all things in an accurate and consecutive manner. The Gospel itself shows an orderly presentation of events from the pre-natal announcements of the birth of Jesus to His death, resurrection, and ascension. There is thus a completeness which is lacking, for example, in Mark. We are able to test the value of Luke's sources, Mark and Q; indeed, there is some reason for thinking that Luke made use of a primary gospel consisting of Q and the material peculiar to Luke, into which, at convenient points, the author inserted excerpts from Mark.[1] This would suggest Luke's care in estimating the value of his sources, especially if he was led to set aside even Mark as his primary authority in favour of a Gospel he deemed to be more authoritative.

Acts would therefore be compiled with the same painstaking care. Luke seems to have been a fellow-traveller of Paul at various times.[2] The apostle's knowledge of the primitive Church would be available for the author's use. He and Paul were once guests of the evangelist Philip, whose personal experience of the primitive Church could be utilized (xxi. 8, cf. vi. 5, viii. 5–13). The local church at Cæsarea where Philip lived could furnish Luke with many data, not the least interesting being the conversion of Cornelius and his reception into the Messianic community (x. 44–48). Luke also seems to have been at Jerusalem with Paul, and there he could obtain first-hand information about the Jewish-Christian church. If Eusebius is right in

[1] For the Proto-Luke theory, cf. B. H. Streeter, *The Four Gospels*, 1924, pp. 201 ff.

[2] This is the most natural explanation of the " we " passages in Acts xvi. 11 ff., xx. 5 ff., xxi. 1 ff., xxvii. 1–xxviii. 16.

supposing Luke to be a native of Antioch (*H.E.* iii. 4), the evangelist's connection with this city would account for his knowledge of the Church developments there. The famous Codex Bezæ has an additional " we " passage at this point (xi. 27), and thus suggests that Luke was with Paul during the momentous happenings in that Church.

In the second place, the discussion on the sources of Acts has produced no sure conclusions. The Semitic colour of the early chapters has led to a search for Aramaic originals.[1] The Semitic features, however, may be due to the primitive Aramaic tradition of the Church, which, when at its oral stage, was translated into Greek for the use of Hellenistic-Jewish converts, thus carrying over its characteristic idioms into the Greek rendering. In this case the Semitic features point to the primitive nature of the tradition underlying the narrative. Until there is more agreement as to the actual documentary sources used in Acts, the Semitic characteristics are better explained by the translation of the tradition into the Greek language. The various source discussions, however, have established the primitive character of the material in the earlier chapters of Acts.

While the literary data do not warrant the too confident judgment that " it is difficult to rate too highly the historical value of the Book of Acts," [2] yet in view of Luke's methods of investigation, and of the primitive nature of the tradition he uses, we may have a fair degree of confidence that Acts is by no means unreliable. The presence of so-called doublets may be merely parallel versions of the same incident ; [3] that there are inconsistencies in the narrative is what

---

[1] Cf. C. H. Torrey, *The Composition and Date of Acts*, 1916.
[2] C. F. Nolloth, *The Rise of the Christian Religion*, 1917, p. 53.
[3] *E.g.* Acts ii. 1–13, iv. 31 : ii. 14–36, iii. 12–26 : ii. 37–41, iv. 4 : ii. 42–47, iv. 34–37.

we expect, while the criticism that Luke prefers the miraculous version of an incident loses force in view of the abnormal phenomena which every religious up-heaval brings to the surface. If Luke was motived in his writing by a desire to present the universal mission of the Gospel from the very outset, or if he wished to present the case for the Christian faith to the Emperor Domitian in view of impending persecution, his work is not thereby impaired in value, for the recognition of any special motive enables us to observe his tendencies, and to allow for them accordingly. If Acts is a historical picture rather than scientific history,[1] the religious experience which inspired it is not thereby discredited, for Acts still presents us with the vital conception " that the work of the Church is a continuation of Christ's energy." [2]

" Two names contain in themselves the primitive history of Christianity : the names of Jesus and Paul. Jesus is himself alone—Paul needs some foundation. What Paul is, he is in Christ." [3] But among the apostle's foundations is the primitive Church, which stands between Jesus and Paul. In several places Paul refers directly to what he had received from the Church prior to him, as in the observance of the Lord's Supper (1 Cor. xi. 23), or in a summary of what the primitive Church taught about the death and resur-rection of Jesus (1 Cor. xv. 3). Such references cannot be dismissed as containing direct revelations to Paul, as is sometimes assumed from his statement that he had received the tradition " from the Lord " (xi. 23). These

[1] A " Geschichtsbild," as W. Mundle describes it, *ZNW*. vol. xxvii. p. 36.

[2] J. Moffatt, *Introduction to the Literature of the New Testament*, 3rd edn. 1918, p. 285.

[3] Deissmann, *Paul*, Eng. Tr. 1926, p. 3.

traditions are referred to as being handed down (xi. 2),
and there is no need to "assume a supernatural
communication when a natural one was ready at hand,"
for "it would be easy for St. Paul to learn everything
from some of the Twelve." [1] Elsewhere there are direct
references to what the primitive Church had handed down,
such as the necessity for Messiah to suffer and be raised
from the dead in accordance with the Scriptures, and that
this Messiah was none other than Jesus (2 Thess. ii. 15, cf.
Acts xvii. 1–3). The received tradition also embodied
religious experience which had power to change the character and conduct of those who adhered to its teaching,
for Paul urges the believers to withdraw from those who
are living unworthily and not according to the tradition
which he has handed on to them (2 Thess. iii. 6). Where
the true results in life are lacking, the tradition is being
set at naught. J. B. Mayor notes that the Christian
tradition "also included rules of action," and cites
this instance accordingly; [2] but what in the first place
gave birth to the rules of action? As the religious
experience of the primitive Church motived the subsequent beliefs or rules of belief, so there is inherent
in it the creative moral force which issues in Christian
character. By Paul's time much of the content of the
tradition is of a somewhat trivial nature (1 Cor. xi. 2,
3–16), and we see the beginnings of the process which
tended to diffuse the creative religious experience into
a series of "delivered instructions," [3] as these modify-
ing processes began to influence the earlier and more
authentic experience. Here we observe Rabbinical
teaching on the status of women, and the social con-

[1] Robertson and Plummer, *Commentary on 1 Corinthians, ICC.*
2nd edn. 1914, p. 242.
  [2] *The Epistle of St. Jude and the Second Epistle of St. Peter*, 1907, p. 63.
  [3] Robertson and Plummer, *op. cit.* p. 228.

ventions of Paul's age are interpreting the primitive
tradition along narrower lines.

The earliest epistle of Paul, I Thessalonians, which
of all his letters is perhaps nearest in spirit as well as
in time to the primitive community, indicates a gospel
which came as an experience of power through the
Spirit, and not simply by word or set of beliefs (i. 5).
The religious experience hinted at is not unlike what we
sense within the Pentecost atmosphere (Acts ii. 1-4,
cf. iv. 31). This may be regarded as indicating what
usually took place when a Church came into being, and
thus reflects the primitive experience. We learn,
further, how the Thessalonians were " to await His
(God's) son from heaven, whom He raised from the
dead, Jesus who liberates from the coming wrath "
(i. 10). Here are references to the primitive Church
traditions of the resurrection of Jesus, the exalted
Messiah's return, this Messiah being none other than
Jesus, who would secure the believers in the imminent
eschatological judgment. Once again the primitive
Church standpoint that the guilt of the crucifixion lies
at the door of the Jew is mentioned (ii. 15). Various
apocalyptic expectations (iv. 13-17, v. 1-3) suggest the
atmosphere of the Church in which Paul dwells.

Indirect hints of what Paul received from the
primitive community may be gleaned by his use of
certain terms, the most significant of which is *euaggelion*,
with its cognate verb. The study of such words, however, yields surprisingly scanty information, if any,
about the primitive Church experience. For the most
part the meaning of *euaggelion* is semi-technical, indicating the " gospel " or the act of preaching the gospel
without reference to the empirical content of the gospel
(cf. Rom. i. 9, 15, ii. 16). The gospel is equated with
the tradition received and passed on (I Cor. xv. 1).

It includes non-Jews within its scope, any teaching to
the contrary being a " different gospel," an illegitimate
one, not in line with the received one (Gal. i. 6 ff.).   The
gospel is attested " in the power of signs and wonders,
in power of the Holy Spirit " (Rom. xv. 19), and includes in its content the confession, " Jesus is Lord "
(Rom. x. 16, cf. ver. 9), the belief that God raised Jesus
from the dead, and exalted him as Messiah.   In all these
instances we are back amidst the primitive Church
experience.   The gospel of salvation in Christ sets the
seal on the faith of the believers in the Holy Spirit of
promise, and the Spirit is the "earnest " of redemption,
the pledge that the promise is to be fulfilled (Eph. i. 13 f.).
Here once more the apostle reflects the experiential
outlook of the Church prior to his creative influence.

We may therefore discern within the epistles of
Paul a cumulative body of references and suggestions
confirmatory of the earlier empirical fundamentals.   It
is true that direct reference to what had been received is
not so great nor so clear as we are sometimes led to
believe,[1] and there is a strange silence about the facts of
the life of Jesus.   Yet there is positive evidence of the
nature of the religious experience and outlook of the
primitive Church, and this may be accordingly summed
up.   The apostasy of Israel was responsible for the
rejection of Jesus the Messiah, and the nation is summoned to repent in order that God may still use it
for the redemption of the Gentiles.   But the nation
itself must first be redeemed before it could undertake
its divinely appointed mission of redeeming the world.
From another angle, it was divine necessity that made
inevitable Messiah's death, as the Scriptures foreshadowed, had Israel but the insight to discern this

[1] Cf. J. Weiss, Urchristentum, 1917, p. 3 ; E. F. Scott, The Beginnings of the Church, p. 7.

truth. The death of Jesus was also connected with the forgiveness of sins, and again according to the Scriptures. All these data centred in Jesus, because He was this divinely appointed Messiah who was crucified and whom God raised from the dead. The exalted Messiah was expected to return almost at any time. A new community of salvation had come into being on the basis of these empirical facts, and this community was invested from the outset with the power of the Spirit as the pledge that salvation in the Kingdom was to be fulfilled. The Spirit's presence was attested by what we would designate abnormal psychological phenomena; abnormal, too, were the Spirit-inspired lives which stood out as extraordinary when placed against the background of the ancient world and its mediocre moral standards. The observance of the Lord's Supper was not only a memorial of Jesus, but also the pledge that the exalted Messiah was soon to return in the divine Kingdom. This cursory summary will find its justification in the course of our investigation, and if so much in Paul's epistles can be traced back to the primitive Church, the probability is that many more elements in his outlook are derived from the earlier years. The teaching of the primitive Church constitutes a background for Paul's thought ; the doctrines which are so characteristically his own are based on the older and simpler ideas he was endeavouring to interpret and elucidate in the light of their implication.

We may, however, use the epistles of Paul in a negative way to afford information about the primitive Church. The developments in the Christian experience which are due to his own creative personal influence and thought are not to be read back into the earlier religious experience.

First, the developed Christology of Paul's thought is in marked contrast to the Jesus of the Synoptic Gospels and the primitive Messianism of the earlier period of the Church. Jesus is now the Son of God (Rom. i. 4), a divine being of the same dignity as God (Phil. ii. 6), the very image of the invisible God, the heavenly being invested with the powers of creation (Col. i. 15 f.), who had surrendered His divine status by becoming a human being and dying that men might be redeemed (Phil. ii. 6-8). This divine Christ is also " the second man, the higher type of humanity, the beginner of a movement towards life in mankind, destined to retrieve the movement towards death which began in Adam; he is not of earthy but of heavenly and spiritual material, and has the power of changing those who believe in him into the same element." [1] Here is a series of ideas not to be discovered in the primitive Church experience, for the believers had not as yet reached out as far as this in their discoveries and affirmations of the unique dignity of Jesus.

Second, the developed Church consciousness of the Pauline era presents features that are not clearly discernible in the earlier period. The Church is now aware of its universal mission, and the Gentiles are legitimately members of the Church along with the Jews (Eph. ii. 22). The Pauline Church has become cognizant of its own distinctiveness over against the traditional Israel. Jews and non-Jews enter its fellowship through the spiritual conditions of faith in Jesus Christ. Admission to the Church is spiritually, not physically, conditioned, and on this basis, the Jew, being justified by faith as was Abraham (Rom. iv. 3 ; Gal. iii. 7 ff.), could feel himself still in line with his ancestral religion, while the Gentile found no racial barrier in the way of his salvation

[1] A. Menzies, *Second Epistle to the Corinthians*, 1912, p. lvi.

experience. The new element was the synthesis of these two streams of religious experience, the Jewish and the Gentile, and the unified Church became something quite apart from the Jewish theocracy. Thus far there was a tremendous advance on the earlier Messianic community which never attained to any such conception of itself. Further, the hints of Church organization, the evolving procedure in Church worship, and the place of women in the Church (1 Cor. xii. 28 ff., xiv. 1–33, 34 f.) point to a growth in church consciousness which is a definite advance. The doctrine of Christ as the head of the Church is enunciated (Eph. i. 22 ; Col. i. 18, 24), the Church is now " The Body of Christ " (1 Cor. x. 16). The primitive community awaiting the advent of the exalted Messiah has now become conscious of itself as the organic spiritual body with Christ as its organic head. These later developments should not be read back into the earlier period. The germs were there, no doubt, but the primitive Church, for instance, never regarded itself as " The Body of Christ," nor in any of these explicit and developed ways.

Third, the ordinances of baptism and the Lord's Supper present new features in the Pauline Church. It is especially important that here we distinguish carefully between the earlier and the later conceptions. With regard to baptism the distinctively new thing is that " it is on the basis of the mystical being-in-Christ, as the centre of his teaching, that Paul explains baptism." [1] In the primitive community the rite marked the admission of the new convert who in the very reception of the baptism was aware of his surrender made to, and accepted by Jesus the Lord whom he confessed and whose name was pronounced over him. According to

[1] A. Schweitzer, *The Mysticism of Paul the Apostle*, Eng. Tr. 1931, pp. 261 f.

Paul, however, the believer re-enacts in baptism the
death and resurrection of Jesus by going down into,
and coming up again from, the water (Rom. vi. 3).   In
the burial-like entrance into the water the convert died
to sin ; his emergence from the water vault was the
realistic rising again to a new life (Rom. vi. 4).

The observance of the Lord's Supper in the Pauline
period, however, seems to follow the lines of that of the
primitive Church.   The uncertainty in the tradition as
to whether the cup preceded or followed the bread is
reflected in Paul, as in the Synoptic Gospels.[1] But the
Christ-mysticism has brought its own influence, for the
mystical union with Christ has become central in the
ordinance, thus preparing the way for the assumption
that Paul was a sacramentarian, viewing the ordinances
ex opere operato.   Even if such sacramentarianism in
Paul's thought were established, we have no more
than a development on the practice of the earlier
period, and it cannot be postulated of the earlier
outlook.[2]

Fourth, the widening of the content of the salvation
experience is a marked feature of Paul, with his many
fruitful interpretations of the death of Jesus and its
significance for Christian experience.   The Cross becomes
a ransom, freeing slaves from the bondage of sin, law,
idols, and death.[3]   The Cross is also regarded as a
sacrificial altar whereon the paschal lamb was offered
up as a " fragrant odour."[4]   The death of Christ was
further a legal penalty suffered by the innocent Jesus

[1] Cf. I Cor. x. 16, 21 with xi. 23–25, and Mark xiv. 22–24 with
Luke xxii. 17–19, and see below, pp. 290 f.

[2] For further notes on this, see below, Appendix I. on " The
Alleged Sacramentarianism of Paul," pp. 345–348.

[3] Cf. Rom. vi. 6, 17, 19 f. ; Gal. iv. 1–7, 8 f ; Rom. viii. 20 ; cf.
I Cor. vi. 20, vii. 23 ; Eph. i. 7, 14 ; Col. i. 14 ; Rom. iii. 24.

[4] I Cor. v. 7 ; Eph. v. 2.

for the sinner who so richly deserved it (2 Cor. v. 21). The Cross, again, is the means of reconciliation whereby estrangement from God is overcome, and religious experience becomes one of reconciliation to God (2 Cor. v. 18–20). The death of Jesus also leads to the " adoption " of the believer as a " child " of God, whereby he is able to say, " Abba, Father! " (Gal. iv. 4–7). We are nearer to the primitive Church in the view of the death of Christ as an " earnest " or " instalment " of the redemption to come ; for the earliest believers it was the prelude to Messiah's exaltation, the " earnest " that He was to bring in final salvation with the divine Kingdom. The new emphasis in Paul is that the real climax of salvation was away from earth and in the heavenly places.

Certain positive streams of influence have joined the main flow of the Christian experience in the Pauline era, and have actively assisted the developments we have noticed.

There was the apostle's own personal religious experience which had a profound influence on the interpretation of the Christian facts. His conversion involved a distinct break with the Jewish law as impotent to secure salvation, and an acceptance of Jesus as Messiah, mightier than the law to save. Paul's experience thus opened up the way for an effective comparison and contrast of the way of Christ with the way of the law, bringing in considerations that were quite absent from the outlook of the primitive Church which was by no means aware of any break with traditional Mosaism. At the same time Paul's own personal contact with the growing liberal movement which had gathered around the name of Stephen may well have given him the germinal ideas of what afterwards came

3

for him to be a thoroughgoing advocacy of the gospel for the whole world, irrespective of Jewish or any other distinctions.

The Jewish elements in the interpretation of the Christian facts according to Paul take their start in that the apostle was a Hellenistic Jew brought up in the strictest Pharisaic circles (Acts xxii. 3, xxvi. 5). He thought in forensic terms such as justification, and as a Christian he still pursued his thinking in such categories, but with his mind now turned upon his experience of salvation in Christ instead of upon the legal obedience unto salvation expected from the Pharisees. If we compare the freedom of Jesus from the law and Paul's bondage to it, we discover that the apostle, though free through his religious experience in Christ, was still in bondage to the law inasmuch as he was psychologically bound to interpret his new faith in terms of the old concepts.   Such bondage proved to be a source of hindrance to the integral understanding of the new experience, and therefore the primitive Church, being relatively free from these Pharisaic limitations, may have preserved elements more clearly than the obscure legal concepts of Paul are sometimes able to do. The effort to interpret the Christian experience as a philosophy of history (Rom. ix.–xi.) utilized the rabbinic categories of predestination which were held in general by the Pharisees, a natural growth of their strict literalism, attributing everything in its origins, even evil, to the far-reaching and far-seeing wisdom of God.[1] The apostle's emphasis on the pre-existence of Christ was primarily " the consequence of his personal experiences and his Jewish mode of thought." [2]

[1] Cf. J. D. Prince, *Enc. Bi.* iv. col. 4324.
[2] Clemen, *Primitive Christianity and its Non-Jewish Sources*, Eng. Tr. 1912, pp. 337 f.

Here is no ideal or abstract inference of pre-existence such as was made by the primitive Church when it identified Jesus with the pre-existent Messiah, but a real one, rooted and grounded in Paul's rabbinic thought applied to Jesus whose significance for his experience was such as to warrant the application to Christ of the highest categories the apostle's own thought and culture could yield. The lofty and noble piety of Pharisaism in its highest classic expression, rather than extra-Jewish influences and ideas, gives the sources of Paul's Christology, and his religious and intellectual development as a Pharisee enabled him to recognize the significance of Jesus as Messiah in a more comprehensive manner than would be possible within the limits of the primitive Church.

The Christian experience passed over into the wider world of ancient civilization, with the result that Greek elements came to be influential in the interpretation of the Christian facts. On his Hellenistic side, Paul was familiar with Greek ways of life and thought. The incoming of countless Gentile converts into the Church accentuated the wider contacts with the thought and ideas of pagan culture as the newcomers brought with them their Hellenistic psychology and general world outlook. One important principle should be recognized here. Whatever the Gentiles read into their Christianity from their former religious experience and understanding should not necessarily be ascribed to the thought of Paul, still less to that of the primitive Church and to the original Christian experience. On the occasions when the apostle used images and ideas from the wider circle of his converts' Gentile outlook, he was doing no more than making use of what they knew to interpret what they did not know, namely, the basic facts of the Christian experience. Analogies do not

denote dependence. If Lightfoot [1] discovers parallels
in the thought of Paul with the ideas of Seneca, this does
not prove that Paul was influenced by philosophical
Ṣtoicism in his interpretation of the Christian facts.
Ideas, like germs, are in the air, and the popular thought
of the time bore as little resemblance to the Stoicism
of Seneca as the modern popular ideas about evolution
do to the actual biological facts, or to the philosophical
implications of evolution. Paul may have made use of
popularized Stoic ideas to light up for the Gentile
believers his message of Christ, but more than this
cannot be assumed. The Stoics could never have said,
" Weep with them that weep " (Rom. xii. 15), nor " If
one member suffer, all the members suffer with it "
(I Cor. xii. 26). But even if Stoicism influenced Paul,
we cannot read it back into the primitive Church experience which had no contact with this or any other specific
Gentile philosophy.

There was, moreover, the influence of Greek language
on the interpretation of the Christian facts. The transition from the Aramaic vernacular, the original language
of the gospel tradition, to Greek was made at an early
date ; the latter language formed a more plastic medium
for the expression of religious experience with its
" unusual number of terms which express moral, religious,
and theological conceptions." [2] This linguistic influence
has led to the theory that Paul depended on the Mystery
Religions for many of his ideas. Identity of terminology
in the Christian Faith and the Mysteries is taken to
imply Paul's dependence on the mystic cults of the
Græco-Roman civilization. Through the apostle the
movement cradled in Jerusalem has become a product

[1] *St. Paul and Seneca*, in Commentary on Philippians, 6th edn.
1890, pp. 270 ff.
[2] H. A. A. Kennedy, *Sources of New Testament Greek*, 1895, p. 8.

of the wider religious syncretism of the world, and the linguistic affinities throw up parallels which are viewed as originating with the wider world movement influencing Paul's thought as it did every form of religion that came within its scope.[1] But the Græco-Roman literature employed to illustrate this thesis is of a much later period, and the religious ideas therein are read back into the earlier period of the Pauline Church. A step farther, and the primitive Church is included within the orbit of the Mystery Religions, and we find Bousset deriving both Paul and the primitive Church largely from their religious influence.[2] The apostle may well have referred to the experience which his Gentile converts had of the Mysteries, to illustrate for them by analogy the operation of the Christian salvation, and while they may have sometimes understood the new faith in terms of mystic cults and such ideas as these presented, it does not follow that Paul, still less the Church before him, actually received any such ideas from the Mystery Religions.[3]

The remaining literature of the New Testament furnishes few data with regard to earlier conditions in the Church. The Pastoral Epistles reflect a type of piety which has its roots in the earliest period, but " it denotes a second stage in the Christian life ; that life has passed through the excitement of conversion . . . the sense of the speedy Parousia of the Lord had passed away." [4] There is a primitive Church tone about the First Epistle of Peter, but the Christology is more developed than in the speeches of Acts. The Church consciousness

[1] R. Reitzenstein is the typical exponent of this view ; cf. his *Die Hellenistischen Mysterienreligionen*, 2nd edn. 1920, p. 66.

[2] *Kurios Christos*, 1913.

[3] Cf. Appendix I. below, pp. 345–348.

[4] W. Lock, *The Pastoral Epistles, ICC.* 1924, p. xv.

reflected is fairly advanced, for the privileges and status
of the old Israel are now transferred to the Church. The
apostle probably inspired the writing of this letter when
it had become clear even to him as the apostle of circumcision that God had transferred his choice to a new
people of God gathered together out of all the nations.
The Epistle of James is looked on as the earliest, and as
among the latest, writings of the New Testament, while
various intermediate dates are suggested.[1] It does not
therefore bear the hallmark of its period and authorship,
yet many scholars have no doubt that it is written by
James, the Lord's brother (i. 1). The superscription,
however, is no evidence that he was the author, who
seems to be one of the unknown personalities of the later
apostolic age. The Jewish - Christian piety reflected is
not that of the primitive Church, but a type which
developed after the long struggle between Paul and the
Judaizers for the soul of the Church, when the Jewish-
Christian section had hardened into a rigid conservatism.
The collection of sayings common to Matthew and
Luke, designated by the symbol Q, is more authoritative
for the " Way " characteristic of the primitive Church
than this epistle (pp. 237 ff.). The Epistle to the Hebrews
is a highly spiritualized presentation of many elementary
Christian facts. The allegorical tone, derived from the
Platonic philosophy in vogue at Alexandria, removes
the epistle from the zone of the more primitive experience. Something, however, may be said for the view
that the type of religious experience reflected is derived
independently from the primitive Church through the
Gentile off-shoot originating with the Stephenite movement. This may have followed its own independent
lines apart from Pauline influence, and found its home

[1] See the " Introductions " to the New Testament by Jülicher,
Moffatt, and Peake.

in some such circle as the Christian Platonism of Alexandria.   This primitive strain may be detected in the
apocalyptic tone of the Epistle, but it is apocalyptic
rapidly becoming spiritualized into the hope of the Kingdom not of this world.   The analogies between Hebrews
and the speech of Stephen (Acts vii., cf. pp. 262 ff.)
do not indicate dependence either way, but the common
ideas are suggestive of some contact with the primitive
Church.[1] The Epistles of John are too remote and
sketchy, the Epistles of Jude and Second Peter too
reminiscent of the second-century experience, to be of
any use for our knowledge of the primitive Church.
The Apocalypse throws back little light on primitive
Church apocalyptic.   Such sources as it uses[2] were
probably available for the earliest believers, but the
phase of the Nero-redivivus myth, with Nero represented
as returning from the abyss as a demon, " combining in
his own person the characteristics of Beliar and the
Anti-Christ,"[3] groups the apocalyptic ideas into a
setting unknown to the primitive Church.

Apart from the New Testament, we have the profound
influence exercised on the primitive Church by the Old
Testament literature.   Both Jesus and his disciples, as
also the earliest converts, were nurtured on the Law and
the Prophets, and drew inspiration from the type of
devotion represented in the Psalter.   Since the Church
was cradled amidst the piety of the Old Testament, it

[1] In both, the history of Israel is reviewed with certain episodes
stressed, the allegorical method interprets the Old Testament, worship
is central, the Law is referred to as being given by angels and the
tabernacle is modelled on a heavenly pattern.   These all go back
to the common tradition of Israel, and are distinctive in their own
right.

[2] Cf. R. H. Charles, *The Revelation of St. John, ICC.* vol. i. 1920,
pp. lxviii. ff.

[3] *Ibid.* p. xcvi.

rests to a large extent on the religious experience which
finds literary embodiment in the Law, the Prophets,
and the Psalms. " It may be said . . . that a knowledge of Apocryphal literature is even more essential
for the study of the New Testament than a knowledge
of the Old Testament itself," [1] and we may add that the
religious experience of the primitive Church cannot be
understood without reference to the ideas and conceptions revealed in the Apocalyptic literature.[2] The
New Testament also has its counterparts in Gospels,
Acts, Epistles, and Apocalypses, which grew up so
luxuriantly during the first few centuries of the Christian
era.[3] Of all these it is sufficient to state that they are
the imaginative products of much later times than the
apostolic age, and are prolific in legends, fantasies,
extravagancies, and absurdities, from which the canonical
writings are comparatively free. The Gospel to the
Hebrews, however, has some claim to consideration,
since in the few fragments preserved of it there seems
to be extant independent Aramaic gospel tradition
which had still lingered within the Jerusalem Church.
As this Church stagnated in the backwater of its conservatism so its gospel faded into insignificance. " Its
anonymity, its primitive character, and the authority it
afterwards enjoyed, point to a very early origin. It
may have come into existence about the same time as
the Synoptic Gospels, and in obedience to some at least
of the same motives as led to their appearance." [4]
The Gospel of Peter is sometimes cited as evidence for

---

[1] H. T. Andrews, *The Apocryphal Books*, 1908, p. 6.

[2] The Book of Enoch (with its Similitudes in xxxvii.–lxxi.), the
Testaments of the Twelve Patriarchs, Jubilees, The Assumption of
Moses, the Psalms of Solomon, are the chief works concerned.

[3] M. R. James, *The Apocryphal New Testament*, 1924.

[4] A. Menzies, in *HDB*. extra vol. p. 343.   Fragments mainly in
Jerome ; cf. James, *op. cit.* pp. 1–8.

the resurrection appearances, but its second-century date and its indecisive contribution cause much hesitation in the use of it for our purpose. P. Gardner-Smith accepts decisively the resurrection evidence,[1] but James Mackinnon rejects it as " a fantastic description of the coming forth from the tomb, worthy of a nursery tale." [2] If Gardner-Smith and Mackinnon reach such diametrically opposed conclusions, where shall the truth of such a document be found ? The Agrapha is a group of some sayings ascribed to Jesus, not found in the canonical Gospels. These may preserve genuine elements of tradition, but no satisfactory solution of their value is forthcoming.[3] Among the writings of the Apostolic Fathers and the Apologists one document alone is relevant to our investigation, the *Didache*, or *The Teaching of the Twelve Apostles*. The problems of its literary origins have not been solved in any way that commands general confidence, but there are very good grounds for supposing that the eucharistic prayers of the *Didache* preserve genuine elements of the primitive Church experience.[4]

[1] *The Narratives of the Resurrection*, 1926, pp. 103 ff.
[2] *The Historic Jesus*, 1931, p. 291.
[3] Cf. M. R. James, *op. cit.* pp. 25, 33 f. for translation, and see H. G. Evelyn White, *The Sayings of Jesus from Oxyrhynchus*, 1920, and R. Dunkerley, *The Agrapha*, for discussions on this question.
[4] Cf. J. V. Bartlet, *H.D.B.* extra vol. pp. 438 ff.

CHAPTER III

THE RELIGIOUS AND PSYCHOLOGICAL BACKGROUND

A LONG religious history, the earlier phases of which are encircled by the mists of myth and legend, lay behind the primitive Church. The Jews looked back to their great ancestor, Abraham, for to be descended from him was the guarantee of incorporation within the Chosen People. This was taken so literally that John the Baptist had to warn his hearers that the racial connection may not always hold good (Matt. iii. 9). Around the significant personality of Moses there was gathered in the course of a long process what was called the "Torah," which took its start from an original deposit of commandments at Sinai. On the basis of the Sinai covenant Moses unified a number of Semitic tribes into the beginnings of a coherent nation, the basis of unity being a common belief in the tribal Yahweh.

The subsequent religious history of Israel is the story of the purifying of this belief. A distinguishing figure in this development is David, who brought about national unification in Palestine under his own sovereignty, and acquired the mountain citadel of Jerusalem where Israel was to erect its national shrine. Future ages, disillusioned by civil strife and political servitude, were to look back on his reign as the golden age of their nation. This age was idealized in Utopian fantasy which forgot the barbarisms and limitations of that time, and the golden age ultimately symbolized the ideal divine sovereignty for which the expectation of the nation yearned. At the same time, aspiration turned on the desire for a deliverer from contemporary troubles, a desire intensely fostered during the exile in Babylon. The deliverer was usually conceived to spring from the dynasty of David.

Thus the germs of two potent ideas destined to come to full expression in the primitive Church are observed in their initial activity in the religious experience of Israel. These ideas are the Kingdom of God and the advent of the Messianic Redeemer.

The prophets were the potent spiritual educators of their nation, as they sought to guide it in ways of obedience to the will of God amidst the world-shaking rivalries of ancient empires which used Palestine either as a buffer state or a cockpit. The prophets therefore were the moral critics of nation and state, as they constantly affirmed the coming of disaster through the divine judgment upon national apostasy and failure to discern the religious implications of contemporary events. On the other hand, the prophets represent a type of religious experience which causes them to be true antecedents of the religion of Jesus.

The final stage of Israel's faith was in the enthronement of the " Torah." The exilic and post-exilic leaders of Israel rewrote and restated the ancient history, traditions, and law codes, and from the days of Ezra and Nehemiah Israel's religion moved more along the lines of closer devotion to precept and statute.[1] The " Torah," and the traditions arising from its interpretation, received so exalted a status that there was created " the illusion which was to last for centuries that the religion of Israel began with a Law." [2] More recent

---

[1] Cf. the P elements in the Pentateuch, and the post-exilic rewriting of 1 and 2 Samuel in 1 and 2 Chronicles ; and see G. F. Moore, *Judaism*, 1927, vol. i. pp. 125 ff.

[2] W. Sanday, *The Oracles of God*, 1891, p. 155.

historical and critical investigation of the Old Testament has exploded the idealization, and has replaced it by a more specific account of the historical facts and the psychological probabilities. Israel's religion is now seen to be a gradual purification of the primitive tribal faith in a tribal deity with whose name there was associated a deliverance from Egypt, and with whom a covenant was made at Sinai. The experience received of God was gradually enlarged until the idea of God inherent in the idealized Torah came to expression with three distinctive values. First, God's personality could not be expressed in any material form, yet was limited by localization to the Holy of Holies. Second, God came to be viewed as the divine sovereign of heaven and earth, and was thus the One God, yet with the limitation that only a selected nation could be regarded as His people. Third, God's moral majesty emerges in its fullest significance, yet this is curiously limited in that He is viewed as One who placed ritual requirements on the same high level as the demands of His moral holiness.[1] These three limitations were to prove decisive points for the growth of the religious experience of the primitive Church.

Alongside this growing legalistic transformation there existed the piety expressed in the many psalms which sang the praise of hearts in a joyous experience of God and obedience to His will and law. The sacrificial system began to develop in a form hitherto unknown, and this was due to an increasing awareness of sin and a corresponding growth in the need and means of

---

[1] If " the majority of the purity laws applied only to priests, or to laymen who had occasion to enter the temple " (I. Abrahams, *Studies in Pharisaism and the Gospels*, 2nd Series, 1924, p. 200), this is another way of saying that to be ceremonially pure is on the same level as moral excellence. Cf. too, C. G. Montefiore, *Hibbert Lectures*, 1892, p. 478.

expiation.[1]   The recognition of this intensified sense of sinfulness in the religious background of the primitive Church is a valuable corrective to the tendency to seek for the origins of Christian salvation in Greek Mystery Religions and their sense of sin.   The Jewish background provides all the necessary categories for interpreting the death of Christ and His redeeming work in connection with sin and its expiation.

The " Servant " passages of the Old Testament were used by the primitive Church to explain the otherwise inexplicable suffering and death of Jesus the Messiah.[2] Despite Sir George Adam Smith's pleading, it is doubtful if the Suffering Servant foreshadowed the Messiah, for the association of suffering with Messiah is too revolutionary for Israel to make.[3]   Indeed, it is not at all certain that there are traces of a suffering Messiah in Hebrew prophecy.   The " Emmanuel " passage (Isa. vii.) reveals no established connection between " Emmanuel " and suffering, while it is doubtful if this prophecy is Messianic in any way.[4]   " Up to the time of Jesus, the Jews did not expect their Messiah to die.   For them, as for Peter, that would have been almost a contradiction in terms." [5]   The fact that the necessity of Messiah's death was so constantly stressed both in the primitive Church and in Paul's apologetic to his fellow-Jews is a sure indication that the idea was a radical innovation for Jewish thought.

It is, therefore, necessary to keep the Messianic idea, or the germs of it in the Old Testament, distinct from the experience of suffering implied in the Suffering

[1] Cf. W. O. E. Oesterley, *Hebrew Religion*, 1930, pp. 296–299.
[2] Isa. xlii. 1–4, xlix. 1–6, l. 4–9, lii. 13–liii. 12 ; cf. with Acts iii. 13, 26, viii. 32–35 ;   1 Pet. i. 19, ii. 22 f., iii. 18.
[3] *The Book of Isaiah*, ii. chs. xvi.–xx.
[4] Cf. J. Skinner, *Isaiah*, Cam.B. vol. i. 1915, p. 67.
[5] W. D. Mackenzie, *ERE*. vii. p. 514.

Servant.   The former took its rise from national aspiration for the return of the glories of the Davidic era, while the latter idea emerged from prophetic insight into the place of suffering in the divine purpose.[1]   The Servant passages may have a close bearing on Messiah's work as seen in Christ, but they were never regarded as Messianic before the time of Jesus.   The Talmud sometimes equates the Suffering Servant with Messiah suffering with His people ;   Justin, in his Dialogue with Trypho (62 f.) makes a Jewish questioner accept the doctrine of the Suffering Messiah.   These later references do not point to a general belief among the Jews, and there is no trace of it in the background of the Gospels.

The inheritance of the primitive Church is Jewish, both in the religious ideas and psychological dispositions which moulded the new faith.   This inheritance carried with it more than religious legalism, theological concepts, and psychological associations ;   it provided a religious experience of God and the soul which, within its limitations, proved to be a noteworthy cradle for the new-born faith.

The religious environment of Jesus, of His disciples, and of the earliest converts to the new community that gathered around His name, is all significant for our investigation.   " It is not possible to distinguish personality from the concrete environing interests and values associated with it." [2]   This is also true if the personality be that of a group or expressive of a social solidarity.   The religious outlook of the primitive Church was in many respects so similar to that of Jewish piety and faith that it was impossible to be in the realm of the one without being to a large degree within the

---

[1] Cf. H. Schultz, *Old Testament Theology*, Eng. Tr. 1898, i. pp. 319 f.
[2] J. S. Haldane, *The Sciences and Philosophy*, 1928, p. 257.

orbit of the other. In its primitive stages it is scarcely possible, in many ways, to distinguish the Church from its religious environment.

The Judaism amidst which the primitive Church came to birth had moved on beyond the simpler limits fore-shadowed by Ezra and Nehemiah. But the ultimate consensus of Rabbinic opinion as to the real content of Judaism, known as Rabbinic Judaism, was not reached for some two centuries after Jesus. Hillel and Shammai were hotly disputing as to what the tenets of Judaism were as the Christian era came into being. The conquests of Alexander, the Hellenistic upheaval in Palestine through Antiochus Epiphanes and the Maccabæan wars, and the incoming of Roman supremacy, all disturbed Israel's religion. The syncretism of the age did not leave the Jewish faith alone, as there mixed with the older Hebrew notions those of Babylonian cosmology, Persian eschatology, the accompanying developments in ideas of good and evil spirits, and the infiltration of the wider ideas of the Hellenistic world. Increasing contacts of the races and peoples through the expanding commerce opened up innumerable avenues of approach among the subject nations of the Roman Empire, and the Jews shared in all these wider developments.

We, therefore, expect to discern advances from the simpler faith of the older religion of Israel. We now come across Pharisees, Sadducees, and Essenes ; we become aware of " traditions " that are associated with the law of Moses, of political Messianism, of angels and demons, of apocalyptic in an advanced form, of syna-gogues for religious worship and instruction in every village and town. But this development does not represent exactly the religion portrayed in the later Rabbinic writings of the Talmud, edited during the long period A.D. 200-500. The religion of the Talmud does not stand for the faith of the people as a whole in the days of Jesus of Nazareth ; it represents that of one section of the Jews, namely, the Pharisees and scribes of the Gospels, or rather, of their successors. Further, the Rabbinism of the later literature came to this expression as Christianity began to come into definite opposition to Judaism, resulting ultimately in the separation of the two religions in the second century. There was a sharpening of divergencies both in Christianity and in Rabbinism. It is, therefore, more than likely that the Rabbinic Judaism of A.D. 300–500 was not quite the same as the scribal Judaism in which Paul was trained. Mr. Montefiore does not find this gap too serious, as he passes easily from the later Rabbinism to the first Christian generation in order to show that Paul was not a pure Rabbinic Jew. " Either the Rabbinic Judaism of A.D. 50 was not the Rabbinic Judaism of A.D. 500 or 300, or Paul at the time of his conversion was no pure Rabbinic Jew." [1] This great Jewish interpreter inclines to the latter alternative, but the former alternative has sufficient truth in it to suggest that the Rabbinic idealization of the later centuries may represent differences from the Judaism of the time of Jesus and Paul, as this in turn portrays differences from the relatively simpler position of the Old Testament.[2]

If the classic Rabbinism of the Talmud is not the typical religious expression of the Judaism of the age of Jesus, where are we to look for this ? The Pharisees and scribes formed a brotherhood into which " they would admit only such as pledged themselves . . . to live in accordance with their fixed rules of piety, avoiding contact with the *Am ha-aretz* and sinners, and especially

---

[1] *Judaism and St. Paul*, 1914, p. 68.
[2] Cf. Appendix II. below, pp. 348–351, " Rabbinic Parallels and the Gospels."

to observe the Levitical laws of purity at their meals." [1]
If they were so exclusive, it is strange that the Pharisees
represented the bulk of the law-observing Jews.[2] The
Pharisees seem more accurately placed by describing
them as " a small minority superlatively embodying a
certain tendency of thought and practice in the Judaism
of Jesus' day, but neither officially nor unofficially in
control of the situation." [3] Jesus' own remarks to them
show that the Pharisees could be opposed or gainsaid or
even sharply criticized, both in public and in private.
Further, there seem to have been degrees of Pharisaism
according to whether more or less rigid forms of tradition
were followed (Acts xxvi. 5). They did not form a
rigid society as did the Essenes, a body which had little
influence on Judaism, and still less on the Christian
Church.[4] The Sadducees were the nobility of Jerusalem,
in charge of the external religious affairs of the nation,
but not typical of the Judaism of their time, nor of any
other time for that matter.

We are, therefore, left with the great mass of the
people who in a general way looked up to the religious
leaders, and regarded their theorizing with respect,
though making little pretence to follow their traditions.
These were the *Am ha-aretz*, the ordinary folk of the
land. Everywhere we see humble family hearths, where
sincere men, faithful to the requirements of the law of
Moses, looked forward to better times. They were
looking for the advent of a new Elijah, at whose powerful
words the spirit of the nation, rent as it was by con-
tending passions, and in rebellion against God, would

---

[1] K. Kohler, *The Origins of Synagogue and Church*, p. 109.
[2] *Ibid*. p. 110.
[3] W. R. Arnold, " The Relation of Primitive Christianity to Jewish
Thought and Teaching," *Harv. Theol. Rev.* vol. xxiii. p. 169.
[4] Dr. Kohler's ingenious attempt to derive Christianity from the
Essenes is not convincing, *op. cit.*

4

be changed. These common people nourished their piety on the simpler requirements of the Old Testament Covenant and the devotion of the psalms. For them, the norm and inspiration were the synagogues rather than the Temple, the Old Testament rather than the elaborate Pharisaic interpretation of it. The types of this more lowly piety are seen in Zacharias and his wife, righteous before God (Luke i. 6); Mary the Jewish maiden finding favour in God's sight (Luke i. 28) ; Joseph, her betrothed, devout and righteous (Matt. i. 19) ; Simeon awaiting the hope of Israel ; and Anna serving God day and night (Luke ii. 34, 36 f.). There were many more like them, both in Galilee and in Judæa, who frequented the synagogues, fed their aspirations on prophets and psalms, awaited the salvation of Israel when He who was to appear should come (Luke xxiv. 21 ; cf. i. 68, ii. 38 ; Acts i. 6), and from whose ranks emerged Jesus, His disciples, and finally the primitive Church.

Galilee was notorious for its militant Messianism. Pilate was finding the Galileans so troublesome that he had to discover a pretext for putting many of them to death during a festival (Luke xiii. 1). One Messianic claimant at least had revealed himself with results catastrophic both to himself and to his clamouring followers (Acts v. 37). It is significant that the fatal rebellion which resulted in the overthrow of Jerusalem and in the ruin of the Holy Temple had some of its origin in the activity of John of Gischala,[1] who, fleeing from his condemned Galilean town, escaped to Jerusalem, there to inspire the fanatical enthusiasms which were to prove so disastrous.

The place and power of apocalyptic in the outlook of the Jews, and especially of the Galileans, is all-important

[1] Jos. *De Bell. J.* iv. 2, 1-4, 3, 1-2.

for the understanding of the primitive Church. The Old Testament provided many of the germinal conceptions,[1] but the movement as such had its real driving origin in the period of trial prior to the Maccabæan revolt when the Book of Daniel was written to fortify the faithful in view of impending persecution.[2] The significant literary and theological movement thus begun in Judaism reached its climax in the Book of Revelation, which encouraged the Christians to stand firm in the persecution resulting from their refusal to acquiesce in Cæsar worship. Amidst this development there emerged the Christian Church.

The psychology of fantasy, with its principle of compensation for evils in the creation of symbols and images expressive of overwhelming victory, is inadequate to account for the power and prevalence of apocalyptic. We may, of course, point to the hardships suffered in the persecution of Antiochus, and readily recognize the disillusionment experienced by Israel after the Exile, when the hopes raised by the Unknown Prophet of the Exile faded away into one bitter disappointment after another. Yet none of these circumstances warrant the conclusion that the average religious mind was only able to discover refuge in fantasy which, " in the dire crisis of the national religious life when the first apocalypses were written, took the form of visions of immortal triumph." [3]

Fantasy is of the realm of psychical reality over against actual reality, and it influences the formation of symptoms in neurosis. The habit of creating fantasy is begun in childhood ; the child reproduces in his individual experiences the true experience of the human race as a

[1] R. H. Charles, *Eschatology*, 1899, chs. i.–iv.
[2] W. Fairweather, *The Background of the Gospels*, 3rd edn. 1920, pp. 95 ff., 219 ff.
[3] Dougall and Emmet, *The Lord of Thought*, 1922, p. 14 f.

whole in its prehistoric experiences. Fantasy enshrines
the history of childhood much as every race weaves
myths about its forgotten early history.[1] On psychological grounds, therefore, we should expect the Jews,
in their desire for psychical refuge from stern reality,
to go back to the past history of their race and find
compensation for contemporary tribulation in the ethnic
and national epics of the agelong past. On the contrary,
however, the essence of apocalyptic is the ardent expectation of a future consummation, accompanied with
fervent, unshakable convictions of ultimate triumph.
Further, fantasy is due mainly to the operation of unconscious processes,[2] but apocalyptic vision is often
consciously motived and indulged in. The faith of
apocalyptic is too deeply rooted to be explained by the
categories of fantasy. Such an inadequate view of the
origin of apocalyptic implies that it was due to individual
and collective subconscious neurosis. The apocalyptic
neurosis of Israel's national life arose through the painful
experience of continual frustration of their highest
hopes. The pain was repressed and buried deeply
within the subconscious mind ; it found compensation
in acute neurotic symptoms such as visions of overwhelming triumph, the very reverse of the actual reality
of unutterable servitude to Gentile powers. The more
stern the experience of the actual reality, the more
fantastic were the compensations in psychical reality.
In view, however, of the incessant disillusionment and
subjection, if the psychological theorizing were the true
explanation, there should rightly take place a psycho-

[1] Freud, *Introductory Lectures on Psycho-Analysis*, Eng. Tr. 1922,
pp. 308 ff.

[2] We are not here thinking of day-dreams, which are fantasies
" in their most conscious phase " (Hadfield, *Psychology and Morals*,
1923, p. 53), but the main ones, which result from the subconscious
mind.

logical breakdown altogether, leaving Israel a broken people seeking complete refuge in fantasy and still more fantasy.   But this is not Israel as history reveals the nation, for there was never any breakdown, since Israel preserved its faith in God, unshakable and sure, all through its experiences.

Not to the delusions of fantasy-making as compensatory of evil must we turn to account for the rise and power of apocalyptic, but to religious experience of a noble intensity, motived by deep-rooted faith in the living God.   Such faith, with its worship and obedience to holy law and precept, convinced Israel that God never failed His people in their need, and that if He ever did so, it would be because of their sin and infidelity.   The phrase of George Tyrrell, " the truth value of vision," [1] is more to the purpose than explanations along the lines of psychological neurosis.   We may allow for any elements of unwholesomeness in apocalyptic in so far as these drifted away from human and historic conditions, or as luxuriant imagination was allowed to be in control irrespective of true religious insight.   It is more probable that the psychology of apocalyptic will get nearer the truth by exploring the psychology of vision with its subjective-objective medium of discovery, and the possibilities it possesses as a channel of truth for the human spirit.

Apocalyptic vision with its picture thinking, its fervent symbolism and luxuriant imagery, finds its real value and truth in the religious experience of which these outward signs are the varied and luxuriant material and colour of their external dress.   Apocalyptic truth does not lie in its characteristic visionary-ecstatic form, but in its religious import, and in its moral and spiritual content as such.   Much of the symbolism is no more than

[1] *Christianity at the Cross-Roads*, 1909, p. 105.

literary device and embellishment, much as a poet adorns
his verse with a luxuriance of decorative imagery. We
have, therefore, to think back to the religious convictions which all the symbols and images seek to express
and to interpret.

It may be largely true that the Old Testament
prophets were mainly preachers of righteousness, but
for their contemporaries the final test of the worth of
prophecy was whether it conformed to actual historical
events. In actual fact, many prophetic promises were
never fulfilled, and their non-fulfilment set up an acute
problem for faith. Some effort had to be made to solve
this real difficulty of Israel's religious experience, and
this took the form of making new prophecies of the
apocalyptic sort which again differed from the older
prophecies in that they aimed at reconciling the golden
promises of the future with the evils of the actual present.
For instance, Ezekiel reinterprets the predictions of
Jeremiah (i. 15, v. 15, vi. 22) and Zephaniah (i. 10 ff.)
which declare that Judah will be invaded from the
north. This foe never showed itself, and the prophecies
were thus unfulfilled. Ezekiel restates them by stating
that " Gog," *i.e.* a mighty company, will one day invade
Jerusalem from the north (xxxviii. 8, 16), and declares that
this is the foe which the earlier prophets foretold (ver. 17).

The sharpest problem raised by the non-fulfilment of
prophecy was the failure of the consummation of the
Messianic Kingdom. Despite Jeremiah's prophecy of
Israel's restoration blessed with the Messianic Kingdom
(xxv. 12, xxix. 10), Ezekiel's elaborate promises of
reconstruction (xl.–xlviii.), the predictions of Haggai
and Zechariah that the rebuilding of the Temple would
usher in the Kingdom (i. 8, ii. 6–9, 20–23 ; Zech. iii.
7–10, vi. 12 f.), the Kingdom did not come. This disappointment had continually to be reinterpreted, and the

Books of Daniel and Enoch (lxxxiii.–xc.) clothe the dead bones of disappointment with the living flesh of apocalyptic expectation as they pronounce the imminence of the Kingdom. Yet the Kingdom still tarried, and the years pass by until we reach the primitive Church which was to enter upon this hope in an enthusiasm inspired by the resurrection and exaltation of Jesus.

The religious environment of the primitive Church was highly coloured by these apocalyptic hopes. While it may not be clear how far they influenced the contemporary outlook of the Jews, it is against the facts to conclude that " the apocalyptic writings lie for the most part outside the line of the purest Jewish development, and often present but the fringe or excrescence, and not the real substance of the dominating religious thought. The fact that the originals of those which were written in Hebrew or Aramaic are nearly all lost partly shows that they had no deep hold on the people, or were off the beaten track of the official religion." [1] One reply to this understatement is that at least there is the Book of Daniel, which itself is an apocalyptic document, and found its way into the Old Testament canon. To this important extent apocalyptic is recognized even by official Judaism. Further, the fact that the apocalyptic writings were translated into other languages is a tribute to their influence and importance, for such translations would be needed for the Jews out in the wider world ; there must have been a demand for the translations, and thus there was definite apocalyptic influence among the Hellenistic Jews. The disappearance of Hebrew or Aramaic originals is not sufficient to indicate that these had no hold on the Jews any more than the disappearance

---

[1] C. G. Montefiore, *Hibbert Lectures*, 1892, p. 467. Much the same position is maintained in his article, " Contemporary Jewish Religion," *P.C.* pp. 618, 624.

of the original Aramaic gospel tradition proves that such tradition had no hold on the primitive Church. As the Gospels were written in Greek to meet the wider needs of the growing Church, so the apocalyptic translations were made to meet the demands for them in the Diaspora. Finally, if apocalyptic be no more than on the fringe of Judaism, how are we to account for its presence in the outlook of Jesus, of His many followers, and of the primitive Church ?

The probability is that no intelligent Jew could have been ignorant of the apocalyptic literature nor unaware of its influential ideas disseminated everywhere. Every pious Jew loved to meditate on the divine justice and on the divine power which guaranteed that justice assumed in the apocalypses. Apocalyptic writings gained so prevalent an influence that the Jewish Rabbis ultimately banned as heresy all belief in a supernatural catastrophe and its accompanying eschatological ideas. Would it have been necessary for official Judaism to proceed to so drastic a measure if apocalyptic had not become dangerously powerful, as the Rabbis supposed ?

We have now to review the leading religious ideas in apocalyptic which have significance for the religious experience of the primitive Church. First, there is the expectation of the Kingdom of God, and this assumes several aspects.

(a) The Kingdom is to be set up on earth under the direct rule of God ; the members of it are to be the righteous Israelites. The blessings of the new era are spiritually conceived, but the expectations of material good are not absent. From this prophetic conception every subsequent development is due to apocalyptic thought. The everlasting Kingdom is set up on earth following the divine judgment at Mount Sinai to which

God comes with myriads of His holy ones (En. i.). Or
the scene is the New Jerusalem on earth (En. xc. 28 f.).
The Judgment is unfavourable to the undeserving
(En. xiii., xxi. 1 f., xc. 26 ; T.S. vi. 6 ; T.L. iii. 2).
For the deserving, both the living and the dead raised
to life, there is to be a blissful life on an earth that has
been cleansed, with many material blessings, and the
enjoyment of God's favour and presence, while there
is to be no more sin (En. x. 17–xi. 2). The risen
righteous become like Messiah (En. xc. 33 ff.). This
may be called the "sensuous" conception of the
Kingdom. The Gentiles left after the Judgment become
righteous, and are found among those who praise and
worship God (En. x. 21); they have opportunity to
repent (En. l. 2), the surviving are converted and make
spontaneous submission to Israel; thus Israel becomes
the channel for the redemption of the Gentiles (En. xc.
30–34). The "sensuous" Kingdom therefore finds a
place for the Gentiles especially in the noble universalism of the author of the Testaments of the Twelve
Patriarchs ; unlike the author of Jubilees, who taught
that there was absolutely no hope for Gentiles, he
was a true scion of the larger-hearted prophets, boldly
proclaiming the salvation of the non-Jews.[1]

(b) The Kingdom is also thought of as being on
earth, but it is to be of temporary duration only. It
emerges in the eighth world-week, when sinners are
handed over to the righteous for destruction (En. xci.
12 ff.). The righteous acquire houses and a temple is
built (En. xci. 13). The righteous judgment is revealed
to the world in the ninth week, and the Judgment takes

---

[1] Cf. Jub. xv. 31, xxx. 7–17, with T.L. iv. 4, viii. 14, ii. 11 ; T.S.
vi. 5 ; T.N. viii. 3 ; T.Ash. vii. 3 ; T.D. vi. 7 ; T.J. xxv. 5 ; T.B.
ix. 2, x. 5. God understands all men (T.N. ii. 5), and the law is given
to lighten every man (T.L. xiv. 4).

effect during the tenth week.   Earth and heaven depart, and a new heaven appears (En. xci. 14–17).   The righteous arise from their sleep (ver. 10), and the wicked are cast into Sheol for evermore (En. ciii. 7 f.).   There are Messianic woes prior to the advent of the Kingdom, according to the Book of Jubilees, where heaven and earth are conceived to be gradually renewed condition-ally upon man's nature being spiritually transformed (i. 26, 29, iv. 26, xxiii. 13 f.).   But it is not here clear whether the Kingdom is eternal or ends with the Judg-ment (xxiii. 30), and the same uncertainty appears in the Psalms of Solomon with its vital Messianic hope. The temporal Kingdom is foreshadowed in the As-sumption of Moses, and even more clearly in the Apocalypse of Baruch (A.D. 50–70) where the King-dom exists for the time being, and endures until "the world of corruption" is at an end (xl. 3, lxxiii. 1), being "sensuous" in idea (xxix. 4 f.).   Messiah returns to heaven (xxx. 1) and "the consummation of the times" comes with the Day of Judgment (xxx. 3, lix. 8, liv. 15).

(c) At this point the idea of the eternal hereafter appears in the Kingdom not of this world.   In some minds the temporal Kingdom leads on to eternal life for the righteous, but the pessimists give up the idea of the Messianic Kingdom on earth, and reach out in hope to the Kingdom which is really " a Hereafter on the earth, so much so that after some modification it is resolved into a Hereafter proper."[1]   The Apocalypse of Baruch is the best exposition of the view which gives up the world as hopeless ; a world is to appear which shall not die (xx. 2, xxiii. 7, xxv., li. 3).

(d) There was further the idea of the Kingdom as temporal, and its exact duration was calculated on the

[1] T. Walker, *The Teaching of Jesus and the Teaching of His Age*, 1923, pp. 99 f.

basis of the seventy years which Jeremiah announced would elapse before the divine rule would be established (xxix. 10). The Books of Daniel and Enoch (lxxxiii.-xc.) are the chief exponents of this view. The Book of the Secrets of Enoch develops the millennium theory which was to become so popular in after years. The world was created in six days, each day a thousand years (Ps. xc. 4), the seventh day being the duration of the temporal Kingdom, now viewed as the Millennium. The Day of Judgment follows, the righteous go to their reward in Paradise, while the wicked are cast into hell. Thus begins the eighth day of eternal blessedness when time should be no more (xxxiii. 1).

Such were some of the ideas of the Kingdom contemporary with Jesus and the primitive Church. There is diversity of outlook, but in all instances the eschatological setting of the Kingdom is very striking. There was also the fervent nationalistic consciousness so vital for the conception of the future golden age. Political liberation and triumph on the one hand, and religious and moral regeneration on the other, are the two aspects involved, as they " run into each other and blend like the two overlapping edges of two clouds." [1]

The second influential idea in apocalyptic which is significant for the primitive Church is that of the Messiah. We need to guard against confusing the personal Messiah with the broader conception of the Messianic era, and taking predictions as Messianic where no personal Messiah is mentioned nor even assumed. In many prophets where the Day of the Lord is foretold, the Messiah finds no place ; he is not mentioned in Daniel nor in eschatological writings such as Isaiah xxiv.-xxvii. The same surprising characteristic is shown in the non-canonical literature, for no Messiah appears in

[1] G. F. Moore, *op. cit.* vol. ii. p. 324.

certain sections of the Book of Enoch, in the Book of
the Secrets of Enoch, in the Books of the Maccabees,
nor in many other works.

The Messiah appears with the Kingdom as a figure-
head only in Enoch lxxxiii.–xc., but in another section
of that book (xxxvii.–lxxi.) we come across a series of
ideas which are significant. The personal Messiah
appears not as a scion of earth nor even of the idealized
Davidic dynasty, but as a supernatural being. The
Messiah is the " Anointed One," *i.e.* the " Christ," and
thus the title which had hitherto been applied to
patriarchs, priests, prophets, kings, and to Israel as
the anointed nation for God's purpose, is now ascribed
for the first time to the Messiah in his ideal, suprahuman dignity in association with the advent of the
divine Kingdom (En. xlviii. 10. lii. 4). He is the
" Righteous One," a title which indicates his nature,
and is significant in being applied by the primitive
Church to Jesus (En. xxxviii. 2, liii. 6 ; Acts iii. 14, vii. 52).
The Messiah is further the " Elect One," a title applied
in this way for the first time, and also significant for
the primitive Church designation of Jesus (En. xl. 5,
xlv. 3 f., cf. Luke ix. 35, xxiii. 35). Finally, the Messiah
is the " Son of Man," a distinct personal designation.
The demonstrative " this " and " that " Son of Man
which occasionally occurs in place of the usual article
" the " is due to the Ethiopian translator who renders
the Greek article by the demonstratives as well as by
the article.[1] Such linguistic data are sufficiently strong
to induce Dalman to resort to the desperate device of

---

[1] En. xlvi. 2 f., xlviii. 2, lxii. 9, 14, etc. The Ethiopic is the extant
version from which our knowledge of this section is mainly derived ;
the Greek version from which the Ethiopic was made is in itself a
translation from either Hebrew or Aramaic. Cf. Charles, *A. and P.*
vol. ii. pp. 173 ff. The linguistic data tell against the view that the
title means no more than " man."

excising the references to the Son of Man as interpolations,[1] for they point definitely to the personal Messiah as known among his distinctive titles by the appellation, the " Son of Man."

The Messiah is viewed elsewhere as a descendant from Levi, a scion of priestly stock, being, in fact, a priest Himself (T.R. vi. 7–12 ; T.L. viii. 14 ; T.J. xxiv. 1 ff.). Here is no suprahuman being, but a doughty warrior against Israel's enemies (T.R. vi. 12 ; T.D. v. 10). He is free from sin, has power over evil spirits, and the highest ethical qualities such as meekness and righteousness are ascribed to Him. He is the mediator for the Gentiles (T.J. xxiv. 1 ; T.L. xviii. 12, viii. 14). In the Psalms of Solomon the Messiah springs from the conventional Davidic dynasty, having special power and endowment from God, being a righteous king, taught of God, pure from sin, and purging Jerusalem from sin. He is the " Anointed One," *i.e.* the " Christ," but in the human sense only (xvii. 23–25, 32, 33, 36, 41, xviii. 6, 8).

From these sporadic intimations of Messiah's personality two strains of thought emerge. There is the " human " Messiah, the wholly righteous representative of God's will. Strictly subordinate to God, His primary duty is to achieve for Israel political supremacy over all the nations ; hence His advent is heralded by wars and rumours of war. The result will be a reign of universal peace in the Kingdom of God on earth. The second series of ideas centred upon the Messiah as " suprahuman " or " heavenly " in essence, a divine personality who emerges from His pre-existent condition, no one knows how. He is indeed " supra-angelic," for angels are His ministers, and He is almost on an equality with God. Things are to become as evil as they may be, when the heavenly Messiah will intervene, and at the close of

[1] *The Words of Jesus*, Eng. Tr. 1909, pp. 269 f.

the age He will set up the Judgment as He acts directly for God. There are not, of course, two Messiahs, but rather two conceptions of Messiah which to some extent overlap each other, for suprahuman qualities are sometimes ascribed to the human, and human ones to the suprahuman Messiah.

In these apocalyptic references to the Messiah there are no associations of suffering with His personality. Whether viewed as human or suprahuman, or a mixture of both, His character is regal throughout, and suffering could never be associated with one so majestic, triumphant, and princely in Himself.

The Messiah is sometimes regarded as being heralded by His forerunner, and He will carry into effect what His herald has announced in His name (Frag. Zad. i. 7, ii. 10, viii. 2, ix. 10, 29, xv. 4, xviii. 8). The prevalent belief was that this forerunner would be Elijah risen from the dead, an apocalyptic idea we see reflected in the gospels (Mal. iii. 1–3 ; Mark i. 2, viii. 28).

The religious expectations inherent in all these Messianic hopes are vital for the primitive Church. It is not essential " to make a picture out of the dissected puzzle of prophecy or out of the eschatological nightmares of the apocalypses." [1] Apocalyptic religious experience is rooted and grounded in the idea of a plan of God operative in the history of the world, evoking the ardent faith that God will carry out His plan to the uttermost. As for anything else, its value lay in that, through imaginary presentation, men were helped to reality for their faith. The cardinal expectation that history has its divine significance is a religious discovery motived by moral and spiritual insight which was to find its sublimest expression in the emergence of the primitive Church and its central faith in Jesus the Messiah.

[1] G. F. Moore, *op. cit.* vol. ii. p. 323.

The third significant element bequeathed to the Church prior to Paul by apocalyptic lies in ideas of resurrection far more advanced than anything given to us in the Old Testament. This latter source presents a slow, hesitating development of the idea, and where it occurs in any clear measure it is in connection with eschatological expectations (Isa. xxvi. 1–19 ; Dan. xii. 2). Under the influence of apocalyptic the ideas of resurrection become more definite. A bodily resurrection is announced in positive, decided terms (cf. 2 Macc. vii, 11, xiv. 46). The earth gives up the body even as Sheol surrenders the soul, and the united body and soul are judged in their oneness (En. li. 1). On the other hand, the bodily resurrection is as definitely and as decisively rejected by other writers in favour of a spiritual resurrection (En. xci.–civ.). This conception attains its most beautiful expression in the Book of Jubilees (xxiii. 31) ; the souls of the righteous enjoy a blessed immortality after death. The Wisdom of Solomon expresses in poetic thought the same expectation (iii. 1–9). A third type of resurrection finds literary expression prior to the Fall of Jerusalem, and is therefore later than the primitive Church, but the belief may well have been held long before its literary statement. The righteous arise with their bodies exactly as they were committed to the tomb, to facilitate recognition, but thereafter the risen bodies will be transformed and made like unto the angels (2 Bar. xlix. 2–li.). A further development of this is seen in Josephus, who states that the Pharisees held that the righteous rise in a body wholly different from the present material one (B.J. ii. 8, 14).

Those who viewed the divine Kingdom in the " sensuous " way were likely to regard resurrection as being of the actual, material body. The more spiritual ideas of the Kingdom carried with them corresponding spiritual forms of the resurrection hope. Even with the bodily resurrection, the risen body becomes a transfigured one, a body of light, for the righteous (En. lxii. 15 f.). In which of these forms did the primitive Church construe their experience of the resurrection of Jesus, or in what combination of such forms ?

The fourth element in the apocalyptic environment of the primitive Church was the " angels," the inhabitants of the spirit world and potent for human life as messengers of God. We have here not so much the " angel of Yahweh " of the Old Testament, a simple theophany of Yahweh in a form that could be apprehended by the human eye ; what we have is rather a multitude of suprahuman beings, probably non-ethical in character, forming the court of the divine majesty of God. The imposing celestial hierarchy which we view in apocalyptic literature may have entered the thought of Israel through Persian influence,[1] but it may be no more than a parallel growth on Old Testament lines through the advance of eschatological ideas. There are fiery troops of great archangels, incorporeal forces, dominions, cherubim and seraphim, thrones and many-eyed ones (Secr. En. xx. 1) ; there is the " angel of the presence " (Tob. xii. 15 ; Jub. i. 27, ii. 2 ; T.J. xxv. 2) ; the nations have their guardian angels (Dan. x. 13, 20 f.) ; other angels are " watchers " (Secr. En. xviii. 1 ; En. xii. 4 ; Dan. iv. 13, 17) ; some have individual names such as Michael, Gabriel, Raphael, etc., each one with his distinctive sphere of authority (En. xx. 3, 5, 7, xl. 9 ; Tob. xii. 15). These celestials were often the mediators of God's will to man (T.D. vi. 2 ; Tob. xii. 15).

The angelic atmosphere meets us in the outlook of Jesus and of the primitive Church. God utilizes angels as His messengers to men, as in dreams (Matt. i. 20,

---

[1] W. Fairweather, *HDB.* extra vol. p. 287.

ii. 13, 19), or in vision (Luke ii. 9, xxiv. 23). They announce Jesus' birth (Luke ii. 9), minister to Jesus in the desert (Mark i. 13), or open a prison door (Acts v. 19). Jesus says that twelve legions of them are at His disposal, thus showing how realistically He shared in the outlook of His age (Matt. xxvi. 53). The angels are to accompany Messiah in His advent, being reapers at the end of all things (Matt. xiii. 39, 41, 49), or sent on beforehand to herald His appearance (Matt. xxiv. 31). The individual has his guardian angel (Matt. xviii. 10 ; cf. Jub. xxxv. 17), and this reveals a further stage in the apocalyptic emphasis on the individual. In the next life the risen are as the angels (Mark. xii. 25) ; Peter's friends, hearing his voice, think it is the voice of his angel, i.e. of his departed personality (Acts xii. 15).

The fifth significant element in the religious environment of the Church before Paul, derived from apocalyptic influence, is the place and power of the belief in demons. A great change came over Jewish faith after the Exile, in that God was conceived to be more and more transcendent, using hosts of angels as His mediators ; in the same way God seemed the more removed from evil, and human suffering and sin were accounted for by demonic agency. The deep-rooted despair of better things apart from divine intervention encouraged the belief in evil spirits as responsible for the evils, whose power was to be broken by the advent of the divine Kingdom. Thus the empirical link between the advent of the Kingdom and the overthrow of the demons was forged in the prevailing faith.

We are amidst a sort of practical dualism based not on philosophy, but on the perplexed findings of a religious experience which, knowing God as the source of goodness and moral worth, ascribed contemporary evil to the intervention of spiritual powers hostile to

5

that source.   Faith had, however, discerned the ultimate victory to be with God.

The demons may be conceived as fallen angels (En. xix. 1), defiling men and leading them into error. Angelic " Watchers " came down to earth to instruct men in righteousness (Jub. iv. 15), but they fell from their celestial dignity by lusting after the daughters of men (Jub. iv. 22, v. 1–9) ; children were born of these unions, the giants, and from their souls went forth spirits that were evil, called demons (Jub. v. 7, 9). These evil spirits corrupt, and finally destroy, the wicked (Jub. x. 2, 6).   At their head is Mastema, or Satan, or Beelzebub, the prince of demons (Jub. x. 8 f.). The work of moral ruin goes on until the prince receives judgment prior to the advent of the Kingdom (Jub. x. 8), or until the Kingdom actually appears in the triumph of God.   Then the prince's power, as that of his myrmidons, will be no more (Jub. xxiii. 29).

While evil spirits are mainly concerned with inciting men to sin (En. lxix. 4, 6), they may vex them with all manner of diseases (Jub. x. 10–12).   They charge men before God with the very misdoings which they themselves have tempted them to do (En. xl. 7), and punish them in various ways (En. liii. 3).   They are largely in control of the air, the abode of spirits, good and evil alike (Secr. En. xxix. 5 ; cf. Eph. ii. 2).   The demons and their demon king rule the world as it is (Mar. Is. ii. 4 ; Asc. Is. x. 29 ; En. liv. 6), and are responsible for the infliction of the human experience of death (Wis. ii. 24 ; Tob. iii. 8 ; En. lxix. 11).

These evil spirits, however, have a limit set to their baneful activities.   The divine Kingdom may come at any time and then the demons are to be destroyed (Jub. xxiii. 29 f.) ; the undoing of demonic influence is a sure sign the Kingdom approaches.

Fear of evil spirits is intense within the religious background of the primitive Church. The plague of demon-possession hangs about everywhere. Jesus came with His proclamation of the imminence of the Kingdom, and His words were attested by the defeat of demons wherever He met their victims.

One experiential principle that is clearly discerned amid the maze of angelology and demonology is the conviction that human life, whether viewed as " personality " or as " self " was readily accessible to the invasive influences of what we to-day would call " supernatural." Here we have the point of departure for the experience of the Spirit so pronounced in the primitive Church. There was no distinction made between the " natural " and the " supernatural " such as modern thought makes, and the transition from " ruach," the actual wind, to " ruach," the windlike energy of good or evil spirits, was easily made. Thus " spirit," taking its start from the actual wind that bloweth where it listeth, receives an inspirational content where the spirit of Yahweh is responsible for abnormal human character or conduct (Judg. xiv. 6 ; 1 Sam. xvi. 15 ; Isa. xi. 2). The term also denotes the principle of life, not dissimilar from the " breath-soul " (*nephesh*), which may include the psychical aspect of human consciousness (2 Kings i. 13 ; Job. xvi. 4). The " Spirit " in human personality, that energy which makes a man a living soul, is " holy spirit," lent as it were for the period of human life, and to be returned to the Creator unspoiled (Test. XII. Patr., App. i. 10, 9). Men may defile their " holy spirit " which has been entrusted to them in their life (Frag. Zad. vii. 12, viii. 20 ; cf. 1 Cor. vi. 19). It is not that the Spirit of God is identified with the spirit in man ; the apparent coalescence suggests no more than the close empirical connection between the two, the latter being so readily accessible to the invasion of the former.

The divine energy described as " holy spirit " operates upon and through human personality ; [1] since such activity had abnormal results in human life, the abnormal phenomena disclosed came in themselves to denote the presence within of the spirit. Normal behaviour did not need any such explanation, but Joseph's extraordinary powers of dream-interpretation caused Pharaoh to refer to him as one in whom the spirit of God was (Gen. xli. 38). Daniel becomes prominent in the court of Nebuchadnezzar, and his genius is accounted for in that he has the spirit of the holy gods in him (Dan. iv. 8, 18). Remarkable craftsmanship (Ex. xxxi. 3 f.), abnormal enhancement of physical strength (Judg. xiii. 25, xiv. 6, xv. 14), success in war (Judg. iii. 10), are all due to the invasive energy of the Spirit. Saul is to become " another " man in the sense of being above the ordinary man, when the Spirit comes on him, and the same power causes the non-ethical frenzy of the same man in an abnormal state of mind (1 Sam. x. 6, 10–12). This power causes conduct that baffles calculation (1 Kings xviii, 7 ff.), and frustrates purposes which thus work out in a way not intended (Num. xxii. 21–35, xxiv. 2 ff.). The " Spirit " invades prophets and accounts for their abnormal condition and insight (Ezek. ii. 2, 3 ff., iii. 12, 14, xi. 1, 5, 24) ; visions, dreams, and the like are symptoms of the same control (Joel ii. 28 f. ; cf. En. lxx. 2). Abnormal wisdom and understanding are ascribed to the same source (2 Chron. xv. 1 ; Neh. ix. 20). Of Israel's coming Deliverer it is said that the spirit of the Lord shall rest upon him, for there is no other way of explaining His remarkable qualities

[1] Cf. H. Gunkel, *Die Wirkungen des heiligen Geistes*, 1909, p. 5. There are very few exceptions to this principle.

(Isa. xi. 2). The Creator plants His "sweet" spirit to guide mortals (Sib. Frag. i. 5, 6) ; Ezra prays for inspiration to restore the Scriptures by saying, "Send into me the Holy Spirit" (4 Ezra xiv. 22) ; extraordinary wisdom and ability would be needed for such a duty, and the Spirit's indwelling would guarantee this. Messiah derives His extraordinary dignity and power from the same indwelling (En. xlix. 3). It is by His activities as apprehended in human experience that Messiah will be recognized. The extraordinary evidences of His power and authority as He comes in the judgment will be due to the operation of the Spirit within His personality. Jesus made this empirical connection as He read in the synagogue and astounded His hearers by applying to Himself the words beginning, "The Spirit of the Lord is upon Me . . ." (Luke iv. 18 f., quoting Isa. lxi. 1 f.). Indeed, this was afterwards the only way of explaining His uniqueness by those who saw and heard (Luke iv. 1). There is thus a definite empirical link between the experience of the Spirit and the coming Kingdom of God. Messiah's powers are inspired by the Spirit to enable Him to bring in the Kingdom, which in itself was the supremely extraordinary event which Israel awaited. In so far as the Kingdom was connected with Messiah, its advent was due to the energy of the Spirit which inspired the Deliverer ; inasmuch as the Kingdom was conceived apart from Messiah bringing it into being, the Spirit produced the abnormal effects in human life which made the advent of the Kingdom inevitable, or was the actual moving energy which brought it about at last. Thus the divine energy known as the Spirit of God was vitally linked up in religious experience with the expectation of the new age.

This empirical deduction is further strengthened in that nothing is more striking than the fact that the normal, matter-of-fact life is never regarded as being due to the Spirit's presence. The normal did not call for explanation. The instances where wisdom is cited as being due to the Spirit may seem to be exceptions to this principle,[1] but such ethical characteristics appeared abnormal and unique when viewed alongside the usual conduct and character of men. In the Book of Sirach, which treats almost entirely of moral conduct and ordinary living, there is no reference to the Spirit as the creative source of this manner of life. The time was not yet when another great Jew was to formulate the energy of the Spirit as the dynamic behind the normal conduct of godly living. This discoverer was Paul, and the primitive Church came between the discoveries of his religious experience in Christ and the circles of religious experience we are investigating.

We therefore carry forward to the study of the religious experience of the primitive Church some significant empirical data with regard to the human appropriation of the Spirit. (1) The Spirit is approached by way of living experience rather than by any system of teaching which is nowhere found in Jewish literature. The phrase of Pfleiderer, " traditional teaching," as applied to the Spirit, is misleading and unhistorical, for there was no such thing. (2) The Spirit's operation is known almost exclusively through human experience as the divine energy invading and dominating human personality. (3) The presence of the Spirit is detected by specific phenomena in human life, by " symptoms " which call attention to the overmastering power that was in possession. (4) The phenomena, symptoms, or effects, are of an abnormal and extraordinary character,

[1] Cf. H. Gunkel, *op. cit.* p. 9.   Cf. 2 Cor. xv. 1 ; Neh. ix. 20 ; Isa. xi. 2, xxviii. 6, xxxii. 15 ff., lxi. 1 ff. ; Wis. ix. 17 ; En. xlix. 3, lxii. 2 ; T.L. ii. 3.

and lead to the conclusion that they are due to the Spirit's presence. (5) The ordinary conduct of men, the ethical or religious life as such, were not ascribed to the Spirit's activity in human personality. (6) The Spirit was the active agency in the creation of human life, and is sometimes regarded as the channel for the existence of the human spirit. Here we see a close relationship with the human spirit so easily accessible to the invasive power of the divine Spirit. (7) The Spirit was conceived to be the energy operative in Messiah's personality, equipping Him with the extraordinary powers and authority needed for His office. (8) The Spirit was the divine power behind the advent of the Kingdom.

The term " corporate personality " [1] as applied to the social solidarity of Israel as a religious unit, although not free from objection, denotes phenomena in religious experience which are central to the nation's faith. It is difficult to conceive of a group possessing personality *per se*, while the word " corporate " would be better replaced by " social." " Social personality " is open to the objection that it is all too easy to associate with the group the characteristics we discern in individual personality.

The distinctive feature of a social unit such as Israel is " solidarity," and the phenomena presented are better described as " social solidarity." At all events, the lack of any ideas of personal resurrection, or of any individual life after death, reveals a defective awareness of individuality. The individual person was thought of and treated as merged in the wider social solidarity of family or clan or nation, whether related to man or to

[1] H. W. Robinson, *The Christian Doctrine of Man*, 2nd edn. 1913, pp. 27–30.

God. The nation as a whole was the religious unit. The breach of taboo is punished by the death not only of the culprit but of all his family (Josh. vii. 24–26), since the family is regarded as one unit. There was no thought of injustice to the innocent members, for all were implicated by social solidarity in the sin of the head, the complete logic of which is seen in the principle, " the sins of the fathers are visited upon the children," which was later to be challenged by the noble individualism of Jeremiah (xxxi. 29) and Ezekiel (xviii. 2 f.). The basis of the Mosaic covenant (Ex. xix. 5 f., Deut. xxvi. 17 f.) is that God chooses the people in their solidarity as the nation set apart for Himself, and this solidarity was never really broken even with the growth of individualism in later times ; the individualism that was the basis of the new covenant of Jeremiah (xxxi. 31 f.) was purely within the limits of the social-religious unit known as Israel ; the Gentiles were to be redeemed, but by conversion to this social-religious unit, Israel, the unified people of God.

Human personality consists of " body " and " soul " or " spirit." In the few cases where a trichotomy, " body," " soul," and " spirit," may possibly be detected, " the writers have not, in their thought, entered the period of the apocalyptists," [1] who seem to make no distinction between " spirit " and " soul." The Hebrew notion of personality as " body and soul," or " body and spirit," persists in apocalyptic without any suggestions of Greek dualism which sets the soul over against the body in an ethical struggle.

As the idea of resurrection and immortality gained ground, moral individualism grew more prominent. Individual retribution for transgressors implies that moral personality is being ascribed to the individual

[1] T. Walker, op. cit. p. 185.

member of Israel.   Men enter the portals of the next world not as a social or national unit, but one by one. The Messianic Kingdom is corporate in its conception, yet the tendency towards the recognition of the individual was none the less significant of the liberating influence of the belief in personal resurrection.

We have surveyed the experiential inheritance and religious environment of the primitive Church.   Within this amalgam, with its many-sided expression and development, there emerged the primitive Church with its distinctive inspiration in the life and personality of Jesus.   Many of the phenomena that confront us in the primitive Church receive clearer interpretation in view of so rich and dynamic a background, apart from which much would remain inexplicable.

PART TWO

THE EXPERIENCE OF THE EYE-WITNESSES

CHAPTER IV

CREATIVE CONTACTS AND IMPRESSIONS

WHEN Jesus Christ entered into the stream of human life and affairs, men of many kinds came into contact with Him, and formed their personal impressions, conscious or subconscious, of Him. From the innumerable contacts, impressions, and experiences, as all of them creatively issued in a vital consummation, there emerged in due time the primitive Church. Our immediate inquiry, therefore, is with these creative contacts, impressions, and experiences arising from Jesus' personal impact upon those who saw and heard. We set out to discover what the eye-witnesses were making of Jesus rather than what He was making of them, although, of course, the latter cannot be arbitrarily dissociated from the former.

What did the ordinary people of Galilee make of Jesus of Nazareth as they saw Him healing some unfortunate sufferer, or heard Him in their synagogues? The Gospel of Mark introduces us to an atmosphere that is electric with astonishment at His words and actions (i. 22). The people ask one another who was this who gave commands to evil spirits and they obeyed Him (i. 27). They were impressed with the manner in which Jesus cast out the demons, for while Jewish exorcists had power to expel spirits by elaborate formulæ, Jesus gave the simple, direct command to " come out of him." The awestruck eye-witnesses spread His fame everywhere through Galilee (i. 28). This is typical of what took place wherever Jesus passed through the province, and Luke sums up the general amazed impression that was formed of Jesus in the earlier Galilean activity ; His fame went everywhere through the region, and a reputation of unique import arose in that He was " being glorified of all " (iv. 14 f.). There was a specific freshness about Jesus' words, and the people were quick to capture the new accents.

Another glimpse of what was happening is caught when the disciples announce to Jesus that all men are looking out for Him (Mark i. 37).   True, the crowds had realized the material blessings He was able to bestow, and their quest was prompted by motives that were very mixed.   As the gospel summaries indicate, Jesus was leaving tremendous contacts, impressions, and experiences everywhere in the lives of countless multitudes (Matt. iv. 24 f.).   Jesus uses occasions of healing for teaching as well (Luke vi. 17).   A further summary of healing activity prompts the idea that Jesus is fulfilling Scripture as one who " bears our griefs and carries our sorrows " (Matt. viii. 17 ; cf. Isa. liii. 4) ; while this may be no more than the comment of the evangelist, the words may well have occurred to the recipients of His healing power.

The stilling of the storm causes men as a whole (Matt. viii. 27) to marvel ; Mark mentions a breathless awe which held those who watched Him (iv. 41) ; the crowds throng Him on the way to the house of Jairus, and the miracle there adds to the growing fame and the popular enthusiasm in which Jesus was held by all (Mark v. 24, 42).

"What manner of man is this ? " epitomizes the wonder of the people.   No doubt it was His power to heal that moved mainly to wonder, and Jesus' fame as a wonder-worker impels the people to pursue Him into the lonely places whither He had retreated for prayer. But when Jesus set aside the traditional requirements of Sabbath observance in the interests of healing (*e.g.* Mark iii. 2 ff.) we may be sure that while the rigidly orthodox would resent it, the ordinary people would wonder at Him all the more. There were serious limitations as far as the influence of the miracles was concerned. The healings in themselves did not create the impressions and results which Jesus had in view, namely, repentance in respect of the imminent Kingdom of God (Mark i. 15). Chorazin and Capernaum were unresponsive and unrepentant in spite of His mighty works, and these towns are compared very unfavourably with the Gentile cities of Tyre and Sidon, the people of which would long ago have repented had similar miracles been enacted there. We must recognize, however, that the new accents of His teaching were arousing attention and astonishment. His fellow-townsmen marvelled at the words of grace that fell from His lips (Luke iv. 22). In the minds of many earnest, pious believers in Israel, a type we have already noticed, there would lodge many a saying or parable ; they would apprehend the new spiritual emphasis and inner meaning of Jesus' words, and many such were to become fruitful soil for the primitive Church. The more specific spiritual and moral elements, however, were received only in germ, to shoot forth in fruitful ways in the religious experience of the Church.

Alongside this quieter enthusiasm went the more popular and dangerous enthusiasm with which Galilee was ablaze for Jesus. This excitement arose also from the militant Messianic fervour for which Galilee was notorious, and Jesus knew that efforts would be made to place Him at the head of a nationalist movement with a mixture of religious and political aims in view. The

Fourth Gospel echoes this peril in the strong determination of the crowd to take Jesus by force and make Him king (vi. 15). A multitude going into the wilderness after a leader was precisely the situation associated with Messianic claimants. The Johannine tradition appears to be at work on an original incident of popular Messianic fervour centring around Jesus, who withdrew from the threatening situation to the lonely hillsides.

The Fourth Gospel presents the impressions received of Jesus chiefly in Jerusalem, where, as we expect from His growing fame, Jesus was much in demand (vii. 11). Opinions about Him were various ; He was a good man, He was no more than a deceiver (vii. 12) ; there is surprise at His wisdom since He was of the common people (vii. 15 ; cf. Luke ii. 47, iv. 22) ; He was truly a prophet, while it was thought by some that He was the Messiah (vii. 40 f.), but this last suggestion causes doubt because of His Galilean connections, and a division of opinion arises (John vii. 41 ff. ; cf. vi. 14). We are reminded of what the people thought of Jesus, according to the disciples, and this turned on the idea that He was a prophet (Mark viii. 28).

It is here that we obtain the clue to what the crowds really thought Jesus was. Jesus was a prophet, a herald of the coming Kingdom of God. He had opened His ministry with the prophetic call to repent, as the Kingdom was imminent (Mark i. 15), and is thus a herald of the divine age. For minds prepared by apocalyptic, as the Galileans were, His casting out of demons was eloquent of His authority as the forerunner of Messiah. It was very apparent, therefore, to the crowds, that Jesus was vitally connected with the advent of the eagerly awaited redemption of Israel in the Kingdom of God. Some were even asserting that He was John the Baptist, who had been viewed as a forerunner of Messiah, risen from the dead, while others went further and designated Him as Elijah returned to herald the kingdom itself (Mark vi. 14 f.). The perplexed inquiry of the Baptist as to whether Jesus was the " one who should come or are we to look for another ? " (Luke vii. 19) refers to the herald of the new reign of God. The recognition of the Messianic status of Jesus by the demoniacs as being something more than that of herald leads Jesus to command them to silence (Mark i. 24 f., 34, iii. 11 f., v. 7), and at least suggests the immense personal impression Jesus was making in His commanding goodness, while the demoniacs would be more than ordinarily suggestible in their insight. The apparent studied reserve Jesus had with regard to His awareness of being Messiah signifies that as yet He did not desire that His dignity should be openly manifest, lest the flames of Messianic militarism should be unduly aroused.

In the triumphal entry into Jerusalem the crowds are acclaiming the herald, of the Kingdom. The exclamatory address, " Son of David," suggests that they were hailing Him as the actual Messiah, but the words are not decisive. Apart from two instances which are parallels to Matthew (xx. 30 f. ; Mark x. 47 f. ; Luke xviii. 38 f.), the title is found in the First Gospel only, which never fails to use any means that will commend Jesus as Messiah to the Jews (xv. 22, xxi. 9, 15 ; cf. i. 1, xii. 23). The quotation, " Blessed is he that cometh in the name of the Lord," is taken from a psalm which welcomes the pilgrim going up to the holy city for the feast (Ps. cxviii. 26, LXX), and is not a description of Messiah. Had the entry of Jesus into Jerusalem been a Messianic one, the Romans would have taken decisive action, while the high priest would have had definite evidence for Jesus' sedition to lay before Pilate. Further, Pilate would not have taken the charge that Jesus

6

claimed to be the King of the Jews so lightly as he di d (Mark xv. 2, 12, 26).

What we have is the enthusiasm of the crowds, including many ardent Galilean patriots, acclaiming the herald of the Kingdom, the new Elijah who was come to restore all things. A simple journey up to Jerusalem is seized upon by the enthusiasts, and Jesus may have been more or less compelled to journey amidst the applauding hosannas of the populace.[1] The situation was unquestionably compromising for Jesus, since " the very fact of a wonder-working prophet approaching the capital with an enthusiastic following could not but suggest . . . that He was aiming at becoming a popular hero who might use His power to incite the thousands of Passover pilgrims to rebellion." [2] It was the national form of the Kingdom, the " sensuous " conception with its admixture of material and spiritual, that the people had in mind, but they were speedily to be disillusioned. The answer to the tribute question (Mark xii. 14–17) must have been very disappointing to the Galilean patriots. The anticlimax of Jesus' arrest and trial before the Jewish and Roman authorities enraged the crowds against Jesus, the Messianic pretender, whose very situation of arrest and trial sufficed to declare that He was not what they had expected. They terrorized the Roman Governor into handing over Jesus to crucifixion even although he had found no reason for death in Him (Mark xv. 12–15). Meanwhile, it had spread around that Jesus had even claimed to be Messiah Himself, and as He hung on the Cross, a most unmessianic situation for any Messiah, the disappointed Galileans hurled abuse at Him (Matt. xxvii. 40).

[1] Cf. T. Llynfi Davies, *Expos. Ti.* 1931, pp. 526 f.
A. H. McNeile, *St. Matthew*, 1915, p. 297.

In addition to the common people, the religious leaders of the nation were forming their impressions of Jesus. Scribes consider He is blaspheming in assuring a man that his sins are forgiven (Mark ii. 7). Luke suggests how widespread is the observation by the leaders in that there were " Pharisees and doctors of the law sitting near, who had come from every village of Galilee, Judæa, and Jerusalem " (v. 17). Pharisees criticize the disciples for an infringement of the Sabbath law (Mark ii. 24) ; unfavourable impressions are received as Jesus sets aside a too scrupulous observance of the law in the interests of humanity (Mark iii. 2). The leaders become convinced that Jesus is a danger to the accepted religion, and they take thought how they may silence Him (Mark iii. 6). Luke, indeed, says that they were " mad " with Him (vi. 11). The cumulative effect of the impressions of blasphemy (Mark ii. 7), legal requirements set aside as secondary to the real issues of religion (Luke v. 33–35), friendship with the outcasts from the law (Mark ii. 16), the more human attitude to the Sabbath (Mark ii. 27),[1] results in specially selected scribes and Pharisees being sent into Galilee to show up Jesus as a mere charlatan, with a view to discrediting Him in the eyes of the populace (Mark iii. 22, vii. 1). They hint, and even openly declare, that Jesus derived His arts from the prince of the demons (Mark iii. 22). This very suggestion, however, is unwitting testimony to something " numinous " in the impression they had received of Jesus, for there must have been some remarkable potency in His personality to suggest supernatural authority, even of the evil order, unless the charge that

[1] The force of this is not to be turned aside by the quotation of a Rabbinic parallel of a much later date, namely, " The Sabbath is handed over to you, not you to the Sabbath " (quoted Kohler, *op. cit.* p. 222), when Rabbinism had to answer the criticism of Pharisaic over-literalness by Jesus, and through Him, by the Church.

He is in league with Satan is to be no more than ridiculous. The Pharisees attack Jesus on the ground that His disciples do not walk according to the tradition of the elders (Mark vii. 5), but His reply penetrates to the springs of inner religion as He calls the crowds around Him to hear the beautiful words about what really defiles a man. At last Jesus retires to the borders of Tyre and Sidon (Mark vii. 24), and the Pharisees thought that they had finally discredited Him. He returns, however, by a circuitous route to the Lake of Galilee (Mark vii. 31), and once more the Pharisees attack Him by asking for a sign, knowing from their observation of Jesus that this was the last thing He would give, and that His refusal would lower His popularity and influence (Mark viii. 11). They attempt to use the patriotic fervour of the Galileans and at the same time trade on His own desire, clearly discerned by them, to refrain from stirring up any premature and dangerous hopes.   Jesus is, therefore, forced to come out a little more into the open as touching His uniqueness and sense of Messiahship (Matt. xii. 39-42, xvi. 1-4), and at the end He is led to the decision to challenge the religious leaders right in the citadel of the national faith (Luke ix. 51), there to bring to its climax His mission along the lines of His victory over the temptations in the wilderness (Matt. iv. 1-11).

The authorities were frankly alarmed by the situation which began to develop when it was rumoured about that Jesus was in Jerusalem. They seek to stem the tide of rising enthusiasm by a direct appeal to Jesus (Luke xix. 39), and even later, when the " hosannas " were ringing within the confines of the temple itself (Matt. xxi. 15 f.). Well might they fear, for the whole city was in an uproar (Matt. xxi. 10 f.). A new verbal offensive is launched against Jesus which seeks to lure Him into statements that could be used as evidence against Him.

This duel culminates in the Parable of the Wicked Husbandmen, the point of which was that, just as the conspiring husbandmen killed the son whom they knew to have greater right and authority than they, so the Jewish authorities, seeking to kill Jesus, thereby acknowledged His higher right and authority (Matt. xxi. 23 ff.).

We cannot go with Lietzmann in regarding the trial of Jesus before the Sanhedrin as unhistorical,[1] nor accept Kohler's view that Jesus was condemned to death by the Romans as a Galilean pretender.[2] The efforts to prove that Jesus was guilty of blasphemy against the temple provided an issue which the Sanhedrin were fully competent to investigate.[3] This issue, rather than Jesus' claim to be the Messiah, seems to have been the specific ground of accusation (Mark xiv. 55–59, xv. 29), and only when the evidence appeared inconsistent did the high priest resort to the charge that Jesus claimed to be Messiah, regarding the confession extorted as blasphemy (Mark xiv. 61 f., 64). What actual law was here blasphemed has never been pointed out. The probability is, therefore, left open that the claim to Messiahship was extorted from Jesus to force Pilate to ratify the sentence of death.[4] Dr. Kohler's judgment placing the responsibility for the crucifixion of Jesus on the Romans fails to take into account the probabilities of religious experience, on grounds of which alone the upholders of the law and the traditions conceived it their duty to silence Him who " made Himself the mediator between God His Father and the rest of mankind." [5]

[1] " Bemerkungen zum Prozess Jesu," in *ZNW*. vol. xxxi. 1932, pp. 78–84.

[2] *Op. cit.* pp. 226 f., 231.

[3] Cf. M. Dibelius, " Das historische Problem der Leidensgeschichte," in *ZNW*. vol. xxx. 1931, pp. 198 f.

[4] As Wellhausen points out, *Das Evangelium Marci*. 1909, p. 124 f.

[5] Kohler, *op. cit.* p. 230.

It is to be noticed that the authorities made no attempt to accuse Jesus on moral grounds. The dilemma they set for Him in the tribute question implied absolute confidence on their part that Jesus at all costs would speak the truth. We have already noted the " numinous " effect Jesus had made upon them, but His uniqueness was felt by the authorities in yet another way. Jesus may or may not have taught anything essentially different from the law, but the mere fact that He was seen so clearly by the scribes to be alongside the law on a footing, at least, of equality in religious authority, is a unique distinction that never befell rabbi, scribe, nor Pharisee. This fact impressed the authorities to such an extent that they saw in the uniqueness of Jesus a danger to the law and the traditions. Yet Jesus produced this impression by being essentially loyal to Judaism. " The whole point of the scathing denunciation of the scribes and Pharisees," says G. F. Moore, " is that they are not true to the religion they profess and their own better knowledge." [1] Far from declaring Israel's faith to be obsolete, Jesus came to fulfil it by going to the spiritual roots of the experience of God it implied. These roots lay, for Jesus, within His own consciousness of uniqueness as the Son of God. If we start from this point to show up the difference between Him and the religious authorities, we see that He was aware that there were differences between Himself and others, the experienced contrasts being of a spiritual and ethical order. This conclusion in the religious experience of Jesus was probably reached only after prolonged reflection and finally accepted at His baptism. From this consciousness of sonship it followed that the true good for others meant their own receiving of His unique knowledge of, and fellowship with, God (Matt. xi. 27).

[1] *Op. cit.* vol. i. p. 183.

The way for others must be His own way, that is,
through experience of His spiritual and ethical uniqueness, as contrasted with their own way, or any other
way they knew, such as the ordinances of Judaism. It
was on such moral and spiritual differentia that Jesus
challenged and fought the Jewish religious authorities
as He focused His own distinctive experience and
knowledge of God against the letter of the law which
viewed God through traditional precept and observance.
This was the essence of His struggle with the Jewish
leaders who were not slow to perceive the crucial import
of His challenge. From their contacts with Jesus, and
their impressions of Him, they realized that " either
Jesus or the Jewish law, as a body of ordinances, had to
be reduced to a secondary place as the organ of the
divine will." [1] The reply of the Jewish authorities to
this dilemma was the crucifixion of Jesus, and through
this, the founding of the primitive Church.

A somewhat special class of eye-witnesses is constituted by the publicans and sinners. Like Lucius
(*Menipp.* par. 11), the Jews placed the taxgatherers
along with whoremongers and sinners. All over the
Roman Empire they were held in reprobation,[2] but in
Palestine they were hated not simply for dishonest
extortion, but as being the agents of the Gentile power
of Rome. Thus they were ranked among the " sinners "
who also included Gentiles, heretics, non-Pharisees or the
wealthy governmental party, and Hellenizing Jews or
renegade Israelites.[3] Many of those who were thus
branded were guilty of no more than abstaining from

[1] Bartlet and Carlyle, *Christianity in History*, 1917, p. 36.
[2] Cf. Plutarch, *De Curiosit.* par. 7, Iamblicus's satire in *Suidas*,
and Chrysostom on Matthew, section xxxi.
[3] Gal. ii. 15 ; Jn. ix. 16, 24 f., 31 ; Ps. Sol. xvii. 6–8 (cf. *A. & P.* ii.
p. 629) ; 1 Macc. ii. 44, 48 (cf. *A. & P.* i. p. 74).

official Pharisaic piety, or followed proscribed occupations, or maybe were of Gentile extraction, or consorted
with Gentiles.[1] The "sinners" included people of
immoral lives as well.

The nature of Jesus' fellowship with these ostracized
classes is shown in the title by which he came to be
known, namely, "Friend of publicans and sinners"
(Luke vii. 34). What did they make of Him as He
fraternized with them? Their experience has to be
interpreted in the light of their own exclusion from
the normal Jewish faith. Being in a state of excom-
munication, only judgment awaited them and the fate
that the Gentiles richly deserved, so far as the God of
Israel's faith was concerned. Since the requirements
of law and statute were not for them, Jesus was able to
make His distinctive appeal to the inner spirit of religion,
and this would impress them greatly. They would grasp
the inner significance all the more firmly in that they
were less bounded by law and tradition. The Jew may
affirm that God did not hear "sinners," but their
contact with Jesus made them discover that the Judaism
from which they were shut out was by no means the only
revelation about God's nature. They realized that
there was joy in heaven over one sinner that repented,
and this was tantamount to saying that God did hear
sinners. This religious discovery acted in accordance
with the two broad types of "sinners" we have discerned. The "sinners" who were outcast because of
occupation, of Gentile extraction, or who refused to
follow Pharisaic piety, welcomed Jesus as one who
spoke with authority and not as the scribes, and followed
Him right to the inner heart of His message. His
moral and spiritual stimulus opened their lives to a
living experience of God such as they had never hitherto

---

[1] H. B. Swete, *St. Mark*, 3rd edn. 1920, pp. 40 f.

imagined. Their thoughts of the divine Kingdom were of a less nationalistic colour. We never hear that they required a sign from Jesus to attest His authority. They drew near " to hear Him " (Luke xv. 1), for His words were sufficient to attest His power in their minds. On the other hand, those who were sinners in the moral sense were influenced into better ways of living ; tax-gatherers notorious for their exactions became honest men (Luke xix. 8), harlots were encouraged to hope for salvation and to " sin no more " (Jn. viii. 1 ff.), and all such sinners found redemption in their personal contact with Jesus as they gained from Him the way of life. In their friendship with Jesus God came very intimately into their lives.

Here Jesus comes directly into touch with definite Gentile elements. The fact that " publicans and sinners " were among those ostracized from Israel's faith and hope places them along with the Gentiles, while many were actually of Gentile extraction and had never been within the Jewish theocracy. The ethically lapsed, such as unchaste women, were chiefly foreigners, and the Jewish refusal to associate with them lay not simply in the fear of unholy desires being aroused ; the intense racial sentiments of the Jew would be defiled by contact with anything Gentile. The sin of the " sinners " was not merely moral, but racial. Jesus in His fellow-ship with them was not seeking to make proselytes to Judaism ; He was indicating to his fellow-Jews their neglected duty to be a light unto the Gentiles. These outcasts were children of the Father whom He was revealing in every word and deed of His ministry, and their overwhelming response proved that exclusion from Israel was no guarantee that they were cut off from fellowship with God.

The Gentile side of Christian experience has its

origin in the direct intercourse of Jesus with specific Gentile elements, and this fact is important in view of the struggle that was to take place within the Church consciousness on the question of its universal mission. Among such circles Jesus was able to speak freely, untrammelled by any Jewish opposition. At such times He could open out His mind to an audience that would not misunderstand Him. From this source there must have originated many recollections of the deeper significance of what Jesus said and did. When Jesus was crucified, the publicans and sinners would mourn not because of frustrated Messianic hopes, but for the beloved friend and teacher whose unique goodness had brought God into their experience in a vital way. Some of them may well have been among those who received experiences of the resurrection of Jesus, and in the primitive Church became the nucleus of the more liberal attitude with which Stephen, and later, Paul, were associated.

The eye-witnesses received their experience of Jesus' uniqueness through His living personality expressed in His distinctive works and words. These carried with them the distinctive quality of one whose vital fellowship with God sprang from His inner consciousness that He stood in a unique relation to God, and was therefore able to express God to those who saw and heard in a manner hitherto unknown. We turn to investigate the religious experience implied in these two aspects.

Did the so-called miracles of Jesus represent certain experiences received of the power of Jesus? Are they due to legendary growth around some distinctive nucleus of experience of Him? Or are they the pious figments of imagination kindled by His presence?

The experience of healing implied in the " healing " miracles has received some illumination through modern psychology, a study which enables some attempts at diagnosis to be made in respect of the patients who were the recipients of Jesus' healing powers, and to suggest the lines along which His cures may have operated. This modern illumination, however, has serious limitations. (1) Functional nervous diseases are chiefly the object of psychological attack, diseases which involve a failure of nervous energy as in the case of a man stricken with paralysis due to the failure of nerve force, although the limbs affected may be organically sound in every way. Blindness may also be caused by neurosis, even if the organ of sight is organically whole. On the other hand, Jesus, while dealing with diseases of this functional nervous type, is seen to heal specific organic disease such as leprosy. Further, Jesus wrought healings at a distance, as in the case of the centurion's servant ; psychology has no light in such cases, nor any power to heal. Father John of Cronstadt (below, pp. 169 f.) is nearer Jesus in his methods than psycho-analysis. (2) The direct response of the afflicted to the healing activity of Jesus stands out in the boldest contrast to the prolonged interviews and efforts at reassociation, characteristic of psychological treatment. Among the many cases illustrated by William McDougall [1] is that of a labourer whose left hand was caught up in some machinery; he was dragged violently up into the air and suspended for some time by his left arm. On release this was found to be " in a condition of complete flaccid paralysis and total anæsthesia." After a year of unsuccessful treatment he came under McDougall's care, and the psychologist treated him accordingly. " With the failure of every attempt at treatment, the patient's conviction that the arm was permanently useless had become more firmly established. . . . The essential step was to shake

[1] *Outline of Abnormal Psychology*, 1926, pp. 242 ff.

and undermine his fixed belief in the permanent nature
of the paralysis." This took many weeks of education,
persuasion, and even hypnotic suggestion. If we place
such a typical case of psychological method alongside the
healing of the man with a withered hand (Mark iii. 1–6),
the direct command of Jesus, " Stretch forth thy hand,"
and the immediate result in healing, we are aware of a
difference due to the impact of vital religious personality
on suffering. (3) The tendency of psychological investigation of the miracles is towards an interpretation
which amounts almost to allegorizing, the miracles being,
as it were, parables which are given concrete embodiment. In the Synoptic Gospels they are materializa-
tions which have petrified, embalmed, and buried the
very spirit and message of Jesus, and to disinter the
vital truths from the holy sarcophagi needs the aid
of psychological insight.[1] The author of the Fourth
Gospel, it is claimed, has seized the symbolic meaning
of the miracles it narrates as in the case of the water
turned into wine, and the raising of Lazarus.[2] The
chief difficulty of such a view is to decide where the
actual ends and the symbolic begins ; it reduces definite
acts to pictorial illustrations of spiritual principles ; the
method is not unlike the somewhat outgrown allegorical
treatment of the Old Testament ; it fails to do justice
to the potency of the personality of Jesus which is not
explained by etherializing His deeds into clouds of
spiritual idealisms.

What we have to do with is the impact of Jesus on
the suffering and the diseased. Having made all allowance for later tendencies to magnify what Jesus did, or
for the growth of legendary elements in the gospel

[1] Cf. G. S. Hall, *Jesus, the Christ, in the Light of Psychology*, 1921,
pp. 592–676, for typical reasoning of this viewpoint.
[2] Thus E. F. Scott, *The Fourth Gospel*, pp. 20, 37, 165, 250.

tradition, we are confronted with a personality possessing unique powers. In the simple instance of Jesus
healing Peter's wife's mother, the fact of Jesus going in
to see her seems to have restored her to health, and
the potency of His personality is vividly demonstrated
(Mark i. 31). The same potency heals leprosy (Mark i.
40 ff. ; Matt. viii. 2 ff. ; Luke v. 12 ff.) : the leper's
words, " If thou wilt, thou canst make me clean," reveal
the widespread reputation of Jesus. Leprosy carried
with it religious associations of the " unholy," and
was therefore looked on as a sign of divine displeasure
due to sin ; such a connection with sin meant that God
must have forgiven the sin before the healing took place,
and forgiveness of sins would be closely associated in
every experience of the cure of leprosy.

The phenomena of demon-possession confronted
Jesus at every turn of His ministry.[1] The minions of
Beelzebub were indeed dreaded. The demons seized,
tore, choked their victims, made them cry out in agony,
and roll about and foam at the mouth (Mark i. 26, v. 9,
ix. 18). The demons clung tenaciously to their human
abode, otherwise they must wander hither and thither,
inhabit unclean beasts, haunt tombs or deserts (Mark
v. 5, 13 ; Luke xi. 24). " Jesus' achievements in this
domain are one of His chief trophies and most potent
suggestions to the world, and there is something here
which the most inexorable criticism must leave essentially intact." [2]

The demoniac in the synagogue at Capernaum
(Mark i. 23 ff.) reveals characteristic features, being in
a state of heightened " numinous " suggestibility, and

[1] " It is clear that Jesus conceived the demons as organized into
an evil kingdom hostile to the Kingdom of God " (T. W. Manson,
The Teaching of Jesus, 1931, p. 165), and cf. Mark iii. 23–27 ; Luke xi.
17–23. Jesus as a Jew shared in the religious environment of His age.
[2] G. S. Hall, *op. cit.* p. 619.

openly recognizing the unique status of Jesus come to destroy demons in the power with which He brought in the divine Kingdom (Mark i. 24). Jesus commands the demon to come out of its victim (i. 25). As though unwilling, yet recognizing that obedience is inevitable, the demon leaves the man, and in so doing " tears " him (i. 26). We have to keep in mind the " objective " character these evil spirits had both for the victims and for the people in general. For them it was no question of psychological condition. An unclean spirit had invaded the man and he was under its control. The man plus the demon was one unit, a demoniac. Recognizing in his suggestible condition that Jesus was not simply the " herald," but the potent One who would bring in the Kingdom and the destruction of evil spirits, the demoniac cried out in protest, " Art thou come to destroy us ? " Objectively, the congregation in the synagogue saw two potencies confronting one another ; at such a moment all believed that Jesus as the " herald " of the Kingdom stood face to face with a minion of the prince of the demons, and the casting out of the demon attested objectively the announcement of Jesus that the Kingdom of God was at hand. On the other hand, demon-possession in all its believed objectivity confronted Jesus with all its terrifying moods and experiences, only to discover that experience of Him resulted in mental fetters broken, multiple personality unified, the enslaved, dormant self awakened to new life and health, the captive imagination set free, fixed ideas broken, diseased wills released from chains, and the general banishment of the ills with which modern psychotherapy has made us familiar.

The religious experience implied in the miracles reveals their attestation of the divine Kingdom as heralded by Jesus whose vital connection with the eagerly awaited

redemption of Israel could no longer be doubted.   Jesus
stood before all as One more potent for good than
Beelzebub was for evil.   The eye-witnesses looked on in
amazement and awaited what was yet to come.

We select the parables as characteristic of the words
of Jesus.   Religious teaching may awaken the religious
consciousness as mere wonder-working is not always able
to do.   The significance of the parable in reflecting the
essential ideas of Jesus should not overshadow the
parallel fact that " it depends for its effectiveness on
the responsiveness of those to whom it is addressed." [1]
This disposes of the primitive Church's inference reflected
in Mark's Gospel that Jesus spoke in parables to prevent
His teaching being understood save by the inner circle
of believers who sympathized with Him (Mark iv. 11 f.).
Jesus intended His truth to go beyond the immediate
circle of His own friends (Mark iv. 9) ; He taught the
people to bring light to their minds about the Kingdom
of God, for this is the central subject of the parables.

We consider first parabolic sayings such as the " Salt
and its Savour," the " Light under a Bushel," and the
"City on a Hill." [2] If these were addressed to disciples only
(Mark), the words are secret counsel to them as uniquely
selected to be the salt of the earth ; if to the crowds,
as is more likely (Matthew and Luke), the sayings refer
to the mission of Israel to the whole world.   The chosen
people are being urged to do their duty of witnessing
to the Kingdom before all the nations, and impart their
soul power and religious experience to savour the world,
as salt has power to give taste, or light to shed radiance
abroad, or the city on a hill to be seen from a far dis-

[1] Manson, *op. cit.* p. 66.
[2] Mark ix. 50 ; Matt. v. 13 ; Luke xiv. 34 f. ; Mark iv. 21 ;
Matt. v. 15 ; Luke xi. 33 ; Matt. v. 14.

tance. The absurdity of a light being kept to itself instead of being allowed to lighten the whole house is no more than that of the nation which would keep the light of its faith all to itself, thus placing its light under a bushel. The crowds would be in no doubt about the identification of the city set on a hill, for Jerusalem was high up on the mountains of Judæa. That city which ought to let the nation's light so shine that it may be seen of all men had become notorious for its exclusiveness and its placing of barriers between the Jews and the rest of mankind. Therefore its outlook on the divine Kingdom is restricted, and Jesus is seeking to widen and deepen it in the minds of the eyewitnesses.

Parables such as the " Children Crying in the Marketplace," the " Mustard Seed," the " Leaven," the " Unfruitful Fig Tree," and the " Wedding Feast," [1] may be viewed as attempts to enlarge the religious experience of the Jews, to deepen their consciousness as God's people with a mission to the world in the Kingdom of God. The children who piped and wailed and those who refused to respond are seen in the references to the Jews as characterized especially in their leaders, and the publicans and sinners. The former took the initiative, the latter, *i.e.* the Gentiles, refusing to accede to Jewish requirements before they could enter the Kingdom of God. The piping and the wailing of the Jews makes no impression on the Gentiles, and the Jews refuse to change their tune or play another game. The parable is thus seen to be a serious effort made by Jesus to awaken His generation of fellow-Jews to their world mission to the Gentiles. Parables such as the " Mustard

---

[1] Matt. xi. 16 ff. ; Luke vii. 31 ff. ; Mark iv. 30 ff. ; Matt. xiii. 31 f. ; Luke xiii. 18 f. ; Matt. xiii. 33 ; Luke xiii. 20 f., 6–9 ; Matt. xxii. 1 ff. cf. Luke xiv. 16–24.

Seed " and the " Leaven " also suggest the expansion
of the Kingdom to a size out of all proportion to the tiny
seed or the amount of leaven concerned, coupled with
the idea of the germinal life at work through the preaching of Jesus and His influence on the disciples.   There
is, however, the additional feature as to what the crowds
were making of this teaching here.   If Jesus were
thinking of the growth of individual moral character,
the eye-witnesses would nevertheless interpret these
parables in a corporate way.   The corporate community
to be blessed with the advent of the divine Kingdom
would be suggested to their minds and they would
instinctively limit that community to Israel.   The
" Mustard Seed," with the figure of the birds nesting in
the branches, would find point in the Old Testament
symbol of the tree and its branches as emblematic of a
mighty kingdom which gave shelter to the nations of
the world (Ezek. xxxi. 6, 12 ; Dan. iv. 12–14, 21 f.), and
there is a Messianic reference which suggests the restoration of Jerusalem and David's dynasty.   The " Leaven "
need not point to the contrast with the " Mustard Seed "
of an intensive character of the Kingdom over against
the extensive ; it carries on the same thought of the
Kingdom as an influence until it has leavened the whole
world of the nations which are thus to find their entrance
into the Kingdom.   With these ideas Jesus is endeavouring to enlarge the religious consciousness of the Jews to
receive the Gentiles as heirs of salvation.   The " Unfruitful Fig Tree " would be heard by those who had
ears to hear the accents of warning to Judaism.   There
was much to be said for the contention that no unfruitful
tree should encumber the ground any longer (Luke xiii. 7).
But the gardener pleads for another chance ; the tree
shall be dug round afresh.   So in Israel there is a
regrettable barrenness, yet the Jews are to have another

7

opportunity of doing their duty by the Gentiles. In the " Great Supper," the self-excuse of those invited in the first place finally places them beyond the possibility of being present (Luke xiv. 24). The very position of the Jews in their religious privilege had made them self-sufficing and exclusive, and Messiah will call in the unprivileged, *i.e.* the Gentiles.

Such parables aim at enlarging the religious consciousness of the Jews. Many did not understand the allusions, for it never dawned on the majority of Jews and Galileans that God had any purpose for the Gentiles. Taxgatherers, sinners, and Gentiles were among the audiences, and these would be quick to capture the new accents and perceive the wider horizons which found their anchor in their freer outlook, and were creative of the spiritual elements which were later to free the primitive Church from its narrower and Jewish self-consciousness.

The imminence of the Kingdom as Jesus taught it evoked parables designed to create the sense of religious crisis within the religious experience of the eye-witnesses. The real difficulty here lay in the nationalist elements and the danger of enthusiasms arising from false ideas of the coming Kingdom. Yet Jesus set Himself to arouse the Jews to a sense of redemptive crisis in a different zone from that of the political, and thus to arouse them to fulfil their true destiny. That is why elements of judgment appear in parabolic sayings such as " The New Patch on the Old Garment " and " The New Wine in the Old Wineskins," " The Divided Kingdom or House," " The Strong Man Armed "—all significantly addressed to the Pharisees as the nation's leaders—" The Blind leading the Blind," " The Master returning from a Marriage Feast," " The Faithful and Unfaithful Stewards," " The Shut Door "—addressed to

the disciples—and " The Rejected Stone," addressed to
all.[1]   These " judgment " elements arise from the crisis of
the imminence of the Kingdom, the reaction to which
will constitute the judgment *ipso facto*, favourable or
unfavourable.

Wellhausen is surely right in asserting that the old
coat and the old wineskin mean no other than a Judaism
which is becoming thread-bare.[2]   The imminent crisis
will show that the old cannot be patched, *i.e.* Judaism
as a system of ordinances and traditional inferences.
The " Wineskins " adds the further idea of a new religious
experience with a new spirit that cannot be contained
in the old vessels, for it would ruin the skins and spill
itself in loss.   Here we receive hints that in view of the
possible inadequacy of Judaism, a new community may
emerge as the outcome of the crisis due to the advent
of the Kingdom.   " The Divided Kingdom " or " House "
illustrates the crisis from another angle.   If the casting
out of demons were due to Satanic agency in Jesus, His
power would be divided against itself, evil being undone
by evil.   These cures, however, indicated that the
source of demonic power was itself being overthrown by
the judgment and power that heralded the Kingdom.
" The Strong Man Armed " points in the same direction,
showing that the demonic prince had met his conqueror
in Jesus.   " The Blind leading the Blind " points to the
inadequacy of both Pharisaic leaders and the people
they were leading ;   the latter are expected to be in a
backward state of enlightenment, but the crisis of the
Kingdom will reveal that the leaders are similarly back-

[1] Mark ii. 21 f. ;   Matt. ix. 16 f. ;   Luke v. 36 ff. ;   Mark iii. 24–26 ;
Matt. xii. 25–28 ;   Luke xi. 17 ff. ;   Mark iii. 27 ;   Matt. xii. 29 ;
Luke xi. 21 ;   Matt. xv. 14 ;   Luke vi. 39 ;   Luke xii. 35 ff. ;   Luke xii.
42 ff., xiii. 24 ff. ;   Mark xii. 10 f.

[2] *Op. cit.* p. 19.

ward and unenlightened, and that therefore other leaders may be needed when the enlightened Kingdom is in being. The series of Lukan parables which concludes these illustrations urges upon the confidential circle of disciples the duty of watchfulness and alert expectancy for the returning Master with the Kingdom, and judgment is implied in approval or disapproval as the case may be. " The Rejected Stone " hints at the way the crisis will work out. It follows the Parable of the Wicked Husband-men, and has in mind the Jewish leaders who were scheming to overthrow Jesus. They would discover that what they had rejected would rise supreme. The crisis would bring forth a new community based on the higher authority of the Kingdom as seen in Jesus. Matthew gives us hints as to the nature of this possible new community. The " others " to whom the vineyard will be handed over in trust are those who will deliver what is expected of them (xxi. 41) ; after referring to the " Rejected Stone," Jesus informs the Jewish leaders that the Kingdom will be taken away from them and given to a community worthy of the trust, just as the vineyard was handed over to others who were more fit to discharge the duty (Matt. xxi. 43). Thus the planning of the death of Jesus by the Jews was really an unwitting preparation for the emergence of the new community of the divine Kingdom. In this sense the crisis would form a judgment on the Jews and their authorities, and at the same time constitute the conditions from which the new community would come into being.

It is unhistorical to regard these hints of a new community for the Kingdom as necessarily referring to the Christian Church, for this was not the case at so early a stage. It is not difficult to read back the later dis-coveries of the primitive Church or those of a later period into these hints. We are amid the faint glimmerings of a newly awakening religious consciousness, and at the moment neither the disciples, still less the eye-witnesses as a whole, were clear as to what might take place. Indeed, they were too likely to construe what Jesus was saying in terms of popular apocalyptic. What we have is the presentation of a crisis that is well-nigh present in the Kingdom of God, with some suggestions that the crisis will cause to emerge a community with a religious experience of a wider character than was the case in the conventional Judaism of the time.

It is clear that the Kingdom as taught by Jesus had a uniquely spiritual and ethical quality. There are parabolic sayings which go right to the inner heart of the individual. Among these are " The Mote and the Beam," a vivid warning against judging others (Matt. vii. 3 f. ; Luke vi. 41 f.). " The Good and Bad Trees " (Matt. vii. 16 ff. ; Luke vi. 43 f.) with its figurative imagery suggests that human conduct reveals the spirit's quality within ; God's truth will reproduce itself through personality, and this will reveal whether a man's life is of God. " The Houses on the Rock and Sand " (Matt. vii. 24 ff. ; Luke vi. 47 ff.) applies to all who hear the words of Jesus, but differentiates those who act seriously on the spiritual affirmations recognized in the soul through the teaching of Jesus, and those whose affirmations of soul do not rise to expression in personality and action. To renounce the vision of reality is to build on the sand and be at the mercy of the storm. The vivid manner in which Jesus atomizes the crowds into thinking and individually responsible beings is further shown by such parables as " The Tower Builder " (Luke xiv. 28 ff.) and " The King Going to War " (Luke xiv. 31 f.), pointing to the need for counting the cost of following Jesus to His Kingdom, even if this means the sundering of the dearest of home-ties (ver. 26).

The renunciation made reveals those who are already in the divine Kingdom, where human life " is reformed on a new plane." [1] The cost involved will find abundant compensation on this higher plane of family kinship with Jesus, on its spiritual side (Mark x. 29 f.). In this sense the "hundredfold now in this time, houses, brethren, sisters, mothers, children, and lands " is tantamount to a parable of family kinship with Jesus in the life of the Kingdom, the kinship being based on the doing of the will of God (Mark iii. 35). Here we get the strong notes of appeal to the individuals who make up the nation with a view to making it worthy of the Kingdom of God. The demands are superhuman, and are suggested rather than defined in detail.[2] The result is that the vital process of religious summons is initiated in the soul of the hearer, and thus the moral individualism set in motion by apocalyptic is reinforced by the unique emphasis of Jesus on individual responsibility in view of the approach of the Kingdom with its judgment.

Jesus seeks the growth of spiritually creative personality into which he inserts the germ of his words and influence, leaving its power of propagating life to bring about the creative personalities who shall be fitting material for the Kingdom. Several parables stress this aspect, namely, " What Defiles a Man " (Mark vii. 14 f.), " The Lost Sheep," " The Lost Coin," " The Lost Son " (Luke xv. 3-32), " The Pharisee and the Publican " (Luke xviii. 9 ff.), and " The Good Samaritan " (Luke x. 30 ff.). The parabolic saying " What Defiles a Man "

---

[1] Hoskyns and Davey, *The Riddle of the New Testament*, 1931, p. 201.

[2] " The standard of this individualism is wholly self-contained, determined simply by its own sense of that which will further its consecration to God. It is bound to go to all lengths in obedience to the demands of the gospel," E. Troeltsch, *Social Teaching of the Christian Churches*, Eng. Tr. 1931, vol. i. p. 55.

makes clear the distinction between the moral and the merely ritual by pointing to the real source of defilement in man's spirit, issuing in unworthy character. This distinction is significant in view of the struggle in the primitive Church to widen its consciousness to include the Gentiles as heirs of salvation needing no Jewish ritual to bring them into the Kingdom. " The Lost Sheep, Coin, and Son " show that divine salvation into the Kingdom is also a matter of repentance and turning to God in faith (Luke xv. 7, 10). The outcasts from orthodox Judaism or the morally unholy may thus enter the new inheritance, and moral individualism is here clearly expressed in the individual aspect of forgiveness presented. " The Pharisee and the Publican " illustrates the despising of the vulgar and the outcast by the Jewish leaders, who were therefore disloyal to their own Levitical law of loving one's neighbour as oneself (Lev. xix. 18), while the catalogue of excellences stands out in contrast to the manner and spirit of the sinner who knows himself so well that he does not judge others, but seeks by repentance the forgiveness of God. " The Good Samaritan " reveals the compassion of true goodness ; a fellow-man in need affords an opportunity for love which does not inquire what minimum must be attained if eternal life is to be possessed. Creative love asks not what are the limits to religious experience and its promptings, but what opportunities for the expression of such personality are afforded. What we have in all these parables is an experience of God stimulated by the imminence of the divine Kingdom as taught by Jesus, expressed on the one hand in repentance and trust, and on the other, in love and service for others. From religious experience so intensely individualized rises religious experience which by implication is intensely universal in the all-

embracing character of the divine Kingdom announced
by Jesus.

The various parables, viewed from the side of religious
experience which was to be creative of the primitive
Church, reveal an outlook with a strong apocalyptic
background and its central feature of the imminent
Kingdom of God.   There is a vivid sense of crisis ; the
chosen nation of Israel will possibly be rejected in view
of its religious faith being too narrowly conceived.   Even
now there are hints that another and worthier community
is secretly being prepared by the impact of the creative
personality of Jesus upon the eye-witnesses, who in
their turn are not unresponsive.   The creative contacts
did not germinate in many who heard, simply because
they stopped at the enjoyment of the story, or the seed
fell by the wayside, or among stony places, or among
the thorns.   The Parable of the Sower (Mark iv. 1 ff.)
is really a parable which explains the parables both in
their spiritual and creative intention and in the types of
reaction to the new experience.   But many kept the
sayings in their hearts, and became fitting material for
the primitive Church.

CHAPTER V

The Growth of the Disciples

WHAT were the disciples making of Jesus as He impregnated their lives by His personal, creative influence?

It is a commonplace of psychology that personality reacts on personality. At His minimum value Jesus was a religious teacher of unique force, whose influence was more significant than the recipients of His personal contacts at the time realized. The receptivity of such influence, however, is largely conditioned by the capacity to take in, and the intake may be at its lowest quality, in which case the teacher has the initial task of enlarging the receptive power of His hearers. Such a preliminary process was much needed for the simple Galileans who accompanied Jesus on His tours (Mark i. 38), with whom He conversed intimately as they with Him (Mark ix. 9 ff.), who were eye-witnesses of His works and hearers of His words, who misunderstood Him as He spoke of His forthcoming agony (Mark ix. 32), and who were overjoyed at the resurrection experience (Luke xxiv. 32, 52). Through their experience of Jesus they were constantly being driven to ask what manner of man this was in their midst, and equally impelled to attempt some answer. Failing in any such attempt they had perforce to let Him answer as time and His spiritual power unfolded and expanded their own spiritual growth, until at last they were able to admit Him within their growing experience.

We are able at once to discover a twofold aspect

in their contacts with Jesus. First, there was the
" positive " side, the actual " plus " to their religious
growth as their impressions deepened in quality, and as
deepening insight enabled them to interpret Jesus
more significantly. Second, we have the " negative "
aspect, the " minus " quantity, that which should have
been there had they reacted appropriately to their
Master, but through ignorance, misunderstanding, or
failure in powers of intake, was lacking in them. Such
a " minus " quantity was influenced by the limitations
of mental and spiritual categories in which they thought
and felt and experienced their normal religious life.
Yet the two aspects should not be too arbitrarily
sundered ; while failing on the cognitive and conscious
sides of their outlook, the disciples were really building
better than they knew as the subconscious levels of
their experience were preparing for a vital consummation in due course. For Jesus was more than a religious
teacher, being in Himself the bearer of a new way of life
which He sought to communicate to the disciples, and
this quickening life was even now working silently and
creatively for what was to come through them in the
emergence of the primitive Church.

The disciples we have in mind are chiefly those designated as the " Twelve," [1] but there were others of almost
equal importance who in some cases knew the mind of
Jesus even more intimately.[2] We hear, too, of an inner
circle of three, or perhaps four disciples (Mark v. 37,
ix. 2, xiii. 3), which may have been more receptive than
the rest of the " Twelve," or may in the first place have
formed a small group of companions with Jesus, which

---

[1] Cf. the name lists in Mark iii. 16–19 ; Matt. x. 2–4 ; Luke vi.
14–16, and Appendix V., pp. 357 ff.
[2] Cf. the Beloved Disciple, who was not one of the Twelve, and
the tradition he inspired in the Fourth Gospel, pp. 17–21.

afterwards in Church tradition was expanded into the
" Twelve." We hear, further, of a larger group sent
out by Jesus to preach the Kingdom of God (Luke x. 1 ff.).
Luke is probably preserving a strand of genuine tradition which pointed to the fact that Jesus had and
actually used a larger body of disciples than twelve.
There were women disciples also, significantly found
alongside the eleven disciples in the Upper Room, who
probably shared in the Spirit's outpouring (Acts i. 14).
The women disciples were eye-witnesses of the Resurrection of Jesus (Matt. xxviii. 1, 9).

According to the Synoptic tradition Jesus called some
Galilean fishermen as they were at work (Mark i. 16–20).
Was His personality so potent as to induce men to leave
all at a moment's notice for His side, without any
previous acquaintance with or experience of Him on
their part ? Without deciding the possibilities here, it
seems more natural to view the call as preceded by
personal intercourse. The informal way in which Jesus
made use of Simon's boat as a point of vantage whence
to address the crowds implies some measure of familiarity
between the two (Luke v. 3). According to the Fourth
Gospel there is a meeting of Jesus with Simon and
Andrew near where John was baptizing, and they are
drawn to Him through conviction of His Messiahship.
This recognition of Jesus as Messiah seems premature
in view of the discovery confessed at Cæsarea Philippi
(Mark viii. 30). There is probably a reading back of
later affirmations into the Fourth Gospel (i. 41), but
what seems to have happened is that some Galileans,
stirred by the reports of the Baptist's preaching the
Kingdom of God, left their occupation for the time being,
and made their journey southwards to join the crowds
listening to John's proclamations. There would be
little use in carrying on with the occupations if the

prophet on Jordan's banks were right. Such at least they would feel about it. Several of them became disciples of the Baptist (John i. 37), and in this way may have come into immediate contact with Jesus, who Himself received baptism from John. They left John and became disciples of Jesus (John i. 37–42). Thereafter they all travelled back to Galilee (John i. 43) and resumed their occupations once more, until Jesus chose His own moment and called them to come after Him (Mark i. 17, 20). However this may be, it is psychologically difficult to feel that there was no prior contact with Jesus.

At all events, the disciples were mainly Galileans sharing in the apocalyptic outlook so characteristic of these people. One came from the "taxgatherers" (Mark ii. 14) amongst whom Jesus was no stranger. One of the circle seemed actually to belong to the patriotic party which looked for the advent of the divine Kingdom in the overthrow of imperial Rome, and the political pre-eminence of Israel. This was Simon the Zealot ; the force of "zealot" is not to be toned down as indicating merely a Jew zealous for the Law. The Pharisees were zealous for the Law as none others were, but they would have objected to being called "Zealots," in view of the political and apocalyptic associations these carried with them. Nor does the device of Dalman in emending the text to avoid the direct suggestion that among the disciples of Jesus there was an enthusiastic revolutionary seem cogent. It is better to take the term for what it stands (Mark iii. 18).

In course of time the Church was to interpret the significance of Jesus in categories which hitherto had been applied only to God. At the same time it came to be more definitely organized and the companions of Jesus were limited in a special sense to twelve and elevated into a sort of apostolic collegium. The disciples, however, had no such exalted position when with Jesus, nor did they perceive in Him from the first what the Church later came to discern. We have to allow for the process of religious growth in them. Along with the crowds they saw in Jesus the " herald " of the Kingdom, they wondered what manner of man this was in their midst, they were spellbound by His miracles, and may have drawn erroneous inferences from what they saw. They may have felt disappointment at the refusal of Jesus to place Himself at the head of the patriotic movement to make Him king, but unlike many who left Jesus, they stood by Him, feeling there was more in their Master yet to be revealed (John vi. 68 f.). Even in their early stages of friendship with Jesus there was growing up an awareness that He was different from any one else they had known, or of whom they had heard. An intimate friendship grew to its flower as He was known in their homes, shared common meals, observed the *Kiddûsh* with them, whether that of the weekly Sabbath or that of some important feast such as Pentecost or Passover. The last meal Jesus and they shared together was a *Kiddûsh* celebration for the Passover.[1] In the common journeys, the intimate talks, and the fellowship daily opening itself, Jesus was impressing upon them the more significant spiritual and ethical aspects of what He was teaching in public ; in their conscious minds the disciples were slow enough to appraise such aspects, yet subconsciously the seed was germinating within them, to reveal its fruit in due season.

Their cognitive attitude to the Jewish Law and the Traditions was undergoing modification. There is evidence here of their growth in this respect in their

[1] On this cf. below, pp. 287, 293.

plucking the ears of corn on the Sabbath (Mark ii. 23 ff.),
and in their disregard of Jewish ritual which required
that the hands should be washed prior to a meal
(Mark vii. 1–5). The disciples were indeed growing
beyond the letter of the law, yet it may be that they
were only following a less strict tradition.[1] When,
however, we take such incidents along with the " Corban "
saying (Mark vii. 11), which led on to the enunciation
of the principle that things cannot defile persons, and
the inner criticism of the traditions expressed in the
Sermon on the Mount, we may conclude that the personal
experience they had of Jesus was making the disciples
less legally minded. This process went on more intensively in some than in others, and the way was being
prepared for their experience of the Transfiguration
where in vision the disciples apprehended the superiority
of the Master both to the Law and the Prophets in that
He fulfilled both, and caught up Israel's faith into a new
and higher synthesis.

Sent out on a preaching tour, the disciples return in
joy that even the demons are subject to them (Luke x.
17), showing at work in them the same healing power
as characterized Jesus, who had to remind them of the
deeper aspects of the Kingdom. They were taking the
evidence of the conquest over evil spirits as too literally
fulfilling the hopes of the Kingdom as they conceived
it (Luke x. 20).

From all the influences radiating from the personality
of Jesus, His commanding goodness, His power over evil
spirits, His preaching, teaching, His words and His
works, and the growing intimacy between Him and the
disciples, the conviction was born in their minds that
Jesus was no mere " herald " of the Kingdom, but

[1] Cf. Büchler, *Der galiläische Am-ha Areṣ*, 1906, ch. iv., and
Montefiore, *op. cit.* p. 476, who show that most of the purity laws
applied only to priests or to laymen entering the temple.

Messiah Himself (Mark viii. 29). This found eloquent expression in the confession of Simon Peter at Cæsarea Philippi. The insight of Peter is not to be limited to the mere guessing of some Messianic secret by recognizing in Jesus the conventionally familiar features of the Messiah of apocalyptic. We have in the confession a grand Act of Faith in the synthesis of Jesus and Messiah made by the disciple, who was giving concrete form to something that had never hitherto been seen. A Messiah who lived among men was, of course, a familiar conception in so far as he was expected to emerge from some kingly dynasty or priestly corporation such as the Davidic and Levitic types of human Messiah respectively foreshadowed. On the other hand, a Messiah nurtured in lowly circumstances, who went about doing good, and gathering disciples round Him as did a prophet or a teacher, was unheard of in Jewish expectation. To this extent Peter had cut adrift from popular apocalyptic ideas, and the ensuing growth in insight was due to his fellowship with Jesus. Peter probably expressed in this confession that Jesus was Messiah not only his own conviction, but also the mind of the disciples as a whole. From their growing experience of Jesus it came to be borne in upon their minds that the ordinary ideas such as " Master," " Teacher," " Prophet," " Herald," did not adequately convey what they discerned in Jesus. They were, therefore, led to apply to Him the highest category, save that of " God," of which their religious experience was capable, and identified Him with the Messiah, the Lord's Anointed in very deed.

The application of this unique category to Jesus implied His superiority both to the Law and the Prophets in the sense of fulfilment ; the prophets pointed to Messiah's advent, the emergence of the Messianic Kingdom carried with it the ideal fulfilment of the law.

This superiority was realized by the disciples in a subconscious way through their experience of a vision they
had shortly after the confession.   While Jesus was in
prayer on some hillside, three disciples who attended
Him saw His transfiguration.   This was an experience
of mystic vision where the truths apprehended by the
subconscious mind and only dimly perceived by the
conscious attention came for the moment to the surface
in vivid symbolism.   This is what we have in the Transfiguration as far as the empirical content of the disciples'
minds is concerned.   The subjective preparation in their
contact with Jesus, their impression of His uniqueness,
their confession of Jesus as Messiah with His implied
superiority to Moses and Elijah as representative of the
law and the prophets, objectified itself in their vision of
Jesus talking with these ancient worthies of Israel.
That these convictions were of a subconscious nature,
and only came to the surface in vision, is further shown
by the shock which the disciples received when Jesus
announced His forthcoming suffering and death immediately after the confession.   To suffer and die was not
what was expected of Messiah in His regal splendour ;
the disciples were typical children of their religious
environment in this respect.   When this fact is emphasized along with Luke's information that Jesus,
Moses, and Elijah were conversing about the forthcoming passion at Jerusalem (ix. 31), then what on the
conscious side of the disciples' minds was a source of
misunderstanding and the cause of serious disturbance
became truth which was intuitively grasped in their
deeper subconscious levels, and this truth came to the
surface in the vision.   The truth so discerned was that
Jesus the Messiah would carry out the divine will in
His death, such obedience being the true glory in Him,
such glory being symbolized by the light and the trans-

figured face of Jesus.   While the idea of Messiah suffering and dying to usher in the divine Kingdom was a cause of offence to the conscious attention, the inner significance came to its rightful place in the vision experience of Peter and his friends.   This significance became clear to the disciples in their contacts with the risen Christ, but at the moment it was realized only in a subconscious manner.   Indeed, Wellhausen is probably influenced by this line of thought to regard the Transfiguration as a post-resurrection appearance of Jesus to the three disciples (*op. cit.* p. 71), but it is not necessary to infer this in view of the explanation given in the operation of religious experience and the creative influence of Jesus working unwittingly in the subconscious minds of the disciples, who seek to clarify what they have experienced as they converse with Jesus on the way down the hillside (Mark ix. 9–13).   Their conscious outlook, however, has come back to its own again in their inability to apprehend what Jesus was saying about His forthcoming resurrection to take place after the suffering and the death.

No sooner had the disciples applied to Jesus the highest category of which their religious experience was capable than we find the " minus " elements of their outlook coming forward.   They viewed Jesus the Messiah in ways drawn from the common stock of Messianic ideas.   They failed to perceive the kind of Messiah Jesus was in Himself.   We return to this aspect later, but meanwhile point the fact out as one element in what may be described as " The Great Misunderstanding " concerning Jesus for which the disciples were responsible, fastening literal eschatological expectations on the primitive Church.   This " Great Misunderstanding " was the effect of a thoroughgoing application of apocalyptic literalism to the nature and function of

8

Messiah as identified with Jesus. This fact is not modified essentially by recognizing the real truth inherent in the apocalyptic forms, images, and expectations, namely, the vindication of God's righteousness in the history of the world. We are, however, face to face with the racial psychology of the disciples in their inherited and environmental world outlook. They could act in no other way than they did in their misunderstanding of Jesus, until the spiritual release of subsequent events and discoveries centring around the resurrected and exalted Jesus began to liberate them from their limitations.

If we are to do justice to the influence of apocalyptic on the primitive Church experience it is necessary to keep distinct the two aspects involved. First, there is the apocalyptic of which Jesus made use as a child of his age appealing to His contemporaries, with the recognition that there was His own unique ethical and religious content in His usage (cf. Appendix VII.). Second, there was the apocalyptic outlook of the eye-witnesses who inevitably interpreted the events of His life and the content of His words and works in apocalyptic ways, even where there was no such association in the mind of Jesus. Eschatology was the point of contact between Jesus and His hearers as He revealed His integral message of the Kingdom and its imminence, or led His disciples to discern in Him Israel's expected Messiah. Unlike Jesus, however, they thought too much within the literalism of apocalyptic and did not penetrate to the inner religious realities in the thought-forms which Jesus was constrained to use.

It was highly significant of the impression Jesus was making that the disciples were influenced to place Him as the dominating figure in their eschatological scheme of events. Jesus may have fulfilled the prophets, as

the primitive Church came to see, but it is still further
true that even now for the disciples Jesus fulfilled all
apocalyptic. This accounts for the heightened tension
that followed the confession at Cæsarea Philippi. The
disciples felt their expectations quickened, and felt
that the crisis of the Kingdom was very near indeed.
But their " Great Misunderstanding " of Jesus at this
critical time arose and clouded their outlook through
two obsessions which dominated them.

First, their ideas of the Kingdom of God were not
His. On the whole, theirs was the " sensuous " form of
the Kingdom with its specific nationalist elements.
Their hope was for the Kingdom on earth with God
reigning in the person of a triumphant Messiah, and
Israel high and lifted up above the Gentiles in political
dominance—a theocratic kingdom, indeed, but not therefore necessarily spiritual. Such were the hopes in view.
All privileges and blessings, material and spiritual,
were reserved for Jews, or such of the Gentiles as submitted and became Jews by circumcision. But the
Kingdom as a spiritual community of citizens irrespective of physical descent as sons of Abraham, or of
hyper-rational and non-moral requirements such as
circumcision, was quite foreign to the characteristic
Jewish outlook in which the disciples shared. This
is the religious background of the disciples in their
approach to the divine Kingdom as Jesus heralded its
advent. Disciples of Jesus indeed, yet still characteristic sons of Abraham. For Jesus, the religious content
of the Kingdom was a spiritual order based on God's
Fatherhood, the Divine Love, redemption of men from
sin to the life of the Kingdom—the sin being not
merely ceremonial or ritual—fellowship with God irrespective of status or race, Jew or Gentile. In such a
way the Kingdom was an experience already present,

the consummation to be looked for as the Messiah, triumphant through suffering, brought in the reign of God. The disciples, however, gained but the smallest glimmer of this spiritual and moral majesty at the time.

Second, the " Great Misunderstanding " was due to preconceived ideas about the Messiah. On the whole, the " human " type of Messiah was dominant among the disciples ; the " suprahuman " ideas were only there in the ideal ; the disciples would tend to regard Jesus as the human Messiah invested with superhuman power. Had not Jesus revealed this superhuman power in the casting out of demons ? And was not this fact one guarantee that when the right moment came Jesus would strike His blow for the Kingdom ? The disciples placed Him in the centre of the apocalyptic picture and viewed Him as the Messianic hero of the apocalyptic drama about to be unfolded. Such a one would choose His time ; they awaited with impatience the great day of the Lord ; they were anxious only about the positions they would occupy when Jesus brought in the Kingdom (Mark x. 37). Regal glory, mighty power, the power of a kingly warrior overcoming Israel's enemies, and royal dignity were looked for in him. All these ideas were implicit for the disciples in the great confession, " Thou art the Messiah."

At this point of confession Jesus announced that His Messiahship was to be fulfilled through suffering and death (Mark viii. 31). The reaction of the startled disciples is illustrated in Peter's attempt to controvert any such intention in his Master's mind (Mark viii. 32). The sharp retort of Jesus, " Get thee behind Me, Satan ! " is not personal to Peter, but is explained by the fact that the disciple, for the moment, had become the un-witting instrument of temptation to Jesus to use the worldly way of achieving His Messiahship. Thus this incident becomes associated with Jesus' experience of temptation in the wilderness, which may well have been related by Jesus to the disciples at this point to explain to them the royal way of suffering He had chosen. The spirited remonstrance of Peter was perfectly justified on his Jewish presuppositions, for it was absurd for Messiah to suffer and die ; not only was such a thought un-intelligible to Jews, but also it was a contradiction in terms, since the apocalyptic Messiah had as His special office the vindication of the oppressed and innocently suffering people of God ; it was His part to reverse a world order wherein the righteous suffer.   Peter's expostulation was the expression of an honest but bewildered mind, which simply could not understand that the Jesus he had identified as Messiah was destined to be a suffering Messiah. As time went on Jesus found it necessary to repeat His intimation of suffering as the way of fulfilment for Him, and each time the disciples failed to understand. It seemed to Jesus that they were at latent cross-purposes with Him on this matter; indeed, toward the end He seems to leave the disciples somewhat alone ; He is found walking alone (Mark ix. 33 f., x. 32), while they no longer talk freely with him (Mark ix. 10, 32, 34).

The last meal Jesus and His disciples had together was the scene of an observance of the *Kiddûsh* for the approaching Passover (Mark xiv. 22–25 ; John xiii. 1 f.). The cup was passed round accompanied with the pledge that Jesus would drink no more of it until He passed it round with them at the Messianic banquet. The disciples understood this eschatological allusion, but when the bread went round with the reference to the body of Jesus to be broken in His forthcoming death, the old perplexity arose once more as they failed to discern the significance of what Jesus intended.[1] When they all went out into the night after the Supper, Jesus said that they would all be " scandalized " by Him (Mark xiv. 27), and that very night too (Matt. xxvi. 31). It is beside the mark to make this a prophecy of what was to happen that fateful night. Psychologically viewed, it was the worst thing Jesus could have announced, for He would have thereby set in motion the suggestive processes that would result in the panic of flight when the critical moment arrived.   The statement is rather indicative of a state of mind which Jesus saw in His friends, for the occasion of stumbling lay in their failure to understand what was imminent in Jesus' suffering. In effect, they were already in the psychological state which would cause them to fall away as the crisis came upon them. They had not yet grown sufficiently in their experience of Jesus to view the trial before Him with the sympathetic understanding needed if they were to be of help in standing firmly by their Master. Jesus knew that He must go to the Cross alone ; let them return to Galilee, and He would come for them there after His Messianic triumph in resurrection. But they could do no other at the moment than be offended in Him. The intimations of resurrection would be meaningless (Mark viii. 31, ix. 31, x. 34) at the moment in view of the perplexity caused by the references to His coming death.[2]

In Gethsemane the agony of Jesus is watched by disciples, but the incidence of their slumber points to the length of the vigil. It may also be that the disciples, not understanding the need that Messiah should so act,

---

[1] On the religious experience involved in the Last Meal, cf. pp. 294 ff.

[2] It may be, however, that the reference to the resurrection (Mark xiv. 28) is due to an insertion in view of Mark xvi. 7. The Fayûm Gospel-Fragment omits it, but it is not certain that this fragment belongs to the Gospel (cf. M. R. James, op. cit. p. 25).

gave up the matter and hoped that it would not turn
out in so tragic a way after all. In their tired state they
slept. Luke records that they were "sleeping for
sorrow" (xxii. 45), but the sorrow was not akin to that
of Jesus, being no more than the sorrow of disappointment that Jesus should think it necessary to suffer in
order to bring in the Kingdom. The motives of Judas
in betraying Jesus have been the subject of much discussion, but if our view of the "Great Misunderstanding"
about Jesus be valid, it is by no means inconceivable
that one of the disciples should hand over Jesus to the
authorities as an impostor. Indeed, the words of Jesus,
"One of you shall betray me," and the response elicited,
"Is it I?"(Mark xiv. 18 f.), seem to suggest how near
to Judas the rest of the disciples stood. Judas shared
in the confession that Jesus was Messiah, and experienced the common disillusionment when Jesus announced His suffering and death. He took Jesus at
His word, helped Him to His predicted death, and at the
time was doubtless convinced that he had done the
right thing. Or else in Judas's view, Jesus was no
Messiah at all, and the motive of revenge for disappointment may have operated as Judas realized that He was
no Messiah in the usually accepted sense. The denial
of Jesus by Peter lights up the same psychology of disillusionment about Jesus. Following the affirmation of
Jesus that the disciples would leave Him to His fate,
Peter declared that He would stand by Jesus to the
end, whatever others might do (Mark xiv. 29). In the
hour of testing he failed to make good his words (Mark
xiv. 66–72), and his retraction is sometimes interpreted as the action of one too weak to make good his
boast. The reason, however, goes deeper down to the
disciple's experience of Jesus. The assertion that He
would stand by Jesus was probably prompted by the

conviction that even yet, despite the talk of suffering and death, Jesus would fulfil His Messiahship in the way they all longed to see. But Jesus was at last in the humiliating and unmessianic position of being on trial before Israel's authorities as a blasphemer. It was obvious that He was no Messiah after all. Peter therefore disowned Him to those who reminded him that he was a follower of the Nazarene, and thus retracted the confession that Jesus was Messiah in view of what to him were facts that belied the Messiahship in every way.

Other indications point to the failure of the disciples to perceive the import of what Jesus said and did. Rivalry with ensuing discord had to be exposed (Mark ix. 33 ff.). They forbid a man to do good in the name of Jesus since he did not belong to their company, and have to be reminded that they had no exclusive monopoly of His name and power (Mark ix. 38 ff.). Some disciples wish to call down fire upon inhospitable Samaritans, and Jesus has to rebuke such a display of vindictiveness (Luke ix. 54 f.). The sons of Zebedee ask for the chief places in the coming Kingdom, and the other disciples are incensed at what they suppose to be an attempt to get in front of them; Jesus contrasts their spirit with His own life of service and sacrifice (Mark x. 35-45).

At the moment of their desertion (Mark xiv. 50) the disciples felt that Jesus was no longer authoritative for them, since He was, as they supposed, no more than a discredited Messiah. All hopes of the Kingdom had now crumbled into the dust; gone were all the visions of glory. While Jesus went to the Cross, the disappointed and disillusioned men were left to their own bitter thoughts.

The root cause of their failure lay in the tendency, which they shared with their fellow-Jews, to look at the letter of the Kingdom instead of regarding the spirit of it. They endeavoured to fit in their experience of Jesus with a too literal interpretation of prophecies, especially in those reinterpretations of unfulfilled prophecy known as apocalyptic. " They were indeed godly men, who had already shown the sincerity of their piety by forsaking all for their Master's sake. But at the time of their call they were exceedingly ignorant, narrow-minded, superstitious, full of Jewish prejudices, misconceptions, and animosities. They had much to unlearn of what was bad, as well as much to learn of what was good, and they were slow both to learn and to unlearn. Old beliefs already in possession of their minds made the communication of new religious ideas a difficult task. Men of good honest heart, the soil of their spiritual nature was fitted to produce an abundant harvest ; but it was stiff, and needed much laborious tillage before it would yield its fruit." [1]

[1] A. B. Bruce, *The Training of the Twelve*, 1871, p. 14.

CHAPTER VI

THE EMPIRICAL SIGNIFICANCE OF THE RESURRECTION

WHAT was taking place in the minds of the eye-witnesses during the silent period between the crucifixion of Jesus and their experience of His resurrection ? The crowds went on their way to celebrate the Feast of the Passover ; all apocalyptic enthusiasms centring on Jesus were now evaporated. Yet a few would recall His attractive goodness ; His words and works, and the experiences these had created in the minds of those who heard, beheld, and received, would linger in many minds. The impelling power of His uniqueness was still dimly discerned, and there were some who found that they could not shake Him away from their minds, even though, as things stood, He had gone down in unutterable defeat. The religious authorities no doubt felt " justified " as they returned to temple or synagogue or home ; the troublesome Galilean was crucified and no more would be heard of Him. The publicans and sinners, and the many Gentile friends of Jesus among them, were in a state of real grief. Apocalyptic expectations were matters of less moment to them, but they knew the change Jesus had made in their lives, and how they who were once without religious hope had received through friendship with Jesus a new experience of God. Was death the final word for such a one ? Did they wait and wonder if anything else would be heard of Him ?

We are more specifically concerned with the disciples, not only the " Twelve," but also the wider circle which included the women disciples, and such men as the Beloved Disciple. Judas had already realized the profound mistake he had made in betraying "innocent" blood; remorse had overwhelmed him, and he was driven in despair to end his own life (Matt. xxvii. 3–5). Such a reaction suggests the probability that other disciples were beginning to wonder whether they were not mistaken in judging Jesus to be a Messiah discredited, and whether, after all, there was not more in the circumstances that faced them than they understood. The creative power of Jesus in their personal lives was silently germinating within the subconscious mind; on the other hand, there was the opposition to this inner creative activity, arising from the consciously accepted Jewish scheme of life and outlook. This was the conflict of religious experience that had to be solved; it was between their disappointed hopes and shattered dreams, and the creative impacts of Jesus at work on the deeper levels of their inner experience.

Jesus' very suffering and death were reinforcing the germinal processes active in the disciples. Although the Cross seemed for them to be a tragic mistake in the collapse of their apocalyptic hopes, yet the self-abandon which Jesus showed could not but impress them on the side of their spiritual apperceptions. Was death the end of Jesus after all? Their conscious reasoning answered " Yes "; all the reinforcement of their Jewish psychology and faith concurred with this conclusion; but deeper down the answer was beginning to be " No." At least there still remained " the unfading vision of Him who had gone straitened, tempted, alone, forsaken, but faithful to the last, to do the Will of the Father." [1] There was more yet to come. The darkness was very dark, but there was some undefined sense that some-

---

[1] N. Talbot, *The Mind of the Disciples*, 1914, p. 86.

thing was to happen, they knew not what. Did they feel with any of the intensity of Job, that through the darkness of their Master's death with its shattering of all their most ardent hopes and aspirations, there would issue a vindication of His personality and that He would know it ? Could each disciple dumbly feel, despite the contrary circumstances, " I know that my Redeemer liveth ? " (Job xix. 25).

Not that the disciples were aware of any such train of ideas in any clear or definite form. There is scarcely any information available for any precise understanding of the experiential processes at work in their minds, but we are entitled to follow the logic of religious experience to its conclusion. We are justified in using the hints afforded by their positive and negative impressions of Jesus, and by the contribution of their characteristic Jewish psychology. That the disciples were in a state of pure bewilderment is undoubted ; yet the very inhibitions caused by the momentary shock of the Cross may well have given free play to the subconscious apprehension of the significance of Jesus and their expectations in Him. Withheld by the very bewilderment from clear conclusions on the normal level of mental activity, the subconscious levels were the scene of creative activity.

During this silent period between the Cross and the Resurrection the disciples were being prepared unknowingly to receive the experience of the rising again of Jesus. They could not shake His personality from them, even if He lay in the tomb. Their trust in Him, the growing conviction that He might be right and that His truth might be vindicated in Himself, His uniqueness and commanding goodness that had impressed them so deeply, these were the spiritual constituents that were gathering force. His personality had invaded them consciously and subconsciously ; His death had created a feud, as it were, between the conscious pre-suppositions and the subconscious realization of Jesus' uniqueness.   The conscious thought was insisting, " Jesus cannot be Messiah because He was crucified " ;   the subconscious mind was all the more deeply moved by His death to retain and allow to germinate all the honour and significance already accorded to Him.   In the end the compelling power of Jesus won the day. The creative power in the subconscious won through to victory when the moment of psychological relief came and brought deliverance from the experiential conflict. Contradictions received their solution, misunderstanding gave place to discernment, the tangled skeins were unravelled, the parts coalesced in the experience of the disciples as this blossomed out into glorious meaning and unified itself in a complete whole.   The first hour of relief coincided with the first hour of the resurrection experience.

While this interpretation of the situation does not imply that the disciples kept all together, for some of them may well have returned to Galilee, the probability is that for the most part they hovered near the scene of their Master's death.   The warning words of Jesus as to their " flight " indicated a change in respect of His personality and their attitude to Him rather than any geographical change of place.   The actual flight was from Gethsemane, but not necessarily to Galilee.   The disciples remained in Jerusalem, for the Passover festival was in being.[1]

What was it the eye-witnesses experienced in the first hour of the resurrection appearances of Jesus ?   They

[1] For the view that the disciples fled to Galilee, the truth dawning on their minds amid the quiet scenes of their homes and thus result-ing in their reassembling at Jerusalem, cf. J. Weiss, *op. cit.* p. 12, and Weizsäcker, *The Apostolic Age*, Eng. Tr. vol. i. 1894, p. 1-4.   Cf. Appendix III. below, pp. 351-353.

had no doubt that the Jesus they had known " was alive again, that some of them had seen Him alive, and that therefore it was worth while going on hoping and believing that He would return again in glory." [1]   It is customary to state that " something " happened, but what that " something " was is not easy to define. What, for example, were the modes of thought in which the disciples received the experience ?   Was it the actual body of Him they had accompanied in Galilee ?   Was the experience construed in vision as an " appearance," with a discerned body more suitably expressive of eternal dignity than the one laid in the tomb ?   Or were the disciples no more than victims of hallucination due to their highly strung condition, influenced by the semi-hysteria of the women who found not His body in the tomb ?   If the actual physical body of Jesus be not the mode by which the disciples became aware that He was alive again, it does not follow that they were the victims of hallucination.   Such an assumption rides too rough-shod over the potential power of revelation through vision where the profounder levels of personality are quickened by some objective influence.   It is not sufficient to characterize any physical resurrection as objective fact, and any other mode of receiving the resurrection as merely subjective ; objective knowledge so-called requires the aid of subjective elements in the " knowing " person before even objective knowledge is possible which in any case is knowledge contained within the mind and derived ultimately from the mind.   Thus what may be erroneously dismissed as pure subjectivism may have some real objective contribution in some causal element.   On the hypothesis of ignored reality that is repressed, there may be circumstances which motive the breaking out of the repressed reality into

---

[1] F. C. Burkitt, *Christian Beginnings*, 1924, p. 50.

conscious attention, so that the resulting vision stands apart from the truth which has become objectified in the vision. We return to this aspect, and meanwhile notice in passing that the alternatives are not the physical resurrection or the experience of hallucination.

The evidence of the Gospels on this point is conflicting and gives no consistent aspect of what was the mode of apprehension whereby the resurrection experience was received. First, we have the actual physical resurrection indicated in the " empty tomb " with the implication that Jesus had risen in the actual body nailed to the Cross ; [1] the disciples were also able to take hold of His feet (Matt. xxviii. 9). Peter refers to the raising up of Messiah " according to the flesh " (Acts ii. 30), but this refers to the physical descent from David rather than to the actual resurrection (cf. Luke i. 32, 69 ; Rom. i. 3) ; even if the reference is to physical resurrection the words are probably a later addition to bring the prophecy into line with the prevailing belief in the bodily resurrection which emerged at a later stage of the Apostolic Age.[2] Second, we have appearances which do not suggest the physical presence of Jesus, as in the appearance on the mountain in Galilee (Matt. xxviii. 16–20). The fact of Jesus speaking here does not necessarily imply His physical presence in His pre-crucifixion body, since voices are a feature of the vision experience (Isa. vi. 8). If Jesus was present as He was actually in Galilee, some would not have doubted (cf.

[1] Mark xvi. 4–6 ; Matt. xxviii. 2, 6; cf. 11–15 with the suggestion of the authorities that the body had been stolen, Luke xxiv. 2 f. ; John xx. 1–10 ; cf. The Gospel of Peter, xiii. 55–57.

[2] The textual attestation of the phrase, " the Christ rose according to the flesh " is inferior, and marks an addition of a later age, being found in D*P 614 and most minuscules along with the Harkleian Syriac. The Revised Version rightly omits it. Peter, therefore, is not a witness to the resurrection " according to the flesh."

vv. 17 f.). The spurious ending to Mark's Gospel
informs us that Jesus appeared " in another form "
(xvi. 12), as though the experience were analogous to
that of the Transfiguration. That the Marcan ending
is spurious does not ·preclude the probability that we
have a genuine fragment of reminiscence embodied here.
Third, other appearances are given which are a mixture
of the material and the non-material. The walk to
Emmaus (Luke xxiv. 13 ff.) shows Jesus walking, talking,
going into a house to spend the evening, sitting at table
and eating food. These physical characteristics are
followed by features which suggest that the risen Jesus
was independent of the material order, for the moment
He was recognized, He vanished from view. The same
mixture occurs again as the two disciples are reporting
their experience at Emmaus. Jesus suddenly stood in
the midst, presumably not entering in at the door ; the
disciples are terrified, since they suppose Him to be a
spirit (Luke xxiv. 36 ff.). Yet Jesus invites the disciples
to look at His hands and feet, to handle Him and see
that He is no spirit, but flesh and bones (vv. 39 f.). In
their presence He eats, to convince them He is physically real (vv. 42 f.). The Fourth Gospel shows Mary
mistaking Jesus for the gardener, and recognition did
not come until Jesus spoke (xx. 15 f.). A material
element may be allowed here, yet the voice may be in
vision once more, and Mary's failure to recognize Jesus
suggests that it was not the familiar pre-crucifixion body
before her ; the request of Jesus, " Touch Me not,"
suggests that Mary was aware of the incorporeality of
the appearance in the garden. Once more Jesus enters
through closed doors, and this independence of the
material is again accompanied by physical demonstration
of His reality (John xx. 19 f.). The scepticism of Thomas
causes these phenomena to be repeated (xx. 26–29).

We have to distinguish the psychological outlook of the eye-witnesses from that of our modern standpoint with its sharply drawn distinctions between subjective and objective, natural and supernatural, and the more recent emphasis on the conscious and the subconscious. The modern distinctions between the physical and the spiritual, the physical and the psychical, and the psychical and the spiritual, were not made by the disciples. We have to keep before us their psychological inheritance, their mental dispositions, and their ways of spiritual apprehension. When we do so, we become aware that a mixture of physical and psychical elements is present in the experience of the resurrection and in the interpretation and explanation of the experience. Such experiences of the risen Jesus as the eye-witnesses received resulted from phenomena which they were able to interpret at one time in a physical, and at another in a psychical way, or yet at other times in a mixture or blur of both. Once more, for the Jew or Galilean, body signified what we mean by personality, *i.e.* the man as a whole. Not a man simply in his physical aspect, but the impression of the life as a whole in all its features, moods, and all that made a man just that one man amidst other men, was the significance of " body." There could have been no resurrection experience without the " body," the personality of Jesus as a whole, the sum of all that they had seen and received in Him as they knew Him in life. It would not occur to them to make sure whether it was the same physical body they had formerly known. It was the recognition of Jesus as Jesus, in His personal entity, that was significant. That is why the physical details which pander to the desire for material proof, as when Jesus eats food to demonstrate His actuality, are not unreasonably suspect as due to the later desire of the

9

Church apologetic to make the proofs of the resurrection watertight, and this has influenced the Gospel tradition as it made its way into Greek-speaking circles. Further, the prevailing ideas of personality as accessible to external influences which we designate " supernatural " suggest that phenomena such as the visions of angels [1] were due not to legendary embellishment. Given the current angelology, and the inner creative influence of Jesus upon the disciples, including the women witnesses, angelic visions are a natural accompaniment, and illustrate the " visionary " character of the resurrection experience. Finally, we have the variety in ideas of resurrection, with the resurrection of the actual physical body, the definite rejection of this in favour of a spiritual conception in which the resurrected ones are as the angels in heaven, and the mixed type where the righteous arise with their bodies as they were committed to the tomb, but glorified. [2]

As for the eye-witnesses of the resurrection of Jesus, the physical mode would fit in with their material views of the Kingdom and its Messiah, and as such would need correction in the same sense as their ideas of the Kingdom needed purifying. If their ideas remained at the old level, their construction of the resurrection would be purely a material one. But we have the educative power of their subconscious awakening to the spiritual significance of Jesus in His suffering, and this would bring in their experience of Him in a non-material mode, as in the hints afforded by the Transfiguration experience. Jesus was now as the angels in heaven. We may therefore conclude that the mode of apprehension

[1] Cf. Mark xvi. 5 f. ; Matt. xxviii. 2 f. ; Luke xxiv. 4 ; John xx. 12 f. In Luke (xxiv. 22 f.) the women eye-witnesses have evidently reported to the disciples that they had seen " a vision of angels which said that Jesus was alive," but that they themselves had not seen Jesus.

[2] Cp. p. 63.

whereby the eye-witnesses received the resurrection of Jesus was that His body had left the tomb, but had appeared to them transformed, like unto the angels, a body such as some of them had a sight of at the Transfiguration. This was why they failed to recognize Jesus on some occasions, when recognition came because of some personal bodily action such as His breaking of bread, or when He spoke in the familiar tones. It explains also the non-material data such as Jesus passing in and out of closed doors, or appearing in another form. Through it all, it was the personality of Jesus which they received in resurrection, as they interpreted the experience in thought-forms material, spiritual, or a mixture of both, according to the progress they were severally making from the material idea of the Kingdom and Messiah to the spiritual.

This conclusion is concerned only with the mental categories in which the eye-witnesses received the experience. It is another question as to what actually happened to bring the experience to them. Did the primitive Church arise from the effect produced by an amazing piece of wonder - working such as the resuscitation of a dead body already beginning to decay in the tomb ? Such a marvel is in itself devoid of the ethical and spiritual power so vital in the emergence of the Church, and constitutes just the very sort of sign which Jesus Himself deprecated as attesting His power and authority. This is the difficulty of the purely physical resuscitation, and its force cannot be turned by the assumption that there is no alternative to it but hallucination. The edge of the actual physical resuscitation is sometimes blunted by the view that Jesus appeared in His transformed body, that is, the raised physical body transformed or transfigured into the heavenly, but this explanation seems to be due to the desire to soften the crudity of the corporeal resurrection.[1]

The religious experience of the eye-witnesses contributes some data for the elucidation of what happened. The resurrection is not a new departure which inspired despairing disciples only ; it is the climax for them of what had gone before. All that Jesus meant to them, the impact of His personality, His fellowship with them, were all of such power that even in His death they were sure that somehow they were not done with their Friend. They were thus led to remain in Jerusalem, waiting for what might even yet happen in vindication. All that they had experienced in Jesus, observed in Him from day to day, His hold upon their inner life, His creative power working within them, becomes the groundwork of the resurrection experience, which came as the inevitable conclusion to a prepared state of heart and mind. It is not at all remarkable that we have no mention of any appearance of the risen Jesus to any hostile mind. Paul was hostile to Jesus, but the appearance to him came when his spiritual struggle ended in victory for the new faith, the influence of which itself had provoked the conflict in him. While recognizing that the argument from silence is not necessarily proof, the likelihood is that no appearance was possible to any one unprepared to receive such an experience.[2]

[1] It should be noted that where the bodily resuscitation is most stressed in the Gospels (Luke xxiv. 36–43 ; cf. John xxi. 5, 12 f.), it is a body that needs food. This food characteristic has to be faced by the view which urges the bodily resurrection ; if the body be the transfigured corporeal one, why was the food necessary, and is it in turn glorified ?

[2] The Gospel to the Hebrews, in a fragment preserved by Jerome (De Illustr. 2), relates that Jesus gave His shroud to the servant of the high priest, and thus implies that the servant saw the resurrection before any disciple. While some weight may be given to the evidence of this Gospel, this instance comes under similar criticism to that of the other purely corporeal aspects of the resurrection.

Paul gives a list of resurrection appearances which he claims to have received from the primitive Church (1 Cor. xv. 3, 5–8). He states that Jesus appeared (1) to Peter, (2) to the Twelve, (3) to more than five hundred witnesses at one time, (4) to James, (5) to all the apostles, (6) to himself. His insistence that this list comes from the Church prior to him, and the fact that 1 Corinthians is much earlier in date than the earliest Gospel, points to Paul's evidence being of greater value historically than what we have actually in the Gospels. The identification of these appearances with what the Gospels state is a matter of some difficulty,[1] but what is significant for our purpose is that Paul seems to have no doubt that the experience of the resurrection which he had was precisely the same kind which befell the other eye-witnesses enumerated in the list. The formula in every case is the same ("he appeared unto . . ." ὤφθη, with the dative). Paul assumes that the common experience in the manifestations, including his own, was of the same nature, namely, vision or revelation (ὀπτασία, 2 Cor. xii. 1). It is at this point that he shows himself to be our best witness as to the nature of the resurrection experience received through the appearances of the risen Jesus.

From the accounts of Paul's conversion (Acts ix. 3 ff., xxii. 6 ff., xxvi. 12 ff.) it is clear that a vision of the risen Christ came to him, accompanied by the bright light and clear audition of visionary experience. Later on he wrote, " I have seen the Lord " (1 Cor. ix. 1), and in the list of resurrection appearances he adds, " He appeared to me also," both statements referring back to the conversion experience. The import of these state-

---

[1] Cf. E. Fuchs, " Die Auferstehung Jesu Christi und der Anfang der Kirche," in *Zeitschrift für Kirchengeschichte*, 1932, i.–ii. pp. 16 f., for a recent discussion of these appearances.

ments is that the apostle had most certainly seen the risen Jesus, who appeared to him as the glorified, exalted Christ in all His heavenly dignity and majesty. Paul's companions saw nothing (Acts ix. 7) ; the experience was exclusive to him alone. Here was a vision of the risen Christ, in which the apostle's spiritual conflict was clarified. The suppressed reactions to the growing influence of Christ were in subconscious conflict with the strongly entrenched Jewish culture and Pharisaic religious experience which were responsible for the suppression of the new convictions Christ was arousing in him. These finally broke forth into conscious mastery of Paul in a vision of the risen Messiah.

When we take this experience along with his discussion of the resurrection body (1 Cor. xv. 35 ff.), we see him in line with the contemporary Pharisaic belief in the spiritual resurrection characteristic of " the cultured Pharisees in the century immediately preceding the Christian era," a view which " was of a truly spiritual nature." [1] His argument from the grain of corn which must die before it can be quickened (1 Cor. xv. 36–38) reveals that in Paul's mind the death of the body is the *sine qua non* of the new spiritual life which the resurrection foreshadows. The new grain may not be different from the old that dies, but it is, in fact, distinct, and the apostle stresses this essential distinction between the old and the new, that which dies and that which comes to new life. The old is the natural body, the new a spiritual body befitting the new existence ; the two bodies are unconnected except in so far as they are the successive organs of the spirit in both the material and the spiritual worlds. The physical body had to be destroyed in death before the spiritual body could be forthcoming. From these ideas we are able to see further into his

---

[1] R. H. Charles, *Eschatology*, p. 295.

reception of the appearance of the risen Christ as a spiritual experience of the spiritual appearance of Jesus to him, the exalted Jesus in His " spiritual " body ; not the earthly body sown in dishonour, but the one raised in glory ; not the one sown in weakness, but the one raised in power ; not the natural body, but the spiritual body ; not the body of the earth, earthy, but that which is of the heaven, the heavenly (1 Cor. xv. 43–48).

These categories he assumes in the case of the eyewitnesses noted in the list of appearances.   There were differences in the content of what was seen, in that the disciples saw the risen Jesus in thought-forms and vision elements drawn from characteristics of Jesus as He had lived and moved about with them, whereas Paul's vision was of the exalted, heavenly Messiah.   To the former, Jesus was the " human " Messiah triumphant in resurrection and exalted to the right hand of God, soon to come again and bring in the divine Kingdom ; to Paul, Jesus was the " suprahuman " or heavenly Messiah, viewed more from the spiritual Pharisaic conceptions. Such a distinction prevents us from reading too much of Paul's spiritual conceptions into the experience of the disciples, while his evidence and experience lights up the nature of the appearances of Jesus as received by the original eye-witnesses.

A conflict was set up within the minds of the disciples. It was due to convictions about Jesus against which all their conscious religious experience revolted.   The creative power of Jesus was active in them, and their growth was now speedily coming to maturity.   All that Jesus was to them was rapidly reaching the conscious surface of their lives, despite the repressing power of the outward facts of crucifixion and the apparent overthrow of their Messianic hopes.   The whole time series was against any suggestion that Jesus had triumphed.

Yet the conviction that every one was wrong, that circumstances were wrong, that Jesus *was* Messiah and likely to triumph, that all He had said and done and predicted would surely come to fruition, could no longer be prevented from breaking through all inhibitions. The conflict was clarified in a series of visions of Jesus risen and triumphant, as they were thus being prepared to be able to receive His own reappearances to them in His spiritual, glorified form. The immediate cause of the new experiences may have been a report which reached the disciples of the finding of the empty tomb by some women who had gone thither to embalm the body of Jesus, and had declared that they had seen "a vision of angels," which said that He was alive (Luke xxiv. 22 f.). The women may have come to the wrong tomb, mistaking the empty tomb for that of Jesus,[1] or Joseph may have removed the body, which had been hurriedly buried in his tomb for the Sabbath, to its own sepulchre at the close of the Sabbath.[2] The Fourth Gospel states that Mary was convinced that the body had been extracted (John xx. 2, 13, 15), and the angels do not disabuse her of her idea (vv. 12 f.). The Synoptics along with the Johannine tradition stress the visionary character of the women's experience by the angelic visions which they narrate, so that, given the women strained by grief and the contemporary angelology in which they shared, we are at the starting-point for the reception of the resurrection experience. This approach will account for the empty tomb on the Johannine theory of the extraction of the body, or else the women mistook the tomb, and in coming across an empty tomb in the garden, supposed this to be the tomb of Jesus ; being overstrained and distraught, their own

---

[1] Gardner-Smith, *op. cit.* pp. 182 f.
[2] Mackinnon, *op. cit.* p. 292.

inner conflict found its solution in the vision of angelic appearances with the message that Jesus was alive, confirmed afterwards by His appearance to them.

We conclude, therefore, that the resurrection experiences were the inevitable flowering of the seed sown by Jesus in the lives of His friends. They are the crown of the religious experience they had shared in as Jesus was with them. The significance of Jesus, suppressed by their conscious mentality, proves in itself to be the needful correction of mere subjectivity, since it was the deeper truth in Him which finally came into the foreground of their lives. Their conscious subjectivity would have prevented such an emergence had it not been overcome by spiritual dynamic of a more potent order. The objective corrective power of vision has already been illustrated by the Transfiguration experience, where the conscious misunderstanding and failure to see what Jesus had signified to them in predicting His coming suffering was objectively corrected by a vision which liberated for the time being the deeper apprehension of His significance found in their subconscious mind. Abundant illustration of the same fact is afforded in the Old Testament, where the prophets find their way to divine reality through vision which released their inner conflict. To say that vision is no more than delusion is to make most of the religious message of the prophets nothing but delusion ; the call of Isaiah (vi. 1 ff.) and of Jeremiah (i. 4–10) would be no more than hallucination, to say nothing of Ezekiel, Hosea, Amos,[1] and the rest. In all these the cause of the visions was the overmastering urge of divine reality which broke down all conscious resistance,[2] producing

---

[1] Cf. " the words of Amos . . . which he *saw* concerning Israel (i. 1)."
[2] Cf. the resistance of Isaiah (vi. 5), the hesitancy of Jeremiah (i. 6).

experiences of vision where the voice of God is heard, and accompanied here and there with various symbolic pictures. The effect was a conscious grasp of divine truth which impelled the recipient to announce what was the will of God to men, and moved him to predict the future with an extraordinary sureness which always seems to accompany truth attained through vision.

Through vision the eye-witnesses reached the truth that Jesus was not held by the power of death. It overmastered them in its spiritual potency. Spiritual experience cannot delude, when men are faithful to it. This is the answer to the view that the vision hypothesis reduces the rising again of Jesus to mere subjective delusion. The spiritual potency of Jesus, when death released Him from earthly limitations, was able to present Him in His glorified state to disciples whom He Himself had creatively prepared to receive the revelations of His triumph over death. This religious experience and discovery, on which was based the primitive Church, stands out clearly in its solidity as a permanent datum of the Gospel concerning Jesus Christ, by the side of which the more doubtful elements such as the empty tomb and the inconsistent evidence of the Gospels appear of a secondary or even a tertiary order.

The weeks subsequent to the initial resurrection appearances seem to have been a period of intense visionary experience. Jesus was seen by various individuals, and by a multitude of over five hundred people at one time (1 Cor. xv. 6) who may well have seen Jesus somewhere in Galilee ; [1] they would include friends' of Jesus, members of His family,[2] publicans and sinners,

---

[1] Cf. J. Weiss, *op. cit.* p. 18.

[2] For the tradition of resurrection appearances to James, the brother of Jesus, cf. "The Gospel to the Hebrews," quoted by Jerome (*De Illust.* 2).

disciples who had returned to Galilee, who renewed their fellowship with Jesus in the resurrection experiences. The wealth of these appearances is hinted at elsewhere (Acts i. 3), and displays the objectivity of Jesus' overcoming of death in that He was able to appear again to so many minds prepared to receive the experience.

The Ascension was a resurrection appearance, and falls within the empirical series in which we have viewed the resurrection of Jesus. It is not altogether accounted for by the primitive expectation of His return from heaven, implying that He must have returned thither before He could come back to earth. It is true that pre-Copernican ideas of the universe with the conception of the earth as flat, the heavens high above, was the prevailing cosmology of the time, but if the ascension experience was a vision experience it would be construed in a series of such ideas, and Jesus would be seen in vision to go right upwards into the sky until He disappeared from sight. That " the Ascension was the disciples' interpretation of the cessation of the Appearances and the special character of one of them " [1] is probably true, but we may modify this view by regarding the Ascension less as a cessation of appearances, and more as the prelude to the ardently desired consummation of all things in the return of Messiah (Acts i. 11).

We have found it necessary to set forth some suggestion as to what we are to think of the resurrection, in view of the emergence of the primitive Church amidst the empirical conditions which directly arose from the eye-witnesses' experience of the risen Jesus. There is more involved than historical evidence. An answer has to be forthcoming that will satisfy the soul of the inquirer into these fundamental issues. We have been

[1] J. F. Bethune-Baker, *The Faith of the Apostles' Creed*, 1918, p. 133.

led by the historical and other evidence to account for
the resurrection phenomena by way of vision and
audition. We would, however, make it clear that this
view is one which also best satisfies the soul since we
are not driven to dependence on a mere outward sign to
attest the truth of the triumphant presence of the risen
Jesus, and thus far we are at one with the attitude and
spirit of Jesus Himself. If the Son of God passed from
the limitations of His earthly life to the presence of the
Father, what is significant is that He had created the
spiritual conditions which enabled the eye-witnesses to
receive direct evidence from the other side of death that
the Jesus they had known in life was all and more than He
had claimed to be and that they had discerned in Him.
The " vision " explanation is also in line with the best
religious tradition of the prophets, and with the issues
involved in apocalyptic and its expectations. The
remarkable sureness characteristic of prophet or apocalyptic seer finds its complement in the extraordinary
certainty which possessed the disciples that Jesus was
risen ; such sureness is an accompaniment of truth
reached through vision ; it seems to be deeper down
than the memory of any sense impression that Jesus
had risen from the dead. The diversity of the tradition
and its details suggests that on the plane of sense the
eye-witnesses were by no means agreed on what had
taken place, but there is unanimity in the deeper sense
of realizing that Jesus had conquered death and had
shown His glorified personality to many of them. The old
objection to the vision hypothesis, that the disciples were
not expecting the resurrection, is offset by the creative
facts and influences of their subconscious preparation to
receive their Lord once more. The psychology of vision
is helping us to appraise the truth value of " vision "
experience as leading to the sure attainment of reality.

The authority of Jesus, lost as it seemed through His death, was not only restored for the disciples, but was discerned in a more potent way than had hitherto been realized. All doubt that He was God's Messiah was removed for ever. The ascension vision was their registering of the conviction that Jesus had been exalted, and that He was soon to return in the same way as He had been seen to depart, namely, in His well-known, recognizable personality (Acts i. 11). Filled with such a hope, which was now intensified beyond measure, the disciples left the scene of the last resurrection appearance, the Ascension, and repairing to Jerusalem, they gathered enthusiastic eye-witnesses as they went, until some hundred and twenty people were together in a mood of glowing certainty that the exalted Jesus would return at any hour. They became eager to share in His triumph as He descended the pinnacle of the temple in glory.[1] Deep joy, expressive of the heightened anticipations, was their mood, and they were continually in the temple, praising God (Luke xxiv. 52 f.), not simply because they were pious Jews, but like the aged Simeon they expected their Messiah to return there, and they desired to be there to meet Him as He came back (Luke ii. 25 f.). It was in such an atmosphere of vivid expectation, motived by a profound religious experience, that, almost before they were aware of what was taking place, the tremendous uprush of creative spiritual power which we call the experience of Pentecost, came upon them.

[1] Cf. Matt. iv. 5-7; Luke iv. 9-12; Mal. iii. 1. Cf. also the Messianic pledge in the eschatological cup of the last meal Jesus and His disciples shared together, pp. 294 f.

PART THREE

THE EMERGENCE OF THE CHURCH

CHAPTER VII

THE EXPERIENCE OF THE SPIRIT

THE enthusiastic and expectant men and women who were gathered in Jerusalem to await what was to come, gave themselves up to prayer (Acts i. 13 f.), worship, and common meditation wherein they recollected much of what Jesus had said and done, and thereby gave the start to the Gospel tradition which merged into our Gospels. During one of their gatherings, at which they had been probably observing the *Kiddûsh* for the Feast of Pentecost, or maybe even as the celebration was being observed, the believers became aware that something extraordinary was taking place in their midst. A sound as of a rushing mighty wind seemed to shake the house where they were all assembled, cloven tongues as of fire seemed to rest on every one present, and with one accord they all broke out into strange, uncontrollable speech. The conclusion they all reached was that they were all filled with "holy spirit" (Acts ii. 1–4).

These abnormal features belong to the thought-forms in which the experience of the Spirit was received. They are parts of the psychological mechanisms involved where minds are accustomed to the idea of the Spirit of God as a wind-like energy invading human life, and might well experience such in the form of the sound of a rushing wind. The vivid inner experience has results on the system of sensation such as to produce vivid auditory phenomena. The "fire" forms the abnormal visual element in the experience; it was, of course, "an early and natural symbol of the energy

10   145

and glory of the divine,"[1] and no doubt pointed to
the Messianic " fire " of Judgment which the believers
felt was so imminent.[2]   Yet we have to allow for the
probability that the " fire " denoted that the Pentecost
phenomena were psychologically determined on the
physical side rather than on the symbolic, being a vivid
sensation of light, a common feature of abnormal
religious experience.   There is no hint of any burning
or heat ; the phenomenon seems to have been no more
than the sensory effect of bright light due to religious
stress operating abnormally upon the senses.   It is
not sufficient to regard the abnormal elements as merely
metaphorical,[3] or symbolical,[4] for the contribution of
over-stimulated senses is very noteworthy.   The abnormal effects were the result of the heightening of
sensation under the stimulus of a tremendous spiritual
experience, but behind the extraordinary auditory and
visual phenomena was a corresponding objective reality
as in the case of the transfiguration and resurrection experiences.   That reality was experience of the invasive
Spirit coming upon minds prepared by their ante-
cedent experience of " spirit " energy as received in the
tradition of their religious inheritance and environment.

As the narrative stands we are given the impression
that the phenomena described as " to speak in (or with)
other tongues " refers to foreign dialects and languages.
Luke, however, under the missionary influence of the
Church's outlook at a later stage, has misinterpreted

[1] J. V. Bartlet, *Acts, CB.* on Acts ii. 3.
[2] Matt. iii. 11 ; Luke iii. 16 ; cf. Mal. iii. 2 f.
[3] As H. T. Andrews, *Acts, WNT.* 1908, p. 47.
[4] R. B. Rackham, *Acts, WC.* pp. 19–21.   E. F. Scott, *Beginnings of
the Church*, pp. 60 f., thinks that Luke is influenced by the story that
when the law was given at Sinai, God's voice assumed the shape of
a flame of fire which divided itself into seventy languages (Philo,
De Decal. 9, 11), but the resemblance is too superficial even to be of
use for symbolic explanation of the Pentecost phenomena.

his facts (or the tradition on which he relies is responsible)
by assuming an actual endowment of miraculous linguistic powers from the first beginnings of the Church.   It
is not probable, however, that any such endowment
took place.   Greek was the general medium of linguistic
exchange in the ancient world and so the endowment
was unnecessary.   The speech of Peter which follows
the Pentecost experience (Acts ii. 14 ff.) makes no
reference to any linguistic gifts, replying only to the
charge of intoxication made by some who had witnessed
the extraordinary speaking (Acts ii. 15), and it is unlikely that speaking in foreign languages would have
provoked such a charge.   The supposed linguistic
endowment of the early Christian preachers failed in
the case of Saul and Barnabas who did not understand
the Lycaonian dialect (Acts xiv. 8 ff.), and according to
Papias, Peter needed Mark as an interpreter (Eus. *H.E.*
iii. 39 ; Iren. *Adv. Haer*, iii. 1. 1. x. 6).   The most serious
difficulty lies in the extraordinary fact that " if the tale
is told so as to suggest missionary effort in strange
tones and dialects," [1] the authors have overlooked the
strange obtuseness of the Twelve to their duty of preaching Christ to the Gentiles, a fact all the more remarkable
if they had been equipped with the power of speaking
in foreign languages for this special purpose.

The strange language is an inspired form of speech
which seems to have been fairly widespread in the
Church during the first twenty years of its existence.
Peter's Jewish friends in the house of Cornelius were
astonished that the Spirit had been poured out on the
Gentiles, a fact attested for them in that the Gentiles
were speaking with tongues (Acts x. 46).   Peter justified
his baptism of Cornelius on the ground that the Spirit
had fallen on the convert and his friends in the same

---

[1] Burkitt, *op. cit.* p. 91.

way as it had come upon the believers at Pentecost in
the beginning (Acts xi. 15). For Peter, at least, the
speech phenomena of Pentecost were similar to what
he saw in the house of Cornelius.   The Spirit descended
upon the believers at Ephesus as Paul baptized them in
the name of Jesus, the attestation again being that they
began to speak in tongues (Acts xix. 6).   Paul refers to
the phenomenon as if it were a usual feature of Christian
worship (1 Cor. xiv. 2 ff.), and its character was such
that it needed interpretation before it became intelligible to those who heard (ver. 27) ; because of the
unintelligibility involved, Paul would rather speak a
few words intelligibly than utter many words in tongues
(ver. 19).   The tongue speech seems therefore to have
been a form of inspired utterance characterized by unintelligibility.   Uncontrollable religious emotion induced
a mood of ecstatic excitement which found an outlet in ejaculatory sounds conveying no meaning to
those who heard.   The primitive Church and the later
Pauline Church were receiving continually new visions
of divine reality, new truths and powers were breaking
in upon the believers, new religious experiences were
frequent, as the tides of the new faith swept in and out.
Men found the usual channels of speech quite inadequate
to express what they were experiencing.   " A man's
mind is full of something which he wishes to express in
words, and instinctively he makes the effort of speech,
but the words that come are nothing but a series of
arbitrary sounds that only resemble words." [1]

There was, however, more than intense emotion
behind the strange speech. For the speaker, at least,
there was meaning in it, for he expressed to God the
praise and worship in his own soul (1 Cor. xiv. 2).   While
the new power could only find verbal expression in un-

[1] E. F. Scott, *The Spirit in the New Testament*, 1923, p. 101.

meaning vocables, " the new religious experience did in
fact create a new language of its own, one of more immediate speech with God in ecstatic prayer." [1]   Even
Paul explored heights and depths of religious experience
which could find expression only in " unspeakable
words " (2 Cor. xii. 4), while there were direct experiences of God because of the Spirit's indwelling which
could be expressed only " with groanings that cannot be
uttered " (Rom. viii. 26).

This is the character of the strange speech of the
Pentecost experience.   We know that prior to the event
the believers were given much to prayer (Acts i. 14) ;
there were the throbbing expectations centring on the
risen Jesus, and ardent hopes of His immediate return.
Even as they were praying they felt that He might be
on the very point of coming through the closed doors,
and saying, " Peace be with you ! " (Luke xxiv. 36).
In such an atmosphere depths of spiritual intensity and
reserves come to be opened up in all their power.   On
one such occasion when they were at prayer, came the
Pentecost experience.   C. A. Scott's phrase, " The
Uprush of Life," [2] serves at least to denote the climax
of all the hopes, the prayers, the aspirations, the impressions, and experiences they had had of Jesus, centred
in Jesus and motived by the creative contact with Jesus,
from the initial contacts and impressions in Galilee to
the triumph of His rising from the dead.   Underneath
the conscious elements of their experiences of the risen
Jesus, and of their eager anticipations of His parousia,
there was the dynamic effect of the character and the
death and sufferings of Jesus creative in the subconscious
of a directed mass of emotion and spiritual force which
had to find its outlet.   The suppressed excitements and

[1] J. V. Bartlet, *The Apostolic Age*, p. 12, note 1.
[2] *The Fellowship of the Spirit*, 1921, title of chapter iii.

quickened spiritual powers could no longer be held in check. The believers were overwhelmed in the flood-tide of the new experience of the Spirit, as their inhibitions were all released. Traditional images and associations came to the forefront in the windlike noise and the tongue-like flames of light, and the effort to express what the believers were undergoing resulted in the uncontrollable outbreak of ecstatic, inarticulate speech. The normal channels of personality were for the moment too restricted and too inadequate to contain the heights and depths of the new experience, and escape had to be made in abnormal ways.

The conclusion reached in the minds of the believers that their experience was due to the Spirit was reached through the mental categories of their traditional Jewish psychology. The abnormal accompaniments were for their minds " symptoms " attesting the Spirit's invasion of their lives. They reasoned back from the effects to the cause and realized that they were filled with the Spirit who had invaded and possessed their spirit. The higher incursion had taken place. The same energy which would operate in the returning Messiah and bring in the divine Kingdom was in them. Thus their present experience seemed to confirm that their eager anticipations were soon to be realized.

What emerges from the Pentecost experience is a group of men and women unified by a vital experience of Jesus and of the Spirit who animated both Him and the believers. They had " a common attitude of mind and will to Him who had been known as Jesus of Nazareth." [1] The abnormal features should not be allowed to obscure this inner content, by regarding them merely as the symptoms of hysteria or pathological dis-

[1] C. Anderson Scott, " What Happened at Pentecost," in *The Spirit*, ed. B. H. Streeter, 1919, p. 125.

turbance.   They were the inevitable accompaniments of
the stirring awakening ; we should have strong reason to
suspect the genuineness of the experience and its
narration if these were absent.   At the minimum we
have " shiftings of character to higher levels " [1] in the
believers, but at its maximum they were lifted up to a
Christ consciousness that resulted in the emergence of
the Christian Church.   The windlike noise is lost in the
dim distance, the tongues as of fire extinguished, the
ecstatic speech no more heard.   These are only the
accidentals of the great experience, having no permanent
quality, their significance infinitesimal for the extraordinary spiritual and moral consequences of Pentecost.
Paul had to warn his churches against mistaking the
accidentals for the real content of the Christian experience (1 Cor. xiv.), but what stands out clearly is the
turning-point of a new religious experience which
centred in the risen Jesus and His creative power upon
the entwined emotions, loyalties, and self-surrender of the
first believers who went forth to their contemporaries
with the news of Jesus the Messiah.

    If we ask, " What was the power actually experienced
at Pentecost ? " we may reply, as would the historian,
" The Holy Spirit."   If we push the question further
back, however, it becomes " Who or What is the Holy
Spirit ? "   Such a question opens up vistas of theological
inference and philosophical speculation the chief feature
of which would be the very vagueness and nebulosity
which a vista suggests.   The Christian Church with its
doctrine of the Holy Spirit seems to be without " the
historic landmarks by which the student of Christology
or of the doctrine of Justification can orientate himself." [2]

---

[1] William James, *The Varieties of Religious Experience*, 1920, p. 257.
[2] H.W.Robinson, *The Christian Experience of the Holy Spirit*, 1928, p.2.

We have to bear in mind Gunkel's caution [1] against looking for any systematic teaching about the Spirit in the primitive Church. Since the coming of the Spirit was vitally connected with what the believers had experienced of Jesus in His resurrection and exaltation we find it necessary to inquire whether Jesus gave any teaching on the Spirit to the disciples. The answer is that there is surprisingly little teaching,[2] but the more important empirical approach has to be considered. Those who saw and heard Jesus in astonishment at His words and works had no hesitation in ascribing those very wonders to the activity of the Spirit in Jesus Himself; the extraordinary nature, the unique power of Jesus, would lead them to postulate the same active energy as caused the contemporaries of Joseph and Elijah to conclude that these were men in whom the Spirit of the Lord was. For Jesus was extraordinary. All He did and said was extraordinary. In Him the Spirit of God must be at work. The fact of confessing Jesus as Messiah carried with it the corollary that in Him was recognized the Spirit's presence, for it was through the agency of the Spirit of God that Messiah would be equipped to bring in the divine Kingdom (cf. pp. 68 f.). Little wonder, therefore, that the Gospels, based on the impressions of the eye-witnesses, account for Jesus' activity and uniqueness by the Spirit. The birth of Jesus is ascribed to a physical generation by the Spirit in the womb of Mary the Virgin (Matt. i. 18–20). Jesus may well have related His own experience of the Spirit's descent upon Himself at His baptism, but the Spirit's coming was for the disciples the key that fitted the lock which opened up for them His

---

[1] *Op. cit.* p. 4.
[2] On this point see Appendix IV., " The Teaching of Jesus on the Holy Spirit,' pp. 354–357.

THE EXPERIENCE OF THE SPIRIT

uniqueness.[1]   It was the Spirit that drove Jesus afterwards into the wilderness (Mark i. 12), and on His return
He is possessed to the full by the same power (Luke
iv. 14).   His extraordinary life produced a perpetual
impression of remarkable power ; indeed, " any one
who wishes to know the New Testament connotation of
' Spirit ' must use his concordance also for the term
' power,' which is its chief content." [2]

From this standpoint, the Gospels, which at first
glance seem to have little reference to the Spirit, are
shot through and through with the Spirit's power and
activity as beheld by the eye-witnesses in the words
and actions of Jesus.   In view of this datum derived
from their religious experience, and applied by them to
Jesus, there was no special need for Jesus to give the
disciples " some such preparatory teaching about the
gift of the Holy Spirit as is conveyed in His last discourses before His passion according to St. John." [3]
The references to the Spirit in these discourses have more
the colour of the later doctrine of which Paul is the
mediator, for the centre of gravity in them is the risen
and glorified Lord whose presence on earth is now
replaced by the Paraclete (John xiv. 16 f., 26, xv. 26,
xvi. 13 f.).   But for the primitive Church there was no
such idea as the coming of the Spirit at Pentecost to
compensate for the going away of Jesus.   The facts point
in another direction.   Sundry groups reacted to Jesus
during His ministry, and with one exception, all would
regard Jesus as the channel of the Spirit's power invading
Him and possessing Him.   This exception is furnished
by the scribes and Pharisees, who, perceiving something

[1] The baptism with the Spirit's descent was " the Divine explanation of the marvellous personality and deeds of Jesus " ; D. S. Cairns,
The Faith that Rebels, 5th edn. 1933, p. 96.

[2] H. W. Robinson, *op. cit.* p. 128.

[3] C. Gore, *The Holy Spirit and the Church*, 1924, p. 111.

of the extraordinary in His powers, ascribed the source of His energy to the prince of the demons, thus falling back on another " supernatural " source to account for Jesus of Nazareth. But for the eye-witnesses in general, as Jesus passes on to the Cross and to resurrection and exaltation, all is viewed as being due to the power of the Spirit. The Spirit was taken for granted as accounting for Jesus ; this is why so little of His activity is actually ascribed in the Gospels to the Spirit. The very expectation of Jesus' return as Messiah with the divine Kingdom is to be brought about by the same power working in Him. This divine power had come upon the believers at Pentecost ; it was inter-related with their experience of Jesus, and had been made possible for them by Jesus.

The immediate result of the new experience of the Spirit's invasion at Pentecost was the witness of a group or community to the life, death, and resurrection of Jesus the Messiah, soon to make His advent. The experience of the Spirit is mentioned explicitly to prove from prophecy that the Spirit's coming in such power indicated that the " last days " prior to the coming of the Kingdom had arrived. The Spirit's descent and the believers' reception of the new power was the sure sign that Jesus Messiah, now in exaltation, had fulfilled His promise, and had sent the Spirit upon them as a pledge of His imminent return in glory (Acts ii. 33).

Analogies may be drawn from religious history to light up the nature of the Pentecost experience. Speaking of Montanus, Eusebius states that he was carried away in (the) Spirit, being "wrought up into a certain kind of frenzy and extraordinary ecstasy, raving, and speaking, and shouting strange things " (H.E. v. 16). It may be that the ecstasy of Montanus was deliberately induced,[1] in which case we have no light from Montanus on Pentecost. It may be, however, that the growing conservatism of the Church caused Montanus to react in an acute spiritual manner, to receive an outpouring of the Spirit which Montanus believed would descend in great power as upon the community at the first Pentecost. The resulting spiritual ecstasy would be due to association of ideas with the Spirit, the " symptom " of whose activity was that very ecstasy, an idea by no means dead in the Church of the second century, despite Paul's warning about it.[2] The further association, characteristic of Montanism, of this ecstatic experience of the Spirit with the expectation of the parousia of the Christ, strengthens the backward reference to the primitive Church wherein the immediate conclusion drawn from the Pentecost experience of the Spirit was that Jesus would make His advent almost at once. Thus there is reflected in this heresy of the second century something of the atmosphere of the primitive Church.

The Camisards of France revealed an intensified religious experience due to the fierce pressure of persecution. During the rising of the seventeenth century, many of the Protestants of Languedoc went into an ecstasy which infected people of all ages. " They heard supernatural voices. They spoke with tongues. Children of the tenderest years were the subjects of most extraordinary manifestations. Quite uneducated persons gave utterance, when ' seized by the Spirit,' to prophecies in the purest French." [3]   Here again we have hints of the Pentecost atmosphere.

---

[1] As H. J. Lawlor thinks, *ERE.* vol. viii., art. " Montanism," p. 828.
[2] Cf. H. M. Gwatkin, *Early Church History*, 2nd edn. 1912, vol. ii. pp. 80 f.
[3] C. Anderson Scott, *ERE.* vol. iii., art. " Camisards," p. 176.

The spiritual atmosphere of the *Journal* of George Fox is very suggestive in this connection. ". . . it was opened unto me by the eternal light and power, and I saw clearly therein that all was done, and to be done, in and by Christ. . . . Then after this, there did a pure *fire* appear in me ; then I saw *how He sate as a refiner's fire* . . ." (pp. 9 f.).[1] Fox attended a large meeting, and " the Lord opened my mouth . . . and the power of the Lord was over them all " (p. 11). " I *saw* the harvest white, and the seed of God lying thick in the ground. . . . The Lord's *power brake forth*; and I had great openings *and prophecies* " (p. 12). " The Lord's *power* began to *shake* them . . ." (p. 13). " I was moved to pray, and the Lord's power was so great *that the house seemed to be shaken* " (p. 13). Again and again we read that " the Lord's power brake through " (p. 15), " wrought mightily," and " was wonderfully manifested " (pp. 15 ff.). The people " wait to feel the Lord's power and spirit in themselves " (p. 45). At Carlisle, as Fox was speaking, " the power of the Lord was dreadful amongst them in the steeple-house, so that the people trembled and shook, and they thought the steeple-house shook ; and some of them feared it would fall down on their heads " (p. 87).

It may be that Fox, either of set purpose, or at the least subconsciously, is reproducing the Pentecost conditions ; " when I had done . . . some said it was now as in the days of the apostles, when the house was shaken where they were " (p. 13). Even so, from the potent religious experience of Fox, conditions were created which bear some analogy to those in which the primitive community felt the coming of the Spirit, and found expression in visionary and auditory phenomena.

[1] References to the *Journal* are from the Tercentenary text, ed. Penny, *EL*.

Religious upheavals have many features in common, whether that of the first Pentecost or that stirred into activity by Fox. It is to miss the point if these abnormal elements in Fox are treated as symbolic only. They are the inevitable outcome of a mind so charged with religious potency that the normal function of sensation is too restricted. If his *Journal* reveals Fox to have " an unstable psychic constitution," [1] his religious experience was far from being disintegrating in effect, for " he has the distinction of being the founder of a religious sect which has for two centuries and a half continued the mystical type of Christianity which he initiated " as he pursued " his practical attempt to revive ' primitive Christianity.' " [2]

If it is held that Pentecost shows a similar " unstable psychic constitution " in the experiencing disciples, it is essentially true that, as in the case of Fox, the new religious power proved too much for the normal mental mechanisms of personality, and found an outlet in abnormal sensory phenomena. The psychologically abnormal is not simply that which has to be explained by psychological causes, and revealing the " something more " which still remains ; it should be viewed as the necessary means by which the spiritual thing comes to be. Visual, auditory, and strange-speech elements due to subjective stimulus, marking stages in the *disintegration* of personality, must have something quite different as their centre from similar phenomena which make for, and apparently are themselves the means to, greater *integration* ; the former may be no more than merely pathological in origin, but the latter, as in the case of

---

[1] *Op. cit.* p. x., Intro. by Rufus Jones. Cf. W. C. Middleton, " The Denunciations of George Fox viewed Psychologically," *JR*. xi. Oct. 1931, pp. 589 ff.

[2] Rufus Jones, *Studies in Mystical Religion*, 1923, pp. 482 f.

Pentecost, Fox, and other examples we proceed to give, have obvious claims to be considered as authentic tidings and marks of the spiritual essence of the universe, that is, of divine reality, since they contain that which makes for deeper integration of personality.

David Brainerd unwittingly affords a medium link for understanding the phenomena involved in the stress of religious experience. "As I was walking in a dark thick grove, unspeakable glory seemed to open to the view and apprehension of my soul. I do not mean any external brightness, for I saw no such thing ; nor do I intend any imagination of a body of light, somewhere away in the third heavens, or anything of that nature ; but it was a new inward apprehension or view that I had of God, such as I never had before, nor anything which had the least resemblance to it." [1] The medium link lies in the distinction that Brainerd makes between the glory he saw and what he did not see. This effort to semi-rationalize a vivid religious experience is a sort of half-way house between the realisms of Pentecost and the modern attempts to rationalize extraordinary religious phenomena. But in his overwhelming sense of the divine presence Brainerd stands with the believers at Pentecost, although they could not have made the distinction as he did.

The Irvingite movement arose from the insistence that the Spirit's remarkable gifts, as manifested at Pentecost and in the apostolic Church, were a permanent possession of the Church, withheld because of the unfaithfulness of Christian believers. A parishioner of the Rev. Mr. McLeod's became an incurable invalid, and spiritual manifestations appeared in her which were of such a nature as to lead her friends to claim them as a reappearance of the tongues spoken in the apostolic

[1] *Diary and Journal*, vol. i. 1902, July 12, 1739.

Church. Other psychical phenomena were reported, and Erskine, after thorough investigation, decided for their genuineness. " They may, perhaps, be classed and judged with similar manifestations in other parts of Christendom. Irving, predisposed alike by character and antecedents, at once accepted them as a baptism of the Holy Spirit and Fire." [1]

" In 1910 I was present at a religious meeting in Chicago," states J. B. Pratt, [2] " in which the brethren and especially the sisters spoke in tongues, but in these cases the speaking was almost invariably confined to exclamations more or less long." " In fact the practice of speaking with tongues is probably to be found in some part of the United States nearly all the time." [3]

Luke may have misinterpreted the facts when he makes the polyglot witnesses of the Pentecost abnormalities say that they were hearing " every man his own language " spoken (Acts ii. 5–12) ; there may, however, be hints of truth conveyed in such an impression. John Woolman once spoke to Indians, and finding the interpreters of little use, spoke in English. The result was that " I believe the Holy Ghost wrought on some hearts to edification where all the words were not understood." [4] In so far as the Spirit-possessed preacher was understood, it may have seemed to such that he spoke in their own language. A clearer instance is cited by C. Anderson Scott in reference to an œcumenical conference of the Salvation Army " at which were present representatives of nations even more numerous and more heterogeneous than those tabulated in Acts ii. A report of one of the meetings contains the following

---

[1] J. G. Simpson, *ERE*. vol. vii. p. 424.
[2] *The Religious Consciousness*, 1923, p. 187.
[3] *Ibid*. p. 186.
[4] *Journal*, June 19th, 1762.

striking sentence : ' Each time the theme (the saving love of God in Christ) was touched upon, it brought forth from the pent-up feelings of the vast assembly a sort of half-sigh of appreciation. Yet many in the audience knew no English, but they felt that the one great truth to them was being announced at this particular moment. Indians, Chinese, Canadians, Peruvians, Swedes, all of them gave the deep emotional response.' " Professor Scott goes on to say that " it would not be difficult to believe that when the speaker on that occasion had finished, representatives of these various races would be found saying, ' We heard him speaking in our tongue the mighty works of God.' " [1] The onlookers at Pentecost may have so caught the spiritual strains of the speaking with tongues that it seemed to every one that the disciples were speaking in the several languages (Acts ii. 11) ; [2] the audience of the œcumenical conference, however, was *en rapport* with the theme of the speaker, whereas at Pentecost we have a surprised body of polyglot people who came across the believers speaking in the languages represented by the onlookers, as Luke reports it. This vital distinction tells against Luke's interpretation, for there was no psychological unity of experience, no necessary spiritual sympathy between the pilgrims and the disciples.

One example of abnormal religious phenomena from non-Christian religious experience may be given. The Chaitanyite Revival in India in the earlier half of the sixteenth century centred round the personality of Chaitanya who, through the stimulus of a heightened

[1] Quoted in " What Happened at Pentecost," in *The Spirit*, ed. B. H. Streeter, 1919, p. 128 f.

[2] The onlookers were foreign proselytes and God-fearers, up for the feast, and as such were susceptible to religious impression.

spiritual experience, became an apostle of Krishna-bhakti. " He sang and chanted Krishna's name for hours together till he became delirious with *bhakti*. . . . The revival which Chaitanya set on foot inspired countless lives of devotion and won converts from every class of society." [1] Here, again, the heightening of the emotions under religious stress, and the intensification of the abnormal in human personality that resulted therefrom, remind us of the Pentecostal atmosphere.

In all these instances cited from Christian religious experience there is powerful suggestion derived from the phenomena of Pentecost. Professor Pratt, however, seems to miss the inner connection of the empirical " symptoms " with the vital dynamic which is their cause, when he explains that " when one is sure 'from the intensity of one's feelings that the Holy Ghost is within one, it comes into one's head to express one's emotions by speaking in an unknown tongue." [2] Those who are worked up in emotional tension do not pause to ask themselves if the intensity of their experience warrants the inference that the Spirit is in possession of them, nor thereupon does a cognitive process supervene and give the " possessed " the idea that they ought to break out into strange speech. The truth seems to be that the mechanisms of ordinary speech are too inadequate for use under the religious stress. Further, the extraordinary religious experience is in being before any likeness to that of Pentecost can be suggested. While the abnormal forms may be suggested by the experience of the primitive Church, yet in so far as they are the genuine indices of the spiritual power in those who manifest them, they are the genuine psychological

[1] A. C. Underwood, *Conversion, Christian and non-Christian*, 1925, p. 56.
[2] *Op. cit.* p. 184.

II

accompaniments of enhanced religious experience as inspired by the Spirit in the sense of Pentecost. While many of these manifestations may be suggested by Pentecost, that very suggestiveness makes them analogous to the primitive Church experience, and helps us to appraise the atmosphere of that momentous occasion.

We should not overlook the influence of the group here. A company of individuals under the same religious stress introduces an element which is in itself a powerful means of heightening the suggestibility of the whole gathering. The mutual " continuing instant in prayer " of the believers in the Upper Room (Acts i. 14) acted and reacted on the individuals there. Each took fire from each ; the whole group became religiously and psychologically infected by the experience of the individual members. After their renewed fellowship with Jesus risen from the dead, and overwhelmingly sure that He was soon to return with the Kingdom, they had returned to Jerusalem to await the promise of the Father in the coming of the power which should descend on them. The crisis was at hand. The days went by, and every disciple influenced the other in earnest desire, which increased the more they met and talked about it ; they encouraged one another in joyful hope, prayed continually, and every one was in a state of preparedness and likemindedness. The fulfilment came about. The big thing happened. The clouds of heaven, as it were, burst upon them, mind and spirit received illumination, the limiting inhibitions which bound them to their religious antecedents were done away as in heart, mind, and will the believers were surrendered entirely to the new power that came upon them. The tides of emotion swept to and fro, and set up psychological abnormalities which have led some scholars to conclude that these were but mythical accretions, but which were rather the historical indices of a vital religious awakening which produced in its new loyalties results unique and life-changing.

The continued activity of the Spirit is revealed in the growing community by the presence of marvellous works which were viewed as " symptoms " of the power operative in the believers. They pray that signs and wonders may be wrought through them that persecutors may be convinced of the truth about Jesus of Nazareth (Acts iv. 30 ; cf. 27–30) ; the prayer is ratified by the attesting Spirit in such power that it seemed as if the very house in which they were gathered were being shaken (ver. 31). The Spirit is indeed active, for the signs and wonders continue (Acts v. 12) ; they form the inevitable accompaniments of the missionary activity of Barnabas and Saul (Acts xiv. 3), while miracles are wrought by God with Paul as the Spirit's medium (Acts xix. 11).   Paul gains so great a reputation for healing that articles touched by his body, when carried to the afflicted, bring healing to them (Acts xix. 12) ; in the same way the shadow of Peter, passing by, falls on the sick, with healing results (Acts v. 15).   Peter heals a lame man, and the cure is attributed not to his own power, but to that of God which had raised up Jesus, namely, the Spirit (Acts iii. 1–7, 12).   The same dynamic was within Stephen, as was seen from the great signs and wonders which he wrought (Acts vi. 8) ; Philip aroused instant attention in Samaria by " signs " in the casting out of demons, and the healing of the palsied and the lame (Acts viii. 6–8) ; Simon Magus is amazed at such potency, and he desires to possess the Spirit to enable him to work similar wonders (ver. 18 f.).

We may therefore conclude that for the believers in the primitive Church these healings were the

" symptoms " of the Spirit's control in the community.
We are not surprised to discover that " healings,"
" gifts of healings," are enumerated among the manifestations of the Spirit according to Paul's list (1 Cor.
xii. 9, 28, 30). The primitive community looked back
to the signs and wonders, *i.e.* chiefly the healing activities
of Jesus as due to divine power approving His ministry
(Acts ii. 22 ; cf. Jn. iii. 2). The attesting power is
further defined when Jesus is set forward as one endowed
with the Spirit, that is, with power, the result of which
was " doing good " in the healing and deliverance
brought by him (Acts x. 38). When we link up these
experiential discoveries of the primitive community
with what we observe in the miracles of Jesus (pp. 92–94),
and view them from the standpoint of religious experience, we reach the conclusion that while in psychological
analysis the healing miracles may be due to extraordinary
therapeutic powers, from the standpoint of religious
experience they are evidence of the operation of the
Spirit in human personality, whether that of Jesus or of
the Christ-conscious believers of the Spirit-possessed
community. All was due to the power of God designated
as the Spirit. The " why could we not cast it (*sc.* the
demon) out ? " (Mark ix. 28) of the halting days prior to
the clarification of the disciples' experience, has now
turned into the confident command, " in the name of
Jesus Christ the Nazarene, walk ! " (Acts iii. 6), or
" Æneas, Jesus Christ heals thee ! " (Acts ix. 34), or
again, " stand upright on thy feet ! " (Acts xiv. 10 ; cf.
ix. 40, xvi. 18). This is the " faith " atmosphere of the
primitive community, the faith of believers in their
power to heal by virtue of the Spirit's indwelling.

This " healing " atmosphere of the primitive Church.
may be illustrated in subsequent Christian religious
history as due to the quickening of religious revival.

The Venerable Bede relates how Bishop John of Hagulstad healed a man that was dumb. "The bishop caused this young man to be brought, and a little cottage to be made for him. . . . When one week of Lent was over, the next Sunday he caused the poor man to come in to him, and ordered him to put his tongue out of his mouth and show it him ; then laying hold of his chin, he made the sign of the Cross on his tongue, directing him to draw it back into his mouth and to speak. ' Pronounce some word,' said he ; ' say " yea." ' . . . The youth's tongue was immediately loosed, and he said what he was ordered. The bishop, then pronouncing the names of the letters, directed him to say ' A '; he did so, and afterwards ' B,' which he also did. When he had named all the letters after the bishop, the latter proceeded to put syllables and words to him, which being also repeated by him, he commanded him to utter whole sentences, and he did it. Nor did he cease all that day and the next night, as long as he could keep awake . . . to talk something . . . which he could never do before. . . ."[1] As in the case of modern psychological cures (pp. 91 f.), so the long procedure of Bishop John is far below the spiritual power of the primitive Church with its " Walk !" or " Arise, and make thy bed ! " (Acts iii. 6, ix. 34).

Bernard of Clairvaux became famous for his healing power. J. Cotter Morison describes, among many other cures, how Bernard healed Canon John, who had been in bed seven months and was expected to die. He was so pitiful an object that his fellow canons thrust him out into the village near by to perish. Bernard had come to the district, and John, hearing of this amidst his tragic distress, implored to be taken to him. "Six men, therefore, carrying him as he lay in bed, brought

[1] *Eccles. History*, bk. v. ch. ii. ellipsis (EL.).

him into a room close to that in which we were lodged. The abbot heard him confess his sins, and listened to his entreaties to be restored to health. Bernard mentally prayed to God : ' Behold, O Lord, they seek for a sign, and our words avail nothing, unless they be confirmed with signs following.' He then blessed him and left the chamber, and so did we all. In that very hour the sick man rose from his couch, and running after Bernard, kissed his feet with a devotion which cannot be imagined by any one who did not see it." [1] Here we are nearer the " Rise, take up thy bed, and walk " stage of healing through religious stimulus. Indeed, the healing atmosphere that encircles Bernard reminds us of, and throws light upon, the primitive Church possessed by the Spirit. " The cures were so many that those who saw them were not able to give them in detail. . . . In one day Bernard healed nine blind people, ten deaf or dumb, eighteen who were lame or paralysed. . . . At Schaffhausen, the number of wonders grew. . . . On Friday they came to Constance. . . . The people with a thousand shouts of ' Kyrie eleison ! Christ uns gnade ! ' ran to meet him, glorifying Jesus Christ." [2] Morison sums up the cures by saying that " the halt, the blind, the deaf, and the dumb were brought from all parts to be touched by Bernard. The patient was presented to him, whereupon he made the sign of the Cross over the part affected, and the cure was perfect." [3]

Francis of Assisi was renowned for his healing. There was a leper in a hospital " so impatient, and so intolerable, and so wayward, that every one believed . . . that he was possessed by the devil, since he reviled with words and blows so shamefully whomsoever waited

---

[1] *Life and Times of St. Bernard*, 1868, Bk. iv. p. 460.
[2] M. Ratisbonne, *Histoire de S. Bernard*, 1843, vol. ii. p. 210.
[3] *Op. cit.* p. 422.

on him. . . . St. Francis, knowing through revelation
that the leper was possessed by an evil spirit . . . prayed
to God devoutly for him." Then deciding to attend
the leper himself, he " at once let water be boiled, and
many odoriferous herbs . . . and began to wash him
. . . and, through a divine miracle, wherever St.
Francis touched with his holy hands, the leprosy departed
and the flesh remained perfectly healed. And even as
the flesh began to heal, so the soul began to heal." [1]
Here the use of intense prayer in connection with healing
illustrates the primitive Church, where prayer often
formed the religious atmosphere wherein the cure took
place (Acts ix. 40). Yet, for St. Francis, " miracle-
working occupies in his life an entirely secondary rank," [2]
thus placing him alongside the primitive Church believers
whose healing powers were the outflow of the Spirit
residing in them rather than wrought for their own
personal glory.

The famous prayer of Luther over the sick Melanchthon and the resulting cure reminds us that the Reformation liberated spiritual energies which outflowed in
healings. Luther found his friend at the point of death,
or apparently so, disfigured, knowing no one, neither
eating nor drinking. Luther turned to the window and
poured out his heart in prayer to God. He came back
to the bed, gave Philip his hand and bade him be of good
courage, saying that he would not die, for the Lord who
could smite could also heal again. The turn came, and
gradually Melanchthon came back to health. [3]

The " Spirit "-aroused energies of George Fox found
an outlet in marvellous cures. Richard Myer " had

[1] The Little Flowers of St. Francis, ch. xxv.
[2] Sabatier, Life of St. Francis of Assisi, Eng. Tr. 1894, p. 192.
[3] Cf. Seckendoff, Ausführliche Historie des Luthertums, 1714, iii.
p. 1882 ; also T. M. Lindsay, History of the Reformation, vol. i. 2nd
edn., 1908, pp. 380 f.

been long lame of one of his arms.   I was moved of the
Lord to say unto him, amongst all the people, ' Prophet
Myer, stand up on thy legs ! ' . . . and he stood up,
and stretched out his arm . . . and said, ' Be it known
unto you, all people, that this day I am healed.' "   Later
he confessed at a meeting at Swarthmoor " how the Lord
had healed him." [1]   After Fox came out from Carlisle
prison he came into contact with a mad woman who
" fell down of her knees and cried, ' Put off your hats,
for grace, grace hangs about thy neck.'   And so the
Lord's power ran through her that she was sensible of
her condition, and after came and confessed it. . . .
I came to another place in Cumberland, where a man's
wife was distracted and very desperate, attempting at
times to kill her children and her husband.   But I was
moved of the Lord God to speak to her, and she kneeled
down. . . . And the Lord's power wrought through her
and she went home well." [2]   The demon-possessed
atmosphere of the primitive Church is here, although
the thought-forms have changed ; we receive the impression that a spiritual power which is called the Lord's
power is operative as in the primitive Church.

One day Fox called at a house in Hawkshead, where
a boy of eleven years of age was still being rocked in
his cradle.   He had grown to almost twice the size he
should be for his age.   " I was moved of the Lord to
lay my hands upon him and speak to him."   Three years
later he called again at the house.   The mother urged
him to alight from his horse : " Oh, stay," she said,
" and have a meeting at our house, for all the country
is convinced by the great miracle that was done by thee
upon my son. . . . After you were gone we came home
and found our son playing in the streets."   " And this
was about three years after she told me of it," Fox

[1] *Journal*, pp. 81 f.   [2] *Ibid*. p. 92.

comments, "and he was grown to be a straight, full youth then." [1] " I came to Twy-Cross. . . . There was in that town a great man that had long lain sick and was given up by his physicians. . . . I went up to him in his chamber, and spake the word of life to him, and was moved to pray by him ; and the Lord was entreated, and restored him to health." [2]

In these ways the leader of a great spiritual revival expresses his mission by spontaneous healings of the sick in body as well as in soul through " the power of the Lord," that is " the Spirit " which inspired the healings of the primitive Church.

The Evangelical Revival connected with John Wesley produced a religious upheaval with the usual healing wonders. " I was desired to visit one who had been eminently pious, but had now been confined to her bed for several months, and was utterly unable to raise herself up. She desired us to pray, that the chain might be broken. A few of us prayed in faith. Presently she rose up, dressed herself, came downstairs, and I believe had not any further complaint." [3] Here the " faith " element in the healing is stressed, faith not only in the sufferer, but in him through whose prayer the cure was made.

Father John of Cronstadt was continually thronged by crowds for his healing power. His book, *My life in Christ*,[4] has many instances of this, and reminds us of the atmosphere of the primitive Church where the believers expressed their Spirit-possessed personality in healing miracles. In the preface to the book there is a record of a cure brought about by the prayer of some one at a distance. Two children in Moscow fell ill of diphtheria, and the illness developed so rapidly that the

[1] *Journal*, p. 93.   [2] *Ibid.* p. 29.
[3] John Wesley's *Journal*, Oct. 16th, 1778.   [4] Eng. Tr. 1897.

doctors decided for an operation on the trachea. The
parents in their despair lost faith in human aid and sent
a telegram to Father John, beseeching his prayers. The
telegram reached him when he was observing early
Liturgy, " and, as he usually does, immediately after
reading the telegram, he addressed his earnest prayer
to God. Meanwhile, what taking place in Moscow ?
. . . already at nine o'clock a.m. (at the very time of
Father John's prayers in Cronstadt, some 500 miles
away) the doctor who remained on duty noticed an
improvement, which progressed as rapidly as the illness
had previously developed." No operation was necessary,
and the children recovered in three to four days.[1]

These instances of healing power suggest the atmosphere of the primitive Church, especially when the ideas
of " Spirit " and " religious power " are correlated. The
healings of the first believers were, of course, more direct,
more spontaneous, than any cases from later religious
history. The reason is their personal connection with
the living personality of Jesus, the first-hand religious
power awakened in them by their contacts with Him :
with the experience of the same Spirit operative in Him
as in them, they share in His healing powers.

Visions and dreams are interpreted as " symptoms "
of the Spirit's operation ; because of this, young men
are to see visions, and old men to dream dreams
(Acts ii. 17 f.). Peter's trance on the housetop is a
typical instance. In this experience the disciple's subconscious conviction that the gospel was for Gentiles
as well as for Jews came to the surface and broke down
the conscious Jewish ideas of salvation. The psychological nature of the case is the best reply that can be
given to those who still question the authenticity of the

[1] *Father John*, Translator's Preface, p. ix.

narrative. The leaders of the primitive Church were
being forced to face the question as to the admission
of Gentiles into the Church. The Jewish law viewed
all non-Jews as unclean, unworthy of the divine favour
unless they became proselytes. A community had
gathered around the name of Jesus the Messiah, yet the
believers were still Israelites with Israel's privileges
before God. Peter was an Israelite indeed, but his
spiritual problem lay deep within his subconscious mind,
and went back to the days following his confession of
Jesus as Messiah, a problem which was temporarily
solved in the transfiguration experience with the perceived superiority in vision of Jesus to Moses and Elijah
(cf. pp. 112 f.). Peter shared in the appearance of the
risen Jesus where in vision the universal mission of the
gospel was received (Matt. xxviii. 19 f). His characteristic Jewish attitude, however, would inhibit any urge
to win the Gentiles for Christ except they first became
proselytes to Judaism. The conflict between the growing
influence of the wider mission and the suppressing power
of his racial outlook found its solution in the vision on
the housetop. Peter is hungry, but the meal is only in
the course of being prepared (Acts x. 10). He glides
imperceptibly into a condition of trance, in which he is
urged to kill and eat of the " common and unclean "
animals before him (vv. 12 f.), a visionary element based
physically on his hunger. Peter refuses to eat because
of the uncleanness of the food (ver. 14). Here is symbolized the issue between the rising subconscious conviction that the unclean Gentiles have the right to belong
to the Messianic community, and the inhibiting Jewish
psychology which would taboo this. The deeper urges
ultimately prevail ; audition comes to the aid of vision
in the voice of God commanding Peter not to regard as
" common " and " unclean " what God has made clean

(ver. 15). The wider conviction as to the admissibility of the non-Jews as acceptable to God won through as Peter knew at last that the gospel was for the world irrespective of whether men were Jews or Gentiles. The " ship " and the " sail " (x. 11) are elements in the vision derived from the physical noting in subconsciousness of a ship out on the blue waters of the sea, visible from the housetop at the seaport of Joppa (Acts ix. 43, x. 5, 9), and suggesting the strange foreign lands where Gentiles predominated. Was the ship with its full sail standing out to sea emblematic of the gospel setting out to the many lands abroad ?

The truth thus clarified for Peter in trance, where all conscious cognitive influences were lulled to sleep, was that the Gentiles were on the same religious footing as the Jews. Therefore they were fitting objects of the saving truth of Jesus the Messiah, and of the Spirit's energizing power, there being no need for the legal cleansing such as the law of Moses demanded. God had cleansed them, and without further requirements they could believe on the Lord Jesus. The Spirit is the impulsive power in this vision, for in Jewish psychology dreams and visions were ascribed to such activity, while the inner monition that causes Peter to descend from the housetop to meet the men of Cornelius is described as " the Spirit saith " (Acts x. 19).

Stephen's dying hour is visited with a vision of the glory of God and the exalted Jesus, the inspiration of it being the Spirit (Acts vii. 55), while the martyr had been known as one in whom the Spirit abode (Acts vi. 8). " It was in the fervour and love which sprang from this abiding state that he was now enabled to turn his soul from men to heaven, and with rapt gaze see, as it were, God's very glory." [1] In Paul's vision on the way to

---

[1] J. V. Bartlet, *Acts, ad. loc.* vii. 55.

Damascus we observe the removal of the inhibitions which had chained him to his inherited religious outlook, and which were in conflict with the deeper impressions being produced by all he knew and discerned of Jesus. The vision marks the end of the spiritual conflict in victory for the subconscious with its stored creative influence of Christ. Here, again, truth is received only at the cost of the pressure of abnormal experiences ; the reserves of personality are strained beyond normal endurance ; the collapse of the conscious Jewish inhibitions is at the same time the breaking in of the new convictions and powers. The Spirit is not expressly mentioned as the prime mover in this case, yet Paul's conversion and its attendant phenomena would be viewed as being due to the Spirit's invasion of the apostle's personality, whose subsequent stress on the experience of the Spirit only confirms this fact. The Spirit gives the impulse to Ananias to bring healing and comfort to the stricken Paul (Acts ix. 10 ff.).

The intense spiritual ferment which produces visions, trances, dreams, and the like, such as the primitive Church with its experience of the Spirit illustrates, may be found elsewhere.

Basilides, a catechumen of Origen's, became a Christian by reason of the appearance to him in a dream of Potamiaena, a martyr to whom he had rendered a kindness as she went on her way to death. Her appearance fortified him so that he, too, did not hesitate to offer himself up (Eus. *H.E.* vi. 5). The heightened tension and spiritual abandon characteristic of persecution with its train of martyrdoms form fruitful soil for visionary accompaniments of religious experience.

Monica, Augustine's saintly mother, frequently had dreams and visions which purported to be the means of divine revelation. To safeguard her son from the dis-

solute ways of debauchery, she prayed every day for a
vision in which God would reveal something to guide
her in arranging for him a suitable marriage, but
Augustine tells us that God heeded not. Indeed, she
had what he describes as fantasy which resulted from
the activity of the human mind alone. His mother had
no confidence in these merely human visions or dreams :
she could even detect, through a cértain taste which
she could never explain in words, whether she was
experiencing a genuine divine revelation in her vision,
or merely dream images resulting from her own mind.[1]
True religious experience, therefore, has the power to
discern the visions it produces, whether these be of
God or not. Just as the primitive Church found it
necessary to " interpret " the tongue-speech, or discern
the spirits in the same way, so the interpretation and
the discernment would apply to the experiences of
visions and dreams. Such power of discernment would
also be the activity of the Spirit in the community.
Paul's hint that spiritual things are discerned " spiritually " (1 Cor. ii. 14), and the item, " discerning of spirits "
(1 Cor. xii. 10) placed among the " gifts of the Spirit,"
points back to the primitive Church and its power of
discerning whether extraordinary spiritual manifestations were from above or not, whether purely natural,
even if strange, or whether they were of the demons.

Canon Streeter cites a dream of St. Francis of Assisi
to illustrate the comforting power which sometimes
comes through vision. The saint had steadfastly
entreated the Cardinal to further his business with
Pope Innocent III. The Pope granted the request and
blessed the new order. " One night when he (Francis)
was gone to sleep he seemed to be walking along a
road by the side of which stood a very lofty tree. That

[1] Augustine, *Confessions*, vi. 23.

tree was fair and strong, exceeding thick and high. And it came to pass that as he came near to it, and stood beneath it, wondering at its beauty and height, he himself grew to such a height that he touched the top of the tree, and taking it in his hand, very easily bowed it to the ground. And so indeed it was done ; since the Lord Innocent, the highest and loftiest tree in the world, bowed himself so graciously to his will and petition." [1] This is a dream where the symbolism has been clearly explicit in conscious life prior to the dream, but the confirmation by revelation is interesting to observe.

St Patrick of Ireland had a vision which reminds us of Paul's experience in which the man of Macedonia called him to cross into Europe (Acts xvi. 9). Having escaped from slavery to his native Gaul, there came to St. Patrick the call to return to Ireland where he had been a slave to render service of another order. " In the dead of night, I saw a man coming to me as if from Ireland, whose name was Victorinus, and who bore countless letters. And he gave me one of them, and I read the beginning of it, which contained the words : ' The voice of the Irish.' And while I was repeating the words of this beginning, I thought I heard the voice of those who were near the wood Foclut, which is nigh to the western sea ; and they cried thus : ' We pray thee, holy youth, to come and live among us henceforth.' And I was greatly pricked in heart and could read no more." [2]

As we expect from the intensity of a religious experience accompanied by Pentecostal psychic phenomena and healing powers, George Fox had his visions. " I was wrapped up, in a rapture, in the Lord's power " (*Journal*, p. 15). " I saw, through the immediate opening of the invisible Spirit, the blood of Christ.

[1] Cited from Celano's " Lives of St. Francis," in *Reality*, pp. 325 f.
[2] *Confessions*, quoted by Rufus Jones, *op. cit.* p. 115.

And I cried out . . . and said, Do ye not see the blood of Christ ? . . . for I saw it . . . how it came into the heart " (p. 14). The occasion of this vision was a discourse on the blood of Christ, which doubtless caused diversity of opinion, and Fox was quick to express his overwhelming sureness in the vision. Receiving the call to go out and preach to the world, he says, " When I came, in the Lord's mighty power, with the word of life into the world, the world swelled, and made a noise like the great raging waves of the sea " (p. 20). " I was come up in spirit through the flaming sword, into the paradise of God. All things were new ; and all the creation gave another smell unto me than before, beyond what words can utter " (p. 17). Here the sense of smell is abnormally stimulated as sight and hearing are in religious vision.

The more recent visions of Sadhu Sundar Singh illustrate the nature of vision inspired by Christian experience of a heightened and intense order. They are of special interest in that many of them help to suggest the atmosphere of apocalyptic so characteristic of the primitive Church. The Sadhu's visions are of Heaven, the Resurrection of the Body, the Last Judgment, and Hell. " The Third Heaven is Heaven proper, as it might be styled. To this all righteous people will ultimately attain ; but it is granted to a certain few, of whom the Sadhu is privileged to be one, to make short visits there during their earthly life. ' I understood,' said the Sadhu, ' what St. Paul meant when he said, " Whether in the body or out of the body I know not," because when I found myself there I seemed to have a body with form and shape, but all made, as it were, of light. But when I touched it. . . . I felt nothing. This is what St. Paul speaks of as a spiritual body.' " [1]

[1] Streeter and Appasamy, *The Sadhu*, 1923, p. 117.

The Sadhu was given to gliding into a trance. "While in the state of ecstasy, which sometimes lasts for several hours, he loses all perception of the external world ; and he has no sense of the lapse of time ; 'There is no past and no future ; everything is present.'"[1] This savours more of the pure mystic type of religious experience, but it illustrates the absence of the "time" element in religious vision, as for example, in the case of Peter's trance.

The apocalyptists were given to visions, but much in their writing is no more than the multiplication of scenic details or literary embellishments. They thought in pictures about the great religious issues, and their picture thinking produced visions with a wealth of images, symbols, and picture forms, involving types of religious autism such as ecstasy, trance, and dream. The primitive Church entered largely into this apocalyptic environment, and the first believers thought through their new experience in pictures. Thus vision, trance, and the like must have occupied a large place in the religious experience of the primitive Church. Far from suggesting the untrustworthiness of Acts, these elements, reflecting the religious background so naturally, indicate a greater degree of historical reliability than is sometimes supposed. Had they not been there, we should have to consider whether a later outlook had not purged the record in the interests of more formal, logical statement. Nor does the presence of the visionary elements take away from the unique worth of the new religious experience in the Spirit which is prompting them. "It is necessary to realize that image and vision do within limits represent a perfectly genuine way of doing things, which is inevitable for deeply spiritual selves of a certain type ; and that it is neither good

[1] Streeter and Appasamy, *The Sadhu*, 1923, pp. 133 f.

12

psychology nor good Christianity lightly to dismiss as superstition or hysteria the pictured world of symbol." [1] Not only where souls are of the appropriate mystic type, but also where men are caught up in religious experience of a unique order, as were the primitive Church believers, with all its urge towards expression in its dynamic vitality, there are abnormal accompaniments such as vision and trance.

When we have sought to account on psychological principles for the visionary phenomena, we are still faced with the "something other"; the profound comprehension of new truth, and the certainty with which it is received as divine truth still remains. " If we bear in mind that Truth is quite a different thing from the particular psychological mechanism by which it is apprehended, and also that any revelation of the Divine must be conditioned by the mental outlook, culture, and general experience of the recipient, we shall not be inclined to deny that Visions may be a genuine revelation of truth." [2] This important principle is our guide through the maze of the visionary atmosphere of the primitive Church experience until the permanent truth elements, apart from the psychological forms, are seen to centre around the contacts and impressions of Jesus in life and beyond death, and the apprehension of divine reality in the activity of the divine Spirit.

We are therefore able to reply to the tendency in the New Psychology to regard these abnormal phenomena as due to pathological or neurological disturbances. Even if this were always true, we have still to inquire what, in the first place, set up the disturbances. Further, both pathological and neurological disturbances result

---

[1] E. Underhill, *The Life of the Spirit and the Life of To-day*, 1922, p. 101.

[2] Streeter and Appasamy, *op. cit.* pp. 114 f.

in the *disintegration* of the personality affected.[1] The psychologist and the psychiatrist, from the nature of their theory and practice, are dealing with abnormal cases presenting psychopathological phenomena involving "all degrees of dissociation, ranging from cases of complete or approximate mental unity down through greater and greater degrees of dissociation, until at last we find several fairly independent and fairly unified separate ' personalities ' or ' complexes ' functioning in one body, or until even these are disintegrated into more elementary groups of psychic states, each narrower, less unified, and less stable than the last." [2] When, therefore, the psychologist turns to the phenomena of religious experience, especially where these assume an abnormal character, the abnormalities become the object of his investigation. In the light of his conclusions drawn from his practical experience in psychotherapy, he explains the abnormal phenomena of religious ferment as " Hallucinatory or pseudo-hallucinatory luminous phenomena," [3] and begins to search for the pathological disturbance responsible. Thus the New Psychology misses the significant fact that abnormal conditions may in themselves be evidence of the *integration* of personality through the religious experience received in visionary accompaniments. When any one thinks habitually of visions and the like in terms of disintegration, it is difficult to reach out to the truth that the abnormality may be motived from a power centre in the mind, and making for integration, instead of being induced by pathological or neurological maladaptation.

[1] " Neurotic disorder is the expression of disintegration or failure of integration of the personality or of character," W. McDougall, *op. cit.* p. 54.

[2] J. B. Pratt, *op. cit.* p. 57.

[3] William James, *op. cit.* p. 251.

This is the inner truth of the primitive Church experience of the Spirit with its visions, auditions, trances, dreams, healings, and inarticulate ecstatic speech. All these phenomena had for their centre a spiritual experience which integrated personality. The resurrection visions reveal the potency of their cause in the risen Jesus by the integration of witnesses hitherto in doubt and fear, with all their expectations apparently nullified, and their minds pathetically divided. The inner conflict that divided Peter's heart received its solution on the housetop in vision, and resulted in the apostle's integration. Paul's conversion vision brought an inner unity which integrated his hitherto divided personality. Similar integrating effects are seen, and thus illustrate the experience of the primitive Church, in the cases of Fox, Brainerd, Monica, St. Francis, St. Patrick, etc.[1]

Hallucination may, of course, enter into the visions inspired by religious experience ; the Old Testament prophets recognized this ; there were " false " prophets whose visions and auditions were discerned as not coming from God (Jer. xiv. 14 f.). The test lay in an integration of life which enabled the prophet to predict, but which passed into the apprehension of true knowledge of the divine will. Jeremiah regards the false prophets as victims of hallucination because he sees the disintegrating effects which will accrue from following their counsels. These principles may guide us for the primitive Church ; what made for integration was revealed to be a firm apprehension of divine reality and truth. Let William James sum up for us in this matter. " To the medical mind," he says, " these ecstasies signify nothing but suggested and imitated hypnoid

[1] For a full discussion of the theory of integration and disintegration as applied to personality and the problems of consciousness, cf. Wm. McDougall, *op. cit.* pp. 537–56.

states, on an intellectual basis of superstition, and a corporeal one of degeneration and hysteria. Undoubtedly these pathological conditions have existed in many, and possibly in all, the cases, but that fact tells us nothing about the value for knowledge of the consciousness which they induce. To pass a spiritual judgment upon these states, we must not content ourselves with superficial medical talk, but inquire into their fruits for life." [1] This is the ultimate test for the primitive Church experience; the vital integration of disciples who went forth boldly to preach Jesus Christ, the emergence of the Christian Church and its agelong witness, the appropriation of the active energy of the spirit whose fruits were " love, joy, peace, long-suffering, kindness, goodness, faith, meekness, self-control " (Gal. v. 22 f.)—these are the abiding realities within the visions and other abnormal phenomena.

Angels are sometimes conceived as the medium through which the divine revelation is received in vision or dream. Cornelius sees an angel in his dream, and calls him " Lord " (Acts x. 3 f.) ; this angel commands the centurion to send for Peter, but the impulse given to the apostle to go with the men of Cornelius is from the Spirit (x. 20). " Angel," " the Spirit," and " God," seem to be ways of expressing the same experience, namely, of the divine intervention in human life. An " angel of the Lord " opens prison doors (Acts v. 19), and again with psychic accompaniments (xii. 7). Peter would have no doubt that his release was due to the activity of the Spirit. An angel instructs Philip to go to Gaza (viii. 26), yet as the chariot of the Ethiopian approaches it is the Spirit who impels Philip to converse with the eunuch (vv. 29 ff.), and it is the Spirit

[1] *Op. cit.* p. 413.

who snatches Philip away (ver. 39).[1] There is an explanatory link which connects the " angel of the Lord " with the " Spirit " in the idea of angels as ministering spirits (Ps. civ. 4 ; Heb. i. 7, 14) ; elsewhere the angels are the spirits that wait on God, whether of the superior order that attends the divine presence, or the inferior class that controls natural phenomena.[2]

By the time that the primitive Church was emerging, the angels seem to be gliding into the unifying conception of the Spirit as the power behind them. The angels, in so far as they remain distinctive, were symptomatic of the Spirit's activity. Just as the demons tended to be brought under the ægis of an arch spirit or prince, and as their malevolent power was symptomatic of this higher evil energy that inspired their doings, so the Spirit of God came to be regarded as the prevailing dynamic behind the angels. There is no evidence that the Spirit was identified with any archangel such as Gabriel or Michael ; indeed, Gabriel is the messenger of the Spirit's overshadowing of Mary (Luke i. 26, 35).[3] The Spirit was the Supreme Power animating angels and archangels.

[1] As the Spirit caused Elijah's movements to be uncertain (1 Kings xviii. 12). The Spirit here seems to exercise a semi-physical function (cf. Ezek. iii. 12–14, viii. 3, xi. 24). The movement of the " mighty wind " in its suddenness accounts for this idea of the Spirit.

[2] Cf. Jub. ii. 2 for an apocalyptic classification of the angels.

[3] The Spirit is actually identified with Gabriel in the Koran (cf. Sura ii. 81). The identification is not explained from the common stock of Semitic ideas in which Mohammed shared, nor through his contact with the Jewish colonies around Mecca, still less from any Christian sects resident in Arabia. It is probably a deliberate rejection, in the mind of Mohammed, of the divinity of the Spirit as set forth in the Christian Doctrine of the Trinity, along with his rejection of Christianity. " The Holy Spirit stands for Gabriel in the Holy Quran. The Divinity of the Holy Spirit is an innovation of the Christians. The Jews never thought of it as a Divine person, nor did Jesus Christ Himself " ; Muhammad Ali, *Translation of the Holy Quran* (without Arabic Text), 1928, p. 17. But where in Jewish or

The Spirit's control of the primitive Church was further shown by the presence of physical marvels. Philip is snatched bodily away; prison doors open of themselves. As the historian sets forth the story, the sudden deaths of Ananias and Sapphira are a retribution for their offence against the Spirit, and the Spirit is the direct cause of their decease (Acts v. 3-5, 9). From the standpoint of those who were present at the scene, the deaths were due to the Spirit whose power was behind the words of the Spirit-possessed Peter.[1] As to what actually took place it is not easy to determine. The principle *post hoc propter hoc* doubtless dominated the eye-witnesses; Peter rebuked the deceitful, and the deaths at once followed. But the deaths, if such there were, probably had no connection with Peter nor with the Spirit conceived to speak through him; they took place after the revelation of the deceit in the presence of the community; we cannot find anything incredible in a death brought about by shock at a grave exposure of deceit such as this was. The death of Herod Agrippa is related from the standpoint of similar ideas. The king died of a disease which reached its climax very suddenly, and the primitive Church view is that an angel interposed and smote him (Acts xii. 23). Since the Spirit was the unifying power behind angelic action, the primitive Church interpreted this timely removal of a persecutor as the activity of the Spirit whose community was being attacked.

Christian thought is the Spirit identified with Gabriel ? It is possible, however, that the identification arose from a confusion between Gabriel announcing the conception of Jesus in the womb of Mary, and the Spirit overshadowing the Virgin (Luke i. 26, 35) ; this may have associated the two in the mind of Mohammed, or in the contemporary thought which influenced Mohammed.

[1] Gunkel, *op. cit.* p. 49, puts the idea clearly : " eine Lüge gegen den Pneumatophoren Petrus eine Lüge gegen den heiligen Geist ist, und den Apostel erproben den Geist des Herrn erproben heisst."

Marvellous physical effects accompany experiences of great religious stress.   John Wesley in his *Journal* cites many instances of religious emotional disturbance with extraordinary physical repercussions.   ". . . a young man was suddenly seized with a violent trembling all over, and in a few minutes, the sorrows of his heart being enlarged, sunk down to the ground " (*Journal*, 21st April 1739).   As Wesley was preaching to a great concourse of people at Newgate he besought God to bear witness to His power, and " immediately one, and another, and another sunk to the earth : they dropped on every side as thunderstruck.   One of them cried aloud.   We besought God in her behalf, and He turned her heaviness into joy.   A second being in the same agony, we called upon God for her also ; and He spoke peace to her soul."   " One was so wounded by the sword of the Spirit, that you would have imagined she could not live a moment " (25th April 1739).   A physician was present at a subsequent meeting thinking that " there might be fraud. . . . To-day one whom he had known many years . . . broke out into ' strong cries and tears.'   He could hardly believe his own eyes and ears.   He went and stood close to her, and observed every symptom, till great drops of sweat ran down her face, and all her bones shook.   He then knew not what to think, being clearly convinced it was not fraud, nor yet any natural disorder.   But when both her soul and body were healed in a moment, he acknowledged the finger of God " (29th April 1739).   At another meeting " I was interrupted . . . by the cries of one who was ' pricked at the heart,' and strongly groaned for pardon and peace. . . . Another person dropped down. . . . A little boy near him was seized in the same manner.   A young man who stood up behind, fixed his eyes on him, and sunk down himself as one dead ; but soon began to roar out, and beat himself against the ground, so that six men could scarcely hold him " (20th May 1739).

The striking physical effects born of strong conviction of sin afford some parallel to what might well have been the case in the primitive Church and the audiences to which the preachers directed their message, and even with Ananias and Sapphira, whose emotional terror reacted on themselves so forcibly. These instances illustrate first that where people are psychologically uncritical, strong religious emotion may work out in striking physical ways ; second, the danger inherent in these phenomena is seen where it is not discerned that the Spirit is not in the jerks and the convulsions. Wesley's warning stands good for all time : " I told them, they were not to judge of the Spirit whereby any one spoke, either by appearances, or by common report, or by their own inward feelings : no, nor by any dreams, visions, or revelations, supposed to be made to their souls ; any more than by their tears, or any involuntary effects wrought upon their bodies. I warned them, all these were, in themselves, of a doubtful, disputable nature ; they might be from God, and they might not " (22nd June 1739).[1]

In the expressions of the Spirit's energy so far reviewed we have dealt with the abnormal. In each case we came finally to a religious " ultimate," which is common to all. This " ultimate " is the " beyond element "[2] in religious experience, or the " numinous ; "[3] its roots lie deeper than any human insight can reach,

[1] For other illustrations of the physically abnormal accompaniments of excited religious emotion, cf. Davenport, *Primitive Traits in Religious Revivals*, 1906, ch. ix.
[2] As J. C. Flower designates it in his *Psychology of Religion*, 1927, pp. 55, 138, 142, 152.
[3] R. Otto's conception in *The Idea of the Holy*, 1923, Eng. Tr., chs. ix.–xii.

and are far more interwoven than psychological analysis can disentangle. The primitive Church, as does the Church of to-day, designated it by " Holy Spirit."

Other important inspirations are ascribed to the activity of the Spirit. This power enables some future event to be predicted, as when Agabus announced that a great famine was coming (Acts xi. 28), or that Paul would be bound (xxi. 11). The Spirit guides the choice of a successor to Judas by its control of the required " lot " (i. 15 ff.). The Spirit is the pen in the hands of those who wrote the sacred Scriptures (i. 16, iv. 25 ; 1 Pet. i. 11 ; 4 Ezra xiv. 22). The Spirit inspires the extension of the Church to the Gentiles (Acts x. 19 f., 45–47, xi. 11 f., 15, 17, etc.). The Spirit directs the decisions of men as seen in Paul's desire to go to Jerusalem (Acts xix. 21, xx. 22), while the attempts to dissuade him are made by others who feel that they, too, are inspired by the Spirit in so doing (Acts xxi. 4). The Spirit fortifies those in trial on behalf of Christ (Acts iv. 8 ; Mark xiii. 11).

We come to more normal activities inspired by the Spirit. Even here we have religious experience of so high a quality that its expression in more specific spiritual and ethical ways is unique, and extraordinary in every aspect. Such expression is conceived as being due to the Spirit's activity in human personality.

The Spirit inspires extraordinary qualities of character and ability such as Wisdom. The qualifications for election to important office are to be " full of the Spirit and of wisdom " (Acts vi. 3) ; the seven deacons are to be men of distinction and above the average level, the Spirit being the energizing power behind such qualities. The Spirit operated within Stephen so mightily that none could withstand his wisdom (Acts vi. 10). The grace and faith for which Barnabas was renowned were accounted for in that he was " full of the Holy Spirit and of faith " (Acts xi. 24). The Christian life derived its power from the Spirit, and it stood so high above the ordinary level of the world as to call for a supernatural cause.

The higher guidance of the primitive Church is through the activity of the Spirit. The Church is inspired by the Spirit to set apart Saul and Barnabas for " the work whereunto I have called them," the Spirit being personalized as " I " (Acts xiii. 2 f.). At the Council of Jerusalem the decision was reached through what was felt to be the Spirit's guidance (Acts xv. 28).

The " Prayer " atmosphere of the Church is inspired in the same way. The empirical climax at Pentecost when the Spirit was experienced in such amazing vitality was prepared for by continuous praying, and prayer, indeed, was what made such an event possible. The initiates into the new community of the Spirit are instructed in the " prayers " of the Church (Acts ii. 42). Peter and John go up to the temple " to pray " (Acts iii. 1), and likewise the believers as a whole (ii. 46), expecting maybe to greet their Messiah as He descended the pinnacle of the temple, or using the occasion to tell their fellow-Jews about Jesus the Messiah and His imminent return in the divine Kingdom. On the release of the apostles from the custody of the Jewish authorities, the assembled community prays that God will not let His work be hindered by threats of persecution, and that the preachers may be empowered to speak boldly (iv. 24–29). The ratification of the prayer is a repetition of the Pentecost experience (ver. 31). The witness

of the apostles included prayer as well as preaching
(Acts vi. 4) ; after the election of the Seven the apostles
pray over them and lay their hands upon them (vi. 6).
There is little doubt that the essential thing in the laying
on of hands was prayer, the rite being, as it were, an
acted prayer (cf. Acts viii. 14 f., where Peter and John
pray over the believers in Samaria, that the Spirit may
be given them). The connection of the laying on of
hands with the giving of the Spirit is not clear. The
Spirit may be bestowed *after* baptism in the name of
the Lord Jesus (Acts ii. 38) without any reference to
laying on of hands ; the Spirit may, however, be received
first, and His presence sufficiently attested as to warrant
baptism into the new community (Acts x. 44–48, xi.
15–17) ; the Spirit may be given after prayer over those
concerned that God will give the Spirit, there is the
laying on of hands and then the gift is bestowed (Acts viii.
15, 17) ; finally, the Spirit is received after baptism in the
name of the Lord Jesus, the laying on of hands follows,
and then the gift with no reference to the prayer (Acts
xix. 5 f.). It is clear, then, that there was no formal
place given to the laying on of hands in the primitive
Church. Where minds were attuned to the quasi-physical
view of the Spirit, the laying on of hands would impart a
strong stimulus by way of suggestion.

In the hour of death, Stephen is possessed by the
Spirit and shows it by his praying (Acts vii. 59). Peter
prays as the needful preliminary to the restoring of
Dorcas (Acts ix. 40) ; in the course of praying Peter
received the vision which educated his sympathies to include the Gentiles in the work of saving grace (Acts x. 9).
The believers pray for Peter as he is in prison, and when
he returns to the house of John Mark's mother the
occupants are all at prayer (Acts xii. 5, 12). Prayer is
the central experience which calls out the inspiration

of the Spirit to set aside Barnabas and Saul (Acts xiii. 2 f.).
Prayer was integral at the " breaking of bread."

At the centre of the prayers of the primitive community would be found the earnest petition that God
would send the Kingdom in the return of Messiah.
Marana tha, "our Lord, come!" (*Did.* x. 6; 1 Cor.
xvi. 22). This petition came into the Christian worship
at a very early stage, as Heiler points out.[1] The Spirit
inspired the prayer and at the same time was the
guarantee that the prayer would be answered, for the
Spirit was the moving power behind the Kingdom and
in the Messiah. Much of the praying would follow traditional Jewish ideas, but the personal influence of Jesus
developed this side in a potent manner. The eye-
witnesses were amazed when, amidst the clamour of the
crowds, Jesus was missing, and they found Him at
prayer in some secluded retreat (Mark i. 35 f.). Again
and again it was noticed how Jesus withdrew from what
were supposed to be great opportunities into deserted
places to pray (Luke v. 16; Matt. xiv. 23). On one
occasion—probably typical of his custom—Jesus " continued all night in prayer to God " (Mark vi. 46; Luke
vi. 12). According to Luke, Jesus went up the mountain-
side to pray, and while He was praying He was transfigured (ix. 28 f.). Once His disciples were so impressed
by His praying that one of their number asked Him to
teach them to pray; the response was to give them a
prayer which the Church came to denote as the Lord's
Prayer (Luke xi. 2–4; cf. Matt. vi. 9–13). Jesus prays
in Gethsemane, and counsels His disciples to fortify
themselves against temptation by praying (Mark xiv.
32–39).

Jesus constantly urged His disciples to prayer.
They were to pray for those who ill-used them (Matt. v.

[1] F. Heiler, *Das Gebet*, 5 Aufl. 1923, pp. 240, 454 f.

44 ; Luke vi. 28) ; they were to pray in private and avoid the ostentation of scribes and Pharisees in public prayers (Matt. vi. 5 f.). They were to make a habit of prayer (Luke xviii. 1). He urged that the best way of preparing for the advent of the Kingdom was by prayer (Mark xiii. 33 ; Luke xxi. 36). Such power in prayer reacted in turn on disciples and believers when the new experience of the Spirit set free their inner aspirations, and laid the foundation of the Church on that vital fellowship of God and man known as prayer. It was prayer vitalized by the Spirit, but it had its roots in the contacts with the living Jesus.

The " power " aspect of prayer within the primitive Church is well illustrated by the famous watchnight service of John Wesley which proved to be the turning-point in his movement. He and some sixty others were praying through the night hours. " About three in the morning, as we were continuing instant in prayer, the power of God came mightily upon us, insomuch that many cried out for exceeding joy, and many fell to the ground. As soon as we were recovered a little from that awe and amazement at the presence of his Majesty, we broke out with one voice, ' We praise thee, O God ; we acknowledge thee to be the Lord.' " (*Journal*, 1st Jan. 1739). The most startling success began to attend the Wesley revival. In the same way the new endowment of spiritual power was made accessible to the primitive believers by their potency in prayer, and they went forth to declare their faith with wonderful results.

The Spirit was again attested by the overwhelming joy which possessed the primitive Church. The believers knew " gladness of heart " (Acts ii. 46), and their radiance found expression in " praising God," as the ground of their sure confidence. People took notice of such joy and love, and looked on the believers with favour, so that many were caught by the joyous contagion and added to the new community (Acts ii. 47). The apostles rejoice that they are accounted worthy to suffer dishonour for Christ's name (Acts v. 41). In so far as believers endured reproach for Christ they experienced all the greater joy in being permitted so to witness (1 Pet. iv. 13 f., 16). Joy inspires Stephen on his way to martyrdom (Acts vii. 55 f.). There was rejoicing in Samaria over Philip's visit, but the joy was motived by gratitude for healings wrought, and lacks the pure spiritual quality of the characteristic radiance of the Church (Acts viii. 8). The Ethiopian goes on his way with joy after his conversation with Philip (ver. 39). The Church at Jerusalem rejoices over Peter's testimony concerning the Gentiles (Acts xi. 18), while Gentiles themselves share in the new-born, conquering joy of the gospel experience (Acts xiii. 46, 48, 52). Barnabas is radiant over the evidence of the Spirit's power in Antioch (Acts xi. 23). The primitive Church cannot be understood unless full justice is done to this radiance that possessed the believers.[1] Paul connects the prevailing joy with the Spirit (1 Thess. i. 6), but the Spirit as the source of the joy was implied from the very beginning, since the new life prompting it was due to the Spirit's presence and power in the primitive community, and finds its place in the later enumeration of the " fruits of the Spirit " (Gal. v. 22).

" The most characteristic of all the elements of the conversion crisis . . . is the ecstasy of happiness produced." [2] One or two instances from religious experience may be given to light up this feature of the primitive Church life. William James records a conversion, through the Spirit's power, which resulted in an overwhelming sense of happiness. " No words can express

[1] Cf. J. Weiss, *op. cit.* p. 29.   [2] William James, *op. cit.* p. 254.

the wonderful love that was shed abroad in my heart. I wept aloud with joy and love ; and I do not know, but I should say I literally bellowed out the unutterable gushings of my heart. These waves came over me, and over me, and over me, one after the other, until I recollect I cried out, ' I shall die if these waves continue to pass over me.' " [1] The Cornish evangelist, Billy Bray, is a most significant instance of the new-born joy of the converted soul. In a friend's house he exhorted those therein to praise the Lord. Speaking of himself, he said, " I can't help praising the Lord. As I go along the street I lift up one foot, and it seems to say ' Glory ! ' and I lift up the other, and it seems to say ' Amen ' ; and so they keep on like that all the time I am walking." [2] " I feel I'd make the very poker and tongs sing Hallelujah ! " he said on another occasion. The Journals of Brainerd, Woolman, Fox, and Wesley are impregnated on every page with the radiance not only of religious meetings, but with the joy of the many whose lives their gospel touched.

Courage of an extraordinary order was a further " symptom " of the Spirit's presence. If we compare the Peter who disowned Jesus with the courageous exponent of the Messiahship of Jesus and the need that Messiah should suffer, we see the change that the new experience had wrought.[3] Peter finds how true it is that in the time of trial the Spirit would give words to speak, as Jesus had said (Acts iv. 8–12 ; cf. Mark xiii. 11). Such superb courage which led the believers to speak the word boldly, despite persecution, arose from their sure confidence in the Spirit that animated their activities.

[1] W. James, *op. cit.* p. 255.
[2] F. W. Bourne, *The King's Son*, 1891, p. 43.
[3] Boldness was required in advocating the need for Messiah to suffer in an environment that knew no such doctrine. Cf. Acts ii. 22–28, iii. 13 ff., 26.

The Spirit brought "comfort" to the growing Church in its need for strength (Acts ix. 31) ; the Spirit inspired the faith of the community amidst its witness, its difficulties, its trials (Acts iv. 8 ff., 31). Such faith evidenced itself in the signs and wonders which everywhere attested the presence of the Spirit. The extraordinary faith of the believers in the return of Jesus the Messiah with the Kingdom is itself inspired by the Spirit, the object of the very faith itself as being the power which would bring these events to pass (Acts iii. 20).

We have now investigated the experience of the Spirit expressed in the extraordinary happenings ; we have extended the category of the extraordinary to include the moral and spiritual qualities revealing themselves in such outstanding intensity and vigour. All manifestations, whether physical, psychical, ethical, or spiritual, are the evidences of an irresistible, invading power which " came upon " believers, " filled " them, " poured out " upon them, " fell " upon them.[1] Viewed from the standpoint of religious experience, the Spirit " speaks " to the possessed ones, crystallizes into some physical form, " dwells in " them as the occupant of a building, " snatches up," blocks the way, " leads out," " gives utterance." [2] In every case the Spirit is the invading power that controls the human personality concerned. The moral and spiritual powers conferred on the believers appear in themselves so extraordinary, so remarkably pronounced over against the normal expression of the ordinary life, that these too are ascribed to the invasion of the same potent, amazing power. It is not a question of any believer so endowed making

[1] Luke i. 35 ; Acts ii. 4, 33, iv. 8, 31, vi. 5, x. 44, xi. 15.
[2] Acts viii. 29, x. 19, xi. 12 ; Mark i. 10 ; 1 Cor. iii. 16, vi. 19 ; Eph. ii. 21 f. ; Acts viii. 39, xvi. 6 ; Mark i. 12 ; Acts ii. 4.

13

up his mind to be bold, radiant, have wisdom, give himself to prayer, or be a man of faith, any more than he decides to experience visions, speak in tongues, or perform acts of healing. The Spirit invades the personality, hence the outstanding wisdom, guidance, prayer, joy, courage, comfort, and faith ; hence the visions, the ecstasy, the healings, the various marvels, all in themselves the outflow from human lives possessed by the Spirit.

The primitive Church has, therefore, laid the foundation for the later development of the spiritual and ethical sides of the Spirit's activity in human life. The personal contacts with the living Jesus had potent religious and moral implications unrealized at first. These synthesized with the empirical activity of the Spirit in the lives of the earliest believers, and began to produce lives that already stood out in marked contrast to the average character of the ordinary life of the pagan world. Paul drew out these implications in their rich content and force, not only as centring in Christ, but as the activity of the Spirit. In solving his own inner conflict of sin by finding final satisfaction in the sufficiency of Christ, the moral categories concerned became clear and enabled him to transfer his empirical discoveries to his experience of, and thought on, the Spirit. The primitive Church had not yet had time to sort out the accidental from the abiding, but the foundation for the later discoveries was nevertheless laid down as the primitive Church brought forth the first-fruits of the Spirit.

Paul reproduces in his own experience all the marks of the indwelling of the Spirit, as we have already noted them. He was a Spirit-possessed personality, speaking in tongues, working signs and wonders, including healings, receiving visions, auditions, photisms, and revelations.[1]

[1] 1 Cor. xiv. 18 ; Acts xiv. 3, 8 ff., ix. 3 ff. ; 2 Cor. xii. 1, 2-4: Acts xix. 11 f., xvi. 9, xviii. 9 ; Gal. i. 12, ii. 2 ; Eph. iii. 3.

As a preacher he was aware of the Spirit's inspiration which enabled him to clothe his gospel in appropriate speech. The Spirit endows him with extraordinary wisdom ; he knows of the Spirit's guidance for the Church in its progress and decisions, the Spirit as the dynamic in the prayer experience, and, indeed, doing the very praying ; Spirit-inspired joy is the keynote of his life, while Paul was a man of extraordinary boldness and courage, receiving from the Spirit strengthening comfort and faith.[1] In all this varied experience of the Spirit as the invading energy, Paul stands on the same empirical ground as the primitive Church. He has, however, drawn out the spiritual and ethical implications, and in so doing has brought the normal life and activity of the Christian believer within the " symptoms " of the Spirit's operation. The normal, joyous, courageous life of the believer with its wisdom, faith, insight, prayer tone, divine guidance, the wonder of a salvation experienced in Christ and the hopes centring in Him, manifested a standard of conduct and fruitfulness of the Spirit which showed up as abnormal and extraordinary when compared with the average pagan standards. Paul's contribution was simply to show what this abnormal standard of the Church implied ; that what was considered to be so outstanding was after all the normal, everyday life and conduct of those under the Spirit's control. Indeed, from the Christian viewpoint, what came to be abnormal was any lapse from this high standard (1 Cor. vi. 1 ff.).

Paul's faith centres in what Deissmann calls a Christocentric mysticism.[2] Viewed, however, from the side of his Spirit-possessed life, Paul's Christocentric

---

[1] 1 Cor. ii. 4, 6 f., 10 ; Eph. ii. 18 ff., iii. 5, iv. 3 ; Rom. viii. 26 f. ; Eph. vi. 18 ; Rom. xiv. 17 ; 1 Thess. i. 6 ; Eph. vi. 10, 19 f. ; 2 Cor. i. 3.

[2] *St. Paul*, Eng. Tr. pp. 23, 123 ; *The Religion of Jesus and the Faith of St. Paul*, pp. 190, 193.

mysticism is mystical experience of the Spirit, and this empirical identity of experience of Christ with experience of the Spirit is abundantly illustrated. We have experience of " justification " in Christ and of " justification " in the Spirit (Gal. ii. 17 ; 1 Cor. vi. 11). There is " speaking " in Christ and " speaking " in the Spirit (2 Cor. ii. 17 ; 1 Cor. xii. 3). Christ " dwells " in the heart and the Spirit " dwells " in human personality (Eph. iii. 17 ; Rom. viii. 9). The Church is " one body " in Christ and " one body " in the Spirit (Rom. xii. 5 ; 1 Cor. xii. 13). The Church is a " fellowship " of Jesus Christ and a " fellowship " of the Spirit (1 Cor. i. 9 ; 2 Cor. xiii. 14). Experiential constituents due both to Christ and to the Spirit alike are, " joy " (Phil. iii. 1 ; Rom. xiv. 17), " peace " (Phil. iv. 7 ; Rom. xiv. 17), " witness " (Eph. iv. 17 ; Rom. ix. 1), " faith " (Gal. iii. 26 ; 1 Cor. xii. 9), " sanctification " (1 Cor. i. 2 ; Rom. xv. 16), " righteousness " (2 Cor. v. 21 ; Rom. xiv. 17). The strongly mystical tone here seems *prima facie* to be a new element introduced by Paul, and has led to the supposition that he is influenced by the Mystery Religions. But the apostle has only followed through to their consummation the empirical elements inherent in the primitive Church, having transferred his experience of Spirit-possession, which he shared with the earlier believers, to his awareness of the presence and activity in him of the Living Christ. " That a person could be in, or have, or be possessed by a spirit was a common belief among both Jews and Gentiles, and this idea Paul applied to Christ." [1] This empirical process leads at last to the identity of Christ with the Spirit (2 Cor. iii. 17). Already in the primitive Church there was a growing awareness of the presence of Jesus (pp. 307 ff.), but what

---

[1] W. H. P. Hatch, " The Pauline Idea of Faith," in *Harv. Theol. Studies*, ii. p. 41.

THE EXPERIENCE OF THE SPIRIT

was as yet holding up the influence of a more intimate and mystical sense was the concrete expectation of Christ's return in glory. Further, there were empirical links between the believers' experience of the Spirit and of Christ. The coming of the Spirit is closely inter-woven with Jesus who, having received the promise of the Spirit from the Father, had bestowed the gift on them as the pledge of the coming Kingdom (Acts ii. 33). Every evidence of the Spirit's activity was thus associated with Jesus triumphant in resurrection, exalted to the right hand of God, soon to return and consummate the work begun by the Spirit. In this manner, experience of the Spirit caused Jesus to impinge on, move in, and witness through the believers, while the gradual fading of the literal eschatological hopes brought forward more prominently the awareness of Christ's presence.

Paul is, therefore, dependent to a large extent on the primitive Church experience of the Spirit and of Christ ; the empirical constituents of his Christocentric mysticism are derived more from the Spirit-possession of the Church before him, and less from pagan sources such as the Mysteries. So also in the ethical emphasis which he places on the fruits of the Spirit in human life. In the nature of things, under the overwhelming sense of spiritual power which came upon the first believers, the enthusiastic character of the Spirit's manifestation was very prominent. This, however, gives no warrant for assuming that the ethical experience of the Spirit was absent in the earlier period, or that the Spirit was received in the physically and psychologically abnormal only.

The " mystic " or " numinous " nature of the primitive Church experience of the Spirit is revealed in the close relation between experience of the Spirit and experience of demon-possession. The extraordinary words and works of Jesus, while accounted for by the indwelling in Him of the Spirit, cause some minds to infer that He was possessed with an unclean spirit (Mark iii. 30), or inspired by the prince of the demons (Mark iii. 22). There must have been a similarity of " symptoms " in Spirit- and demon-possession, otherwise the criticism shows the scribes and Pharisees to be unspeakably foolish, a charge which cannot be made of them (pp. 83 f.). John the Baptist was regarded as being possessed by the Spirit from his mother's womb (Luke i. 15), but some Jews ascribed his activity to demonic influence (Matt. xi. 18 ; Luke vii. 33). " Thou hast a demon," " say we not well that thou art a Samaritan, and hast a demon ? " were said to Jesus by some of His contemporaries (John vii. 20, viii. 48), or else they summed Him up by asserting that " He has a demon and is mad " (x. 20). It is beside the point to regard these words as no more than vilifying insult. While phenomena inspired by the Spirit may be taken as due to demonic indwelling, on the other hand what was really demonic was sometimes misread as coming from the Spirit. Prophets may be held to be Spirit-inspired, whereas they are only false deceivers, inspired by demons (Matt. xxiv. 11, 24). The " discernment of spirits " (1 Cor. xii. 10) points to this possibility : " There is always need of proving that which is spoken under spiritual influence, because a lying spirit, sent by the devil, can also inspire man and deceive the Church." [1] The similarities between the respective phenomena would easily influence the unthinking and the undiscerning into ascribing to the Spirit what was essentially demonic.

Human personality is the scene of activity for Spirit and demons alike.[2] As the Holy Spirit is sometimes

[1] B. Weiss, *Biblical Theology of the New Testament*, Eng. Tr. 1882, vol. i. p. 304.

[2] The noteworthy exception to this is the entrance of evil spirits into the swine at Gadara (Mark v. 13).

regarded as the principle of life in human personality
(p. 67), so demonic agency may be the same principle
(En. xv. 8 f., 11).   Human personality becomes for the
time being the habitation of either the Spirit or evil
spirits (1 Cor. vi. 19 ; Luke xi. 24–26) ; this indwelling
is brought out by a similarity of phraseology used to
express the respective experiences, namely, " in the
Spirit of God " (Matt. xii. 28), " in an unclean spirit "
(Mark i. 23).   Human personality is the passive recipient
of the numinous energy, whether the Spirit or the
demons.   The Spirit speaks, the organs of speech are
the medium ; [1] so also an indwelling demon may use the
organs of speech for its use in the demon-possessed.[2]
The Spirit active in man causes him to cry out " Abba,
Father ! " (Rom. viii. 15) ; the demonic power causes
its victim to utter startling cries of another kind (Mark i.
26, etc.).   The Spirit impels men to action independent
of their own willing ; Paul's way is hindered (Acts xvi.
6–8), he is impelled across to Macedonia (ver. 10) ;
Jesus is " driven out " into the wilderness " (Mark i. 12).
Similar irresistible urges are the result of being possessed
with demons ; the demon " seizes " and " holds " its
victim (Luke viii. 29), or drives him out from human
habitation (ver. 29), the propulsion being not unlike to
that of the boat impelled by the oars, or forced out to
sea by the wind in its sails (Mark vi. 48 ; John vi. 19).
Or the victim was flung into convulsions (Mark ix. 20),
or irresistibly compelled to throw himself on the ground
and dash himself about (ver. 18).   As the Spirit " binds "
Paul and gives him no choice but to go to Jerusalem
(Acts xx. 22), so the demon " binds " its victim who

[1] 2 Chron. xx. 14 ; Matt. x. 20 ; Luke xii. 12 ; Acts ii. 4, iv. 8,
vi. 10, xiii. 9 f., xxi. 11 ; Rom. viii. 15 ; Gal. iv. 6.

[2] Mark i. 34, iii. 11 f., v. 7–10, 12 ; Acts xvi. 17 f., xix. 15. This
aspect has a negative side ; where the demon-possessed does not
speak (Mark ix. 17, 25), it is the demon in him that is silent.

becomes a passive instrument in the power of the evil spirit (Luke xiii. 16). Possession by the Spirit resulted in marvels of the physical order, while a demon-possessed man could snap the chains that bound him (Mark v. 4), or overcome seven men at one time (Acts xix. 16). As ecstatic conduct was a sign of the Spirit's presence, so demon-possession has its parallel in the victim being " beside oneself," or " mad " (Mark v. 3–5 ; Acts xxvi. 24). The Spirit conferred superhuman insight and wisdom, and an unnatural discernment resulted from demonic agency (Mark i. 24, 34 ; Acts xvi. 16 f., xix. 15).

These resemblances between the two orders of " spirit " experience are accounted for by the psychology of a religious experience which viewed both Spirit and demon-possession as an invasion of a supernatural, overpowering energy into human personality. As man believed himself to have the Spirit, so a similar con- viction held him at other times that he was demon- possessed. Both Spirit and demons were recognized by symptoms, extraordinary and abnormal, which had similar features. We are faced with more than merely belief in demons. We may grant that " the forms and phases in which insanity manifests itself always depend upon the general state of culture and the ideas current in the social environment, so that whenever the religious life is in a state of agitation, and a firm belief prevails in the sinister activity of evil spirits, ' demon-possession ' still breaks out sporadically." [1] But what we have to consider is religious experience which presented pheno- mena of which no doubt existed that demons were the cause, while the existence of demons under the rule of their prince was taken as axiomatic, and all in open enmity with God and the Spirit of God.

[1] Harnack, *Mission and Expansion of Christianity*, Eng. Tr. 1908, i. p. 125.

In the demoniac of Gadara (Mark v. 3–5 ; Luke viii. 27, 29) we have the typical case of an insane man.   He is dominated by superhuman power which enables him to perform extraordinary actions impossible in normal life.   In the case of the dumb demoniac (Mark ix. 17, 25), a deep, silent melancholy has descended upon the victim, and under the settled depression the personality is helpless.   Some evil power, foreign to him, had taken possession.   The madness is accompanied by physical afflictions which baffle understanding, the origin of which no one could account for, the healing of which was beyond human skill.   The whole man was out of himself, and demons were in charge—fearsome, strange powers.

The primitive Church had to deal with this painful and aggressive problem, and it arose to its opportunity inasmuch as it had a counteracting power in the energy of the Spirit of God.   Just as demons could invade personality, so they could be expelled, provided there was a power which would prove too much for the sinister invader.   The Spirit of God was regarded as just that very power to master the demons.   Those who were possessed by the Spirit had in them the very spiritual energy to bring healing to the demon-afflicted by casting out the demon and substituting for it the mightier Spirit.   In the very substitution itself the act of healing took place, for human personality could not be possessed at one and the same time by the Spirit and by a demon, and the demon had to give way as the Spirit, in purest incompatibility, expelled it.   The controlling demon in possession of the personality was aware that in the approach of Jesus it was faced with one in whom operated mightily the Spirit.   Hence was uttered the cry that Jesus would spare, even before he had uttered one word (Mark i. 24).   The disciples possessed the same power to replace the malevolent activity of demons

with the Spirit's creative life. The change that had
to be made was from the experience denoted by " he has
a demon," or " he has an unclean spirit," to the blessed
state pointed to in the words " the holy Spirit is upon
him," from the insanity of a demoniacal condition to
the " right mind " which the Spirit brought, from demon-
possession to Spirit-possession.

As in the experience of the Spirit, so demon-
possession brings us to a something " beyond," a
" numinous," an ultimate which defies analysis. We
only push the mystery further back when, in reaching
the limits of psychological and historical discussion, we
leap beyond them to postulate, as did the Jews, a Satan
as the prince or overlord of demons. But for the
primitive Church there was no dualism in the sense of
two superhuman entities of good and evil in opposition,
for the Spirit was always victorious over the evil
myrmidons. The final triumph of the Spirit was at
hand, for at any moment the divine Kingdom, through
His impulsion, would arrive.

The similarities between the experience of the Spirit
and of evil spirits are not accidental, for there are vital
connecting links. Both series of ideas were at one time
ascribed to the agency of God, who sends an evil spirit
which stirs up the men of Shechem to deal treacher-
ously with Abimelech (Judg. ix. 23); an evil spirit
conceived to come from God causes Saul to attempt
David's life (I Sam. xviii. 10). God was supposed to
send a " lying " spirit into prophets that they may give
deceitful counsel (I Kings xxii. 23) ; indeed God Himself
could be that very lying spirit (ver. 22). The repetition
of these ideas in Chronicles shows that the revisers of
Israel's history held much the same view at a later
period, since they allowed the explanations to stand
(2 Chron. xviii. 20–23). The Levites pray and call to

mind how God gave his " good " spirit to instruct the
people in the wilderness ; does this suggest that God
could give an "evil" spirit if he wished? (Neh. ix. 20 ;
cf. Ps. cxliii. 10). The transcendence of God, however,
became prominent after the Exile, and the reference
back of evil spirits to God tended to cease. At last, a
century or so prior to the coming of Jesus we have a
whole series of evil spirits responsible for the moral
catastrophes of men. The " spirit of deceit " (T.S. vi. 6),
the " spirit of desire " (T. Jud. xvi. 1), the " spirit of
envy " (T.S. iii. 1), the " spirit of fighting " (T.R. iii. 4),
the " spirit of filthy lucre " (T. Jud. xvi. 1), the " spirit
of fornication " (T.R. iii. 3 ; cf. Hos. iv. 12, v. 4), the
" spirit of hatred " (T.G. i. 9), the " spirit of injustice "
(T.R. iii. 6), the " spirit of insatiableness " (T.R. iii. 3),
the " spirit of jealousy" (T. Jud. xiii. 3, cf. Num. v. 14,
30), the " spirit of lust " (T. Jud. xvi. 1), the " spirit of
lying " (T.R. iii. 5), the " spirit of obsequiousness "
(T.R. iii. 4), the " spirit of pride " (T.R. iii. 5), the " spirit
of profligacy " (T. Jud. xvi. 1), the " spirit of sleep "
(T.R. iii. 1), the " spirit of vainglory " (T.D. i. 6), the
" spirit of wickedness " (T.D. v. 6). All these delin-
quencies are abnormal, and cannot be ascribed to God, so
they are accounted for by the invasion of demons.

Hints of the divorce between the two kinds of spirit
influence may also be seen. As the evil spirits are being
dissociated from the divine source, there is a parallel
movement which tends to remove the experience of the
divine Spirit from association with demonic effects. The
links in this movement are further shown in " the spirit
of wisdom " (Isa. xi. 2), the " faithful spirit " (Prov. xi.
13), the " spirit of humility " (Prov. xvi. 19), an " ex-
cellent spirit " (Dan. v. 12), the " spirit of judgment "
(Isa. iv. 4), the " spirit of understanding " (Isa. xi. 2),
the " spirit of might " (*ibid.*), the " spirit of knowledge "

(*ibid.*), a " new spirit " (Ezek. xi. 19), the " spirit of
grace " (Zech. xii. 10), the " spirit of supplication "
(*ibid.*). This process goes on until a century or two
before Christ we find that as the demons are sorted out
with their demonic source, so the projections towards
experience of the Spirit are clarified in their source
being clearly seen in God. Thus we have the " spirit
of faith " (En. lxi. 11), the " spirit of wisdom " (Ps.
Sol. xviii. 8), the " spirit of patience " (En. lxi. 11), the
" spirit of mercy " (*ibid.*), the " spirit of judgment "
(*ibid.*), the " spirit of peace " (*ibid.*), the " spirit of
goodness " (*ibid.*), the " spirit of insight " (En. xlix. 3),
the " spirit of life " (En. lxi. 7), the " spirit of power "
(En. lxxi. 11), the " spirit of understanding " (T.L. ii. 3),
the " spirit of might " (En. xlix. 3), the " spirit of
truth " (T.Jud. xx. 1, 5 ; cf. John xiv. 17), the " spirit
of sanctification " (T.L. xviii. 7). The Spirit's presence
was ultimately found in activities and qualities which
could be derived only from a godly source ; those of the
baser sort could have no other origin than in the base,
demonic sources. " By their fruits ye shall know them,"
was the final principle in religious experience which
sorted out what manifestations were of the Spirit and
what were of the demons.

Therefore, amid the many similarities between the
two kinds of spirit experience, there are vital differences
to be more clearly discerned. The activities of the
demons are injurious to human life. Demon-possession
" grievously vexes " (Matt. xv. 22), brings the horrors
of lunacy (Matt. xvii. 15) and untold misery to its
victims. But possession by the Spirit produces blessing
and joy, restoration and healing. No demon ever opened
the eye of the blind, but divine power can do so (John ix.
33). Further, demon-possession leads to the disintegration of personality (Mark v. 2 ff., 9) ; the Spirit's

indwelling unifies human life.   Again, demon-possession
is unclean and unholy, appertaining to the dominion
of evil, but the Spirit is holy and the manifestations
inspired are holy.   The demon-possessed dread the
presence of Jesus, for they know that he has the power
to cast the evil spirit forth.   But it is the Spirit that
inspires Jesus and enables him to strike terror into evil
spirits.   The demons are hostile to the rule of God.
Pagan deities are called " idols " (Ps. xcvi. 5) and become
identified with demons (Ps. cvi. 37 ; En. xix. 1 f. ; 1 Cor.
x. 20 f.).   Idol worshippers are worshippers of demons,
and they stand over against the divine Kingdom, as the
demonic objects of their worship also do.   The Spirit,
however, is recognized as the active power in the divine
Kingdom, and is thus set over against the pagan deities
identified with the demons (Jub. i. 11, 23).   Demons
are thought of as the spirits of evil men (Sib. Or. III. 723),
or as the spirits which influence the actions of evil men
(Gen. vi. 2, 4 ; En. xv. 8 f.) ; the Spirit is never thought
of as inspiring evil.   Demons induce an atmosphere of
terror, hysterical paroxysms, delusions, and insanity ;
those possessed by the Spirit carry with them an atmosphere of peace, harmony, trust, and joy.   The demons
are active in the name and by virtue of the power of
Satan (Mark iii. 23–27) ; the Spirit is felt to be direct
from God and even to be the energy and power of God,
so that the mention of God's name or Christ's name
evokes that divine power (1 Cor. xii. 1–3).   Those who
confess the name of Christ are divinely inspired, and
become channels for the Spirit's operation, but to cry
" Jesus is anathema " is indicative of demonic inspiration ; to name Jesus as Lord is to be possessed by the
Spirit.   Demon-possession forces its victim away from
God ; the Spirit brings him so close to God that he is
able to address God as Father.   Demons inspire false

teachers and make them appear as angels of light (2 Cor. xi. 14 f.) ; but the true apostles, prophets, and teachers, as their words and lives reveal, are of the Spirit.

"By their fruits ye shall know them." This is the final test. "Not every one that speaks in the Spirit is a prophet, but only if he has the ways of the Lord. By their ways therefore the false prophet and the true shall be known." Thus the *Didache* (xi. 8) reflects this guiding principle of the primitive Church. The "ways" are the "symptoms" the possessed one shows.

The primitive Church was a community possessed by the Spirit. In the believers the Spirit worked, and produced extraordinary phenomena which in themselves were the "fruits" of the indwelling power. The inheritance so rich in ideas of Spirit-possession, the environment potent in creative religious life, above all the personal contacts with the Spirit-possessed Jesus, all endowed the Church with extraordinary potentiality for the operation of the Spirit. From this standpoint many of the perplexing phases of the life and experience of the believers are unified when regarded as expressing the activity of the indwelling Spirit of God. Everything found its central inspiration in the experience of the invading, superhuman, divine power. The Kingdom, ardently awaited, was guaranteed by the manifest operation of the Spirit. "Those earliest believers were lifted above the world of the present and felt that they bore their part in a supernatural order. They constituted the new community, in which the Spirit moved like a mighty rushing wind." [1]

[1] E. F. Scott, *The Beginnings of the Church*, p. 83.

CHAPTER VIII

The Self-Consciousness of the Primitive Church

IN the early chapters of the Acts we have what are no more than detached vignettes of a community under the control of the Spirit, throbbing with vivid expectation of a divine consummation centring in the exalted Jesus whom the believers had known on earth, and who had renewed His contacts with them in the resurrection. Prior to Pentecost the group numbered some one hundred and twenty men and women (Acts i. 13 f.), but there may well have been many others. The five hundred brethren to whom came a resurrection experience may have been an assemblage in Galilee, but it is more likely that they were the expectant Messianic community gathered in Jerusalem, the scene of Messiah's return.[1]

As the records stand, an action is reported on the part of the community which implies a degree of self-consciousness beyond what we naturally expect at this stage. The number of the Twelve is made up, Matthias being chosen to fill the place of Judas the betrayer (Acts i. 21–26). That the completion of the apostolic collegium precedes the outpouring of the Spirit is itself significant, for, if the Twelve occupied the official position at this time which was ascribed to them by the Church of a later period, then it is obvious that their official authority was not derived from the endowment of the Spirit. The Western Text actually represents Peter, not the community, putting forward the two candidates

[1] Cf. E. Fuchs, *op. cit.* pp. 16 f.

for the apostleship ; this " does not seem to be a case of accidental variation, and the Western Text is remarkably like some forms of later ecclesiastical elections." [1] Are we in the presence of later Church theory influencing the tradition, not only in an enhancement of Peter's official position, but in the election of a successor to Judas ? The problem is not merely one of ecclesiastical theory and organization, but whether at this stage there was any " Church " to be expressed in organization. Was the community sufficiently self-conscious to warrant such a completing of an apostolic collegium, or is the collegium itself the reading back of later theory, thus to be discounted as far as the primitive Church is concerned ?

Jesus seems to have chosen " twelve " from among his followers " to be with him " (Mark iii. 14), the number being influenced by the eschatological aspect of the disciples' function. Jesus chose twelve as a parabolic declaration that his message of the Kingdom concerned Israel as a whole, and they were to be assessors at the judgment in their corporate eschatological function (Matt. xix. 28). The significance of the number, therefore, lies not in ecclesiastical selection but in apocalyptic association, as far as Jesus was concerned ; so, too, in the primitive Church. As the Church grew and developed, the number lost its parabolic meaning, yet it retained its place and other meanings had to be found for it. The " Twelve " became a sort of " shadow " cabinet of ecclesiastical government, the beginnings of which are seen in the later decades of the apostolic age. These later meanings are embodied in the Luke–Acts tradition, the Twelve have become the apostolic collegium, while the effort has been made in the tradition,

---

[1] *The Beginnings of Christianity*, ed. Foakes Jackson and Lake, vol. v. 1933, p. 52, referred to henceforth as *BC*., ed. FJ. and L.

not very successfully, to weld the Twelve and the apostles into one and the same unit.[1]

The election of Matthias, if historical, was due to the desire to complete the number in view of the imminent Kingdom, that the chosen assessors might be ready for their eschatological duty in judging Israel. This is the empirical probability underlying the story. The community was sufficiently conscious of itself as a Messianic body to take this step.

The coming of the Spirit was the pledge for the community that the last days were at hand. Jesus of Nazareth, crucified in the purpose of God by the Jews, had overcome death, was exalted in glory, and as the divinely designated Messiah was soon to appear. Meanwhile He had sent " the promise of the Father " in the Spirit as the earnest of His advent. The time was urgent ; those who hear the news are urged to repent and acknowledge Jesus as Messiah (Acts ii. 37–40). Such are the central ideas of Peter's speech which followed the Pentecost experience. It may be no more than a summary of ideas common in the primitive Church, yet it is none the less valuable as an index of the way the community regarded itself in relation to Jesus. We may be in " danger of arguing in a circle, since our ideas of early Christianity, with which the speeches in Acts are said to conform so exactly, are derived in large part from those very speeches," [2] but they are full of traditional Messianic conceptions which we can check with what is found in the religious environment of the Church.

The community is aware at this stage that salvation is to extend to all Israel (Acts ii. 36) ; the burden of the earliest preaching is that " the acceptance of Jesus

---

[1] These summary statements are dealt with in detail in Appendix V., " The Twelve and the Apostles," pp. 357–60.

[2] H. J. Cadbury in *BC.*, ed. FJ. and L., vol. v. pp. 416 f.

as Lord and Christ is an essential condition of the salvation of Israel." [1] Israel's sin lay in its rejection of
Jesus the Messiah; let the nation accept Him in true
contrition, and inherit the Kingdom even now being
prepared for it.   These ideas were forcefully proclaimed
on many occasions.   The community began to grow in
numbers ; the three thousand converts made through
Peter's Pentecostal speech is a statement of progress
during an initial period of active witness rather than an
invasion of the community on one specific occasion
(Acts ii. 41).   We learn of the spiritual routine followed
by the new believers (ver. 42) ; some time, however,
must have elapsed for the community to become so
distinctively aware of itself as to possess a more or less
authoritative corpus of teaching,[2] or know itself as a
fellowship expressing its consciousness in a rite known as
the " breaking of bread," and in the prayers centring
around the immediate return of Jesus in the divine
Kingdom.

The believers are becoming aware of the significance of the suffering of their Messiah, and they had
to find a reason on the conscious plane for what had
been long apprehended subconsciously.   They ascribed
it to the purpose of God, and began to search the Old
Testament for proofs of this.   Jesus had fulfilled the
divine will in the Suffering Servant.[3]   Christ's death,
however, was viewed in other ways beside the eschatological aspect.   Paul says that he received from the
primitive Church tradition the fact that Christ died for
sins according to the Scriptures (1 Cor. xv. 3).   In some
measure, therefore, there were redemptive aspects being

---

[1] J. Mackinnon, *The Gospel in the Early Church*, 1933, p. 14.

[2] For this teaching, see pp. 237–43.

[3] Cf. Luke xxiv. 26 ; Acts ii. 23 ; Luke xxiv. 27 ; Acts iii. 18,
13–16, viii. 35.

discerned; the remission of sins incurred in rejecting Messiah carried with it forgiveness of the sins and salvation from the coming Messianic Judgment. Such aspects, however dimly perceived, would be connected with the death on the Cross as the essential prelude to the coming Messianic glory.

Persecution sharpens the group self-consciousness; the return of the arrested leaders is heralded by corporate prayer which deepens and consolidates the faith and determination of the believers to witness courageously (Acts iv. 23–31). No opportunity was lost to preach Jesus the Messiah (v. 41 f.). The more drastic persecution that followed the martyrdom of Stephen gave the new community a tremendous impetus, for the scattered believers simply carried the gospel with them, and began the process which led to the witness for Christ " in all Judæa, and Samaria, and unto the uttermost parts of the earth." The new experience shows itself to be creative in every way; many small communities begin to arise here and there, some having a good mixture of Gentiles among their adherents. These communities are known as " ecclesiai," each with its reverence for the mother Church at Jerusalem, but as yet too taken up with their own spontaneous religious vitality to be concerned about their relationship to one another or to the parent community. We are in the presence of no formal organization at all; it is the creative power of the religious experience centred in Jesus Christ spontaneously influencing the emergence of the " ecclesiai " in many places. The eye-witnesses, fresh from their contacts with Jesus, spake what they had seen and heard; the spiritual elements embodied in them through such contacts awoke response; the seed of the gospel was taking root in good ground, and communities of believers were showing themselves. The local Jewish synagogues proved too restricted to contain these new groups, and new independent communities, known as " ecclesiai," in contradistinction to the synagogue, began to spring up in the cities, the towns, and the villages of the ancient world.   Problems were inherent which were ultimately to rear their heads and demand solution, and to these we return at a later stage.

The members of the primitive community are aware of themselves as " the disciples" over against those who were not of that category, namely, the Jews whose enmity had crucified Jesus.   We learn that the number of " the disciples " was growing rapidly, until they could be described as a " multitude " (Acts vi. 1 f.). The community of " the disciples " was thriving and extending its influence ; we hear of " the disciples " at Damascus ; Saul has become aware of " the disciples of the Lord " as a distinct group demanding extirpation before it became too prominent (Acts ix. 1 f.).   After his conversion he stays with " the disciples," namely, the Christian community there (ver. 19) ;   arrived back in Jerusalem he asked to be attached to " the disciples " (*i.e.* the church) there (ver. 26).   In Joppa the community is known as " the disciples " (ix. 36, 38) ; so also at Antioch where " the disciples " were to receive the name which ultimately was to designate the believers in Christ, namely, " Christians " (xi. 26). As Paul pursues his missionary journeys we hear of the emergence everywhere of groups of " the disciples " (Acts xiii. 52, xiv. 20, 22, 28, xviii. 23). Peter in pleading for a liberal attitude before the Council of Jerusalem, urged that no unnecessary burden be placed on " the disciples," *i.e.* the Gentile communities here and there (Acts xv. 10).   " The disciples " in Achaia, *i.e.* the community there, are urged to receive Apollos

(Acts xviii. 27). The hostility of the Jews causes Paul to separate " the disciples " from the synagogue (Acts xix. 9), a significant hint of the emergence of " the disciples" as a distinct and self-conscious community; this must have happened very frequently, in the developing church. The members of the community, " the disciples," refuse to allow Paul to hazard his life in a tumult at Ephesus (Acts xix. 30). There are communities at Troas, Tyre, and Cæsarea known as " the disciples " (Acts xx. 7, xxi. 4, 16).

The designation, " the disciples," indicates the primitive Church extending everywhere. The term denotes the Messianic community or the " ecclesia " in its local significance. " Ecclesia " was to be used to indicate the whole Church at large, of which these groups of " the disciples " were the local offshoots. In so referring to themselves as " the disciples " the believers reveal their vague awareness of their relationship to the community as a community, and that what counted at the moment was their personal relationship to Christ. This consciousness of relationship to Jesus preceded the consciousness of their relationship to the community or Church as such. It is this awareness of a vital and personal connection with Jesus the Messiah that lies behind the frequent reference of the Messianic community to itself as " the disciples." This fact is all the more clearly brought out if it be true that Luke is editing his material to show that the Church as a definite organization was intended from the beginning for the whole world, for it is curious how he omits using the term " ecclesia " where it would have so fittingly come in. Instead, he constantly refers to the local communities of Christ as " the disciples." It seems as if Luke is faithful to the tradition in that he retains this elementary mode of referring to the groups as " the disciples," despite his

natural inclination to substitute the more ecclesiastical
term.

While believers expressed their intimate consciousness of Christ in their awareness that they were His
" disciples," they showed the nature of their intimate
relationship to one another by referring to themselves
as " the brethren." The members of the Jewish theocracy
designated themselves as " brethren." [1]   Within the
primitive Church, however, not only is the term used
of a Jew who has entered the new Messianic community,
in referring to a fellow-Jew who may or may not belong
to the community of Christ ; [2] the Gentiles are looked on
as " the brethren" by Jewish disciples (Acts xv. 23), and
the Gentile members look on themselves as " brethren "
(Acts xviii. 27).   Paul's epistles use the term to denote
believers in Christ whether Jew or Gentile (Rom. i. 13 ;
Eph. vi. 23, etc.) ;   distinction of sex is not allowed to
interfere with the conception of brotherhood (Rom. xvi.
1, 15 ; 1 Cor. vii. 15, ix. 5) ; similar considerations apply
to slaves (Gal. iii. 28).   This experience of brotherhood
is more than sentimental humanitarianism, for it is
rooted in the new kinship, spiritually conditioned,
foreshadowed by Jesus (Mark iii. 35).   It was more than
the mere grouping of men around the name of some great
leader in pursuit of an ideal inspired by the leader's
personality ; there was more in the experience than the
spirit of love and mutual helpfulness to hold the scattered
Christian groups struggling in a pagan and even hostile
environment.

In the first place, at the very centre of the new brotherhood lay the awareness of the eye-witnesses, that their
fellowship was grounded in their contacts with Jesus

[1] Ps. l. 20; Isa. xli. 6; Jer. xxxiv. 14; Ezek. xxxiii. 30; Mic. vii. 2;
Matt. v. 22 24, 47, vii. 3–5.
[2] Acts ii. 29, iii. 17, 22, vii. 2, ix. 17, xiii. 26.

in the flesh ; such contacts had impressed upon them in a vital manner what may be called " the Communism of Love," [1] which came to be so characteristic of the primitive community. The place of love in the words of Jesus, above all in His own works of mercy, and His protests against religious exclusivism, combined to set up a fellowship of love, spiritually inspired, the very bond of union between Him and those who followed Him, which was to be the unifying vitality among the followers themselves.

In the second place, these principles, derived at first hand from Jesus, became translated to a growing extent into the life of a community which gathered around Christ's name. The primitive Church proceeded to try out in practical life and organization its Master's spirit of love, and its experience of that love as observed in Him and in His own dealing with men. His love to the disciples had evoked their love for Him and for their fellow-men. Thus there was fostered that love of the brethren which is so conspicuous in the primitive Church.[2] We are told that believers have purged their souls in obedience to the truth through the Spirit, unto unfeigned love of the brethren, and are urged to love one another fervently from the heart (1 Pet. i. 22).

In the third place, the new believers represented in their corporate experience a new society, namely, the divine Kingdom yet to be consummated but even now at hand. The eye-witnesses had learned from Jesus, and through them the new converts made the same discovery, that they were to prepare for the coming of the Kingdom by moulding their lives together *en rapport* with the fundamental purpose of that Kingdom. The

---

[1] E. Troeltsch, *Social Teaching of the Christian Churches*, Eng. Tr. 1931, vol. i. p. 63.

[2] Cf. the " brotherly love " (Rom. xii. 10 ; Heb. xiii. 1).

old order was soon to give way to the newer divine order in which the doing of God's will confers on the believers the status of kinship in the spiritual family of the Christ. The new order demands a new spirit; the old relationships are to be transfigured on a new level. The convert did not simply attach himself to a new organization; he became a member of the new family, the kinship of which was not physical descent as with the Jews or in ordinary family life, but was determined by moral and spiritual affinities and likenesses to Christ. The primitive Church tried to give corporate expression to this inner family experience as it realized that all its members were brethren.

These ideas were not fully realized on the conscious levels of thought and practice, yet they were inherent in the religious experience of the believers, and proved to be quickening motives of their enthusiasm and witness. The " brotherhood " came to vivid practical expression as the believers had " all things in common," and distributed from the common store as each had need (Acts ii. 44 f., iv. 32, 34-37). The writer, who " has been called the socialist among the evangelists," [1] has had his narrative of the " communism " called in question. Much is made of the way Luke portrays the care of Jesus for the delinquent, His sympathy for the poor, and His emphasis on the duty of those who have wealth towards those who have it not. It is therefore not unnatural that the " communism " of the primitive Church is sometimes viewed as an idealizing of the practical life of the community, due to Luke himself. It is true that idealization enters when age-long tradition is being passed on; but the " social " emphasis in Luke's writings is not due simply to some predilection of his own mind, or shaping the narrative to bring out

[1] H. J. Cadbury, *The Making of Luke-Acts*, p. 260.

the " socialist " aspects of the words of Jesus. Why does Luke cease to put forward his " social " theories in the later chapters of Acts ? An author does not usually follow a favourite line of thought and suddenly discontinue it. The answer is that the social emphasis is due not so much to the author's predilections as to his fidelity in following the facts of the tradition of which he made use. The " communism " is due, not to any Lucan theory of what ideally the Church ought to have done, but to the fact that the having all things in common was the practical expression of the brotherhood emphasis in the experience of the Church. ·

The fact that no believer was under obligation to sell all his possessions and contribute what these realized to the common store (Acts v. 4) has led to the supposition that what we have in the " communism " is no more than the customary charity of the Jews repeated in the primitive Church.[1] This, however, is to overlook the enthusiasm of a religious vitality which produced a spiritual detachment where material things were concerned, and at the same time produced the brotherhood of the corporate spiritual life. The " communism " should not, of course, be understood in the modern political sense. There does not seem to have been a common purse ; distribution was made as each had need ; there was no pooling of wages, but probably those who could earn nothing and had no one to earn for them were maintained from a fund provided by the proceeds of property realized by more wealthy members. The fund would include gifts made from time to time by those who were able to earn money in various ways. The whole idea was governed by the voluntary principle ; there were no binding regulations ; the sin of Ananias

[1] Cf. " The Communism of Acts," by K. Lake in *BC.*, ed. FJ. and L., vol. v. pp. 148 f.

was not that he refused to join the scheme, but that, having declared that he had realized his all he yet withheld a part. It was the sin of hypocrisy coupled with deceit. The real new thing in the " communism " was the consumption of capital for the common need.

We are not concerned with the precise sociological implications of this " communism " ; from the standpoint of religious experience it symbolized the inner attitude of the Church consciousness as made up of individuals aware that they stood as " brethren " to one another. Such a spirit was prepared for in the place of renunciation in the lives of the eye-witnesses as they went about with Jesus. The Galilean disciples left all to follow Him (Mark x. 28) ; Peter left his house, the boat, and the nets (Mark i. 18-20) ; while Levi renounced his livelihood at the receipt of custom (Luke v. 27 f.). A man seeking eternal life is advised by Jesus to sell all that he had, give it to the poor, and follow Him (Mark x. 21) ; Jesus urged His listeners to sell their possessions, and give alms (Luke xii. 33). The religious motive behind such renunciation is that detachment from the possessions and the rewards of the world is the best condition of freedom to pursue the life of the divine Kingdom. The " communism " of the primitive Church rests on this foundation. There was a detachment from worldly possessions inspired by love of the brethren and by the desire to be ready for the new order soon to come. It was only a matter of days, or, at the most, weeks, before the old order came to its end, and the believers could prepare for their Lord's advent in no better way than to share their worldly goods with their brethren. Awaiting the new order soon to be inaugurated, they detached themselves from the old and the vanishing. Yet these eschatological considerations do not account for the " communism " as such, for the spiritual renunciation implied was vitally in earnest, inspired by love of the brethren in the kinship of the family of Christ. That the experiment ultimately broke down does not imply failure in the love and the brotherhood ; it was rather due to the non-fulfilment of the eschatological hopes centred in Jesus. But as an early expression of the spirit of the community as a society preparing for the Kingdom of God, the " communism " is eloquent.

The members of the primitive community were aware of themselves as " friends." Paul is allowed to go ashore at Sidon to visit his " friends," and Harnack rightly refuses to see in this a reference only to the personal friends of the apostle. He regards it as denoting Christians in general.[1] Friendship held a high place in the Greek schools of philosophy, of which Aristotle and Socrates with his intimate contacts with his pupils form the most notable examples. If Luke has imbibed Greek culture, he " has permitted himself this once to use the classical designation " of the Church fellowship, and this once only.[2] Yet the designation is by no means unnatural when viewed in the light of the Jewish environment of the Church ; Jesus calls the disciples His friends (Luke xii. 4) ; Abraham was known as the friend of God (2 Chron. xx. 7). In the same way the believers in the Church stood in a similar relation to God as did Abraham. They had been brought into close friendship with God through their experience of Jesus.

The primitive Church was also self-conscious as the body of " the believers." The object of the belief consists of variants around the central fact of Jesus the Messiah, such as the imminent Kingdom, or forgiveness in His name. The belief may be in the gospel such as

[1] *Mission and Expansion*, i. p. 421.
[2] *Ibid.* Cf. also J. Moffatt, *Love in the New Testament*, 1929, p. 47.

Philip preached (Acts viii. 12), the contents of the preaching, as in the case of Peter's (Acts ii. 22 ff.), the coming order in the advent of the exalted Jesus. Or the object of belief may be that Jesus the Messiah is the Son of God, but there is some textual uncertainty about this passage (Acts viii. 37).   Belief in Jesus implies a definite change of life in conversion and surrender to Jesus (Acts xi. 21).   " The believers " are brought into a state of acceptance before God such as the law could not effect, any more than it could bring the peace of heart which such acceptance carried with it (Acts xiii. 39 ff.), a theme to be developed later by Paul.   Attempts were constantly being made to enforce Jewish status through circumcision upon non-Jewish believers as essential to salvation through the community (Acts xv. 5), but these broke down because Gentiles were discovered to be capable of receiving the new experience in Christ independently of Jewish requirements (ver. 7). It was the grace of Christ that brought salvation to the believers (ver. 11). Harnack summarizes the self-consciousness of the Church as expressed in the designation of themselves as " the believers " by saying that they " felt that the decisive and cardinal thing in their religion was the message which had made them what they were, a message which was nothing else than the preaching of the one God, of His son Jesus Christ, and of the life to come." [1] We need to modify the " life to come " to indicate the fact that this was the life of the new age to be ushered in by Jesus the Messiah.

The community is further conscious of itself as consisting of " those who are being saved " (Acts ii. 47). This participle is rare, but the few instances we have suggest a semi-technical reference to a specific element in the religious life of the Church.   Paul contrasts

[1] *Op. cit.* p. 404.

" those who are being saved " with " those who are perishing " (1 Cor. i. 18), probably with the meaning that there are those who are on their way to salvation just as there are those on the way to perdition. The eschatological consummation of the divine Kingdom is yet in the future, and the salvation is thought of as being, by anticipation, already present. The religious experience implied is the confident anticipation of being among the " saved " in the coming crisis of the Messianic Judgment. The " saved " will pass on to the life of the new order. The primitive Church is thus conscious of itself as forming the nucleus of those who look forward to this blessing, guaranteed for them by the presence and operation of the Spirit as the " earnest " of what was to follow in its time.

The believers looked upon themselves as " the saints." This mode of self-designation, while common in Paul's epistles, is rare in Acts (ix. 13, 32, 41, xxvi. 10), but it is not necessary to infer that it was a later term that arose from the developed consciousness of the Church as the Chosen People of God. The primitive believers were mainly Jews, and would therefore not find it at all strange to refer to themselves as members of the Messianic community as " the saints." [1] The primitive Church thus showed its awareness of being " separate " unto God and the Kingdom to be ushered in through the exalted Jesus who had called the believers in this way. The Godward reference of the term, namely, the being holy or separate unto Him was not lacking (1 Pet. i. 15 f.). The very power used to cast out the unclean or unholy demons was indicative of the holy nature of the calling of the Church in the Holy Spirit that worked in the believers.

[1] The members of the Messianic Kingdom are " saints " ; cf. Ps. xxxiv. 9 ; Isa. iv. 3 ; Dan. vii. 18, 22 ; Tob. viii. 15 (LXX).

A few collective terms, applied to the primitive community by outside observers, such as " Nazarenes " or " Galileans " (Acts xxiv. 5, i. 11, ii. 7), while unimportant, show how the community is connected with Jesus of Nazareth or Galilee, in the eyes of the world. The term " Christian," however, indicates how the new movement had centred around Jesus the Messiah whose followers were claiming exalted status for their Lord (Acts xi. 26). If the term took its origin as a nickname, it ·proves the truth of the proverb that " many a truth is spoken in jest," for no name could be more truly applied to the members of a community whose faith, so observant pagans had noticed, had to do with one who was claimed by His disciples to be the Christ.

We have obtained some glimpses into the self-consciousness of the Church reflected in the varied and spontaneous names by which the believers were known among themselves. We turn to discuss this consciousness of itself as seen in two important references, the second of which was destined to become the permanent name of the community in Christ. These two ways of denoting itself were " The Fellowship " and " The Ecclesia."

The Church became early aware of itself as " The Fellowship," " the earliest, and in some respects the most characteristic form which this self-consciousness took." [1] The interests of later ecclesiastical theory were the cause of the mistranslation, " the apostles' teaching and fellowship" (Acts ii. 42, A.V.); [2] the correct rendering of the Greek, τῇ διδαχῇ τῶν ἀποστόλων καὶ τῇ κοινωνίᾳ is, of course, " in the teaching of the apostles and in the fellowship." The relation of the apostles to the community

[1] C. Anderson Scott, *The Fellowship of the Spirit*, 1921, p. 69.
[2] Cf. C. F. Nolloth, *op. cit.* pp. 427 f. for the view of the Church implied in the mistranslation.

was as yet too fluid and undefined for them to be regarded as the constitutive basis of authority for the Fellowship. The origins of " The Fellowship " go back to the circle of friends formed by Jesus and His disciples ; such a circle constituted a " Chabûrah," [1] an Aramaic term in current use " to describe a group of companions or partners, sharers in a common life." [2] The unifying bond was usually religious ; about the gatherings there was a definitely religious atmosphere, the topics of conversation being mainly of a spiritual character. The " Chabûrah " formed of Jesus and His friends observed the weekly meal which gave opportunity to celebrate the *Kiddûsh* for the Sabbath, and the farewell meal they had together was a *Kiddûsh* for the Passover. During the observance of the *Kiddûsh* for the following Pentecost the Spirit came upon the believers ; the " Chabûrah " was still in being, namely, the risen Jesus and His friends.

If this theory be justified, the " Chabûrah " meets us again in the reference to the primitive Church as " The Fellowship " the *Koinonia*. Whether *Koinonia* was used to denote the community or not, is secondary.[3] What is significant is that the mutual religious experience centred in loyalty to Christ worked out in vital fellowship, as the corporate expression of the spiritual attitude of the believers towards one another as " brethren." We come across the corporate word " brotherhood " only once (I Pet. ii. 17), but there was no need for it

[1] From " Chaber," a " comrade," a " companion," or a " friend " ; cf. W. O. E. Oesterley, *The Jewish Background of the Christian Liturgy*, 1925, pp. 167, 172.

[2] C. Anderson Scott, *Christianity according to St. Paul*, 1927, p. 160.

[3] Harnack does not deem the term sufficiently important to mention it among the names by which the early Christians were known (*op. cit.* pp. 399 ff.), while Cadbury dismisses any idea that it denotes the Messianic community with a wave of the hand (*BC.*, ed. FJ. and L. vol. v. pp. 389 f.).

since "The Fellowship" expressed this idea. "The Fellowship " stood for the community of those who were aware of being "brethren," fellow-heirs of salvation who rejoiced together and praised God together, who found themselves caught up into a higher spirit of unity on a common basis of love whereon "all human relations were transfigured, raised to a new power of dignity and sweetness."[1] They were aware of their oneness in fellowship as they waited for the return of their Lord.

We have seen that the community was under the complete control of the Spirit. The community was thus "The Fellowship of the Spirit," ruled by the Spirit, shot through and through with the Spirit's presence and power. This experiential factor interprets Paul's later reference to the community as "The Fellowship of the Holy Spirit " (2 Cor. xiii. 14), or "a Fellowship of the Spirit " (Phil. ii. 1). The community is "The Fellowship" called into being and inspired by the Spirit. The famous dictum of Lietzmann that no dexterity in exegesis is able to afford certainty as to the exact meaning of " The Fellowship of the Holy Spirit "[2] lends colour to Menzies's alternative meanings for the phrase as " the participation in the Holy Spirit coming from God or from Christ, which all believers have . . . or the fellowship with one another into which the Spirit brings them, or the intercourse with the Holy Spirit which all Christians enjoy."[3] The second of these alternatives best fits the empirical facts of "The Fellowship," added to which is the awareness that the Spirit is the vital power behind that Fellowship, the very existence of which is yet one more evidence that the Spirit is in control of the community.

[1] J. V. Bartlet, *The Apostolic Age,* p. 464.
[2] In *Handbuch zum N.T.*, 1907, *ad loc.* 2 Cor. xiii. 14.
[3] A. Menzies, *2 Corinthians,* 1912, p. 107.

Paul takes his start from the primitive Church as
" The Fellowship of the Spirit " and draws out the
implications in the light of his own experiential discoveries.
The community is a Fellowship of Christ, belonging to
and named after Christ, implying further an awareness
of being in fellowship with Christ as with the Spirit
(1 Cor. i. 9). Paul joins *Koinonia*, " the Fellowship,"
with his favourite metaphor for the Church, " The
Body of Christ," and speaks of " The Fellowship of the
Body of Christ " (1 Cor. x. 16), or of " The Blood of
Christ " (*ibid.*). We are not concerned here with the
sacramentarian controversies which had gathered around
this famous passage. The point for recognition is that
the original fellowship experience is at the very centre
of the " fellowship " of the Body or the Blood of Christ,
the very communion or participation in which assumes
the existence of a common fellowship both with Christ and
mutually among the participants attached by common
loyalty and devotion to Christ. The community as
" The Fellowship of Christ," was, of course, no new
discovery of Paul, for the primitive Church was intensely
Christ-conscious and essentially Christocentric.

We proceed to consider the self-consciousness of the
community as revealed by the name which was to
prevail over all other designations, namely, "The
Ecclesia." Harnack regards the use of this word to
describe the new community as " a masterly stroke." [1]
It was already an accepted mode of designation by the
time Paul began to write his epistles. " Ecclesia "
denotes the local Church (1 Cor. i. 2) ; in the plural,
" ecclesiai," it refers to the community or communities
of a district or region (Gal. i. 2, 22 ; 1 Cor. xvi. 19 ;
2 Cor. viii. 1) ; it may signify the actual congregation
assembled in worship (1 Cor. xiv. 19, 23) ; it may stand

[1] *Op. cit.* p. 407.

for the Church as a whole (1 Cor. x. 32, etc.). The term must have been in use prior to Paul, since he refers to his former persecution of the " ecclesia " (Gal. i. 13). The term is found in Acts (v. 11, etc.), and save for one possible exception,[1] the reference is to the local community. If Luke is setting forward the universal scope of the Church, it is noteworthy that he has not reached the use of " ecclesia " to denote the Church as a whole ; this has to await Paul's thinking before it is given its universal and its cosmic content. We are, however, in the atmosphere of the empirical in religious life, where men are in the presence of the extraordinary and not knowing exactly what to do with it or what to think about it. The propagating power of the new religious experience resulted in an " ecclesia " here, in an " ecclesia " there ; there was no time nor inclination as yet to think out the implications, still less to reach out to the unifying principle of the universal Church of which the local churches were the visible expression. Even the exalted theorizing about the " ecclesia " reflected in the Pauline Epistles is probably the personal thinking of the apostle himself, rather than the prevailing opinion of the Churches to whom he writes.

At the same time there was an experiential unity among the " ecclesiai " as these multiplied themselves. The unity was the experience of a common life and witness based on devotion to Jesus Christ, and centred in the expectation of His advent with the Kingdom. It was the dynamic inherent in the gospel message which caused the " ecclesiai " to emerge, and it was only after a long process of discovery that the conception of the

[1] Acts ix. 31, " the Church (ecclesia) throughout the whole of Judæa and Galilee and Samaria " ; even here there is localizing to two or three provinces ; moreover, in the Old Latin MSS we have the reading " churches," as in the majority of later MSS, and thus there is uncertainty as to the text.

Church for the whole world, the Church idea, the *Ding an sich*, came to the forefront of the Church consciousness.

What specific religious experience was denoted by this term " ecclesia " ?   Why did not the term, " The Fellowship " suffice ?   Evidently " ecclesia " expressed religious elements which " Koinonia " did not ;   the latter did not cover the empirical connection with the People of God as revealed in the history of Israel ;   the former term brought this vital aspect into the foreground of the self-consciousness of the Church.

Ecclesia usually translates the Hebrew word *qāhāl* in the Septuagint.   The general meaning of *qāhāl* is " assembly," " convocation," or " congregation."   The remnant of Israel are to be gathered together, and as a great *qāhāl* (company) they will return (Jer. xxxi. 8). There are, however, more specialized meanings.   First, the *qāhāl* was the assembly specially convened, or conceived as such in thought.   Jacob's sons are warned against entering the *qāhāl* of Simeon and Levi (Gen. xlix. 6).   The *qāhāl* (assembly) may be convoked to expose wickedness (Prov. xxvi. 26), or it was a gathering for war (Num. xxii. 4), or the massed assembly of the nations united for the attack on Babylon which would liberate the exiles of Israel (Jer. l. 9).   The *qāhāl* again may be the company of exiles returning to their native land (Jer. xxxi. 8).   The *qāhāl* (convocation) of Israel may come together to hear God's word (Deut. v. 22), or to decide what is to be done to Jeremiah for prophesying disaster and exile (Jer. xxvi. 17), to supplicate the Lord in the presence of danger (2 Chron. xx. 5), to make a great sacrifice (xxx. 25), to listen to Nehemiah's plans for reform and to confirm them (Neh. v. 13), to hold a special fast (Joel ii. 16), to praise the Lord for His goodness (Ps. cvii. 32).   Second, the *qāhāl* is the specifically organized community, self-conscious as the assembly

of the Lord (Num. xvi. 3), a reference back of the later
stage when the priestly rewriting of the nation's traditions
revealed this advanced idea mediated by the prophets
(Mic. ii. 5). We read of " Israel, the *qāhāl* (congregation)
of the Lord " (1 Chron. xxviii. 8), which one may enter
or from which one may be excluded (Deut. xxiii. 2–4).
The *qāhāl* is thus the assembly or congregation of the
people of Israel gathered in the name of the Lord. We
see a people corporately aware of its status as the chosen
people of Yahweh, suitably organized on its ritual side
in the sacrifices and worship of the temple, and guided
by seer, prophet, or wise man revealing Yahweh's will
to the people. The basis of this organized theocratic
community was the original covenant relationship
wherein Yahweh became the people's God and Israel
God's people. The *qāhāl* was the religious unit ; in
virtue of the individual's membership within the *qāhāl*
he had the right to approach God.

The Septuagint carries forward these ideas into the
word *ecclesia*. Israel is assembled for some purpose,
called together under divine authority to express the
divine will for the community. It is doubtful, however,
whether the ideal unity of Israel before God, though not
necessarily assembled, is indicated by *qāhāl* or the Greek
word *ecclesia* which translates it,[1] for there is another
term in Hebrew, namely, *'ēdhāh*, which " is properly,
when applied to Israel, the society itself, formed by the
children of Israel or their representative heads, whether
assembled or not assembled." [2] *'Ēdhāh* signifies a
company assembled by appointment or acting in a
concerted manner as a constituted body ; for instance,
over two hundred representatives of the assembly

---

[1] As R. Sohm thinks (*Kirchenrecht*, p. 16, quoted by A. J. Mason
in *The Early History of the Church and Ministry*, 1918, p. 6).

[2] F. J. A. Hort, *The Christian Ecclesia*, 1914, p. 4.

come together to remonstrate with Moses (Num. xvi. 2). There are more special usages of the word. First, it denotes certain companies such as the congregation of 'Ēl, a company of angels (Ps. lxxxii. 1), the congregation of peoples (Ps. vii. 7), of the righteous (Ps. i. 5) ; Job refers to his devastated dependents as my 'ēdhāh (company) (Job xvi. 7). The 'ēdhāh may be evil, a congregation of evil-doers (Ps. xxii. 16), an 'ēdhāh under some leader such as Korah (Num. xxvi. 9). Second, 'ēdhāh is used of Israel elsewhere, as the whole gathering of the people (Hos. vii. 12), of the whole congregation assembled before Solomon and the ark (1 Kings viii. 5 ff), of the assembly at Shechem which elected Jeroboam as Israel's king (1 Kings xii. 20), also the congregation in its ideal unity to which Jeremiah speaks (vi. 18) ; there is the technical sense of 'ēdhāh as the community of the Exodus, and the congregation of Israel based on this community as such, and identified especially as the congregation of Yahweh (Num. xxvii. 17, xxxi. 16 ; Josh. xxii. 16 f). The emphasis in 'ēdhāh is one of appointing, as its connectiou with the verb yā'adh shows, especially with its Niphal form denoting the reflexive use of " meeting at an appointed place," such as Yahweh meeting Moses at the Tent of " Meeting " (Ex. xxix. 42 f.) ; or in the sense of meeting by appointment (Amos iii. 3) ; or again, to gather, to assemble by appointment, as kings do for a campaign (Josh. xi. 5), or the congregation at the express appointment of Yahweh (Num. x. 4). This short analysis helps us to confirm the conclusion that 'ēdhāh is derived " from a root y'dh used in the Niphal in the sense of gathering together, especially gathering together by appointment or agreement." [1]

[1] Hort, *op. cit.* p. 4 ; cf. H. J. Cadbury in *BC.*, ed. FJ. and L., vol. v. p. 387, n. 7.

The Septuagint renders this Hebrew word, as it does
qāhāl in the earlier books of the Pentateuch, by *sunagōgē*
(synagogue). *'Ēdhāh* is very rare in the later Old
Testament literature ; it occurs for the congregation of
Israel no more than two or three times in the prophets
and psalms. There is a similar paucity as far as *qāhāl*
is concerned, but in the late books of Ezra, Nehemiah,
and Chronicles the references are very numerous. It
looks as if *qāhāl* came to be the usual word for the " congregation " of Israel in the later period of Israel's history
as it led up to the Christian era. While *'ēdhāh* (synagogue) indicates the congregation assembling by appointment, *qāhāl* (ecclesia) has the more precise connotation
of assembling by " calling " or " summoning." This
hint would influence the use of *ecclesia* to translate
qāhāl, since the Greek word stood in secular usage for
the summoning of Greek citizens by means of the
herald's trumpet to the assembly of the city.[1] This
aspect needs to be stressed to avoid reading into the
Christian use of *ecclesia* the notion that it means a group
called out of the world ; this idea may have been
prevalent at a later stage of the apostolic age, but it is
foreign to the self-consciousness of the primitive Church.
The sense of being " called out " to form a New Israel
could have hardly arisen until it was apparent that the
old Israel had finally rejected the call of Christ. Not
yet did " the disciples " feel themselves called out from
an apostate Israel to form a new Israel. They were too
concerned to win Israel from its rejection of Christ and
calling the nation to its salvation in the Kingdom.

In adopting *ecclesia* or its Aramaic equivalent to
denote itself, the primitive community showed that it
was self-conscious as vitally belonging to the earlier

[1] Cf. Num. x. 2–6 for the summoning of the assembly of Israel
by similar means.

" ecclesia " of Israel, the Chosen People ; it was aware
of its social solidarity with the People of God.   The
believers were not conscious of themselves as being
apart from their fellow-Jews nor of standing apart as
a distinct unity over against Judaism.   They worshipped
in the temple, or at the synagogues ; they kept the law,
observed the feasts, hallowed the Sabbaths in their
Kiddûsh gatherings, and in all things worshipped the
same God of Israel, being in fact typical Jews of their
age.   Yet there was an influential factor which in
reality distinguished the primitive Church from Judaism,
and was, indeed, to detach finally the Church from the
theocracy of Israel.   In the primitive Church the centre
of faith and salvation was Jesus the Messiah, regarded
as a crucified pretender by Israel, who by the very
action of putting Him to death had disowned any claim
He had to Messiahship.   But, as yet, it is to misinterpret
the facts to infer that the primitive Church was aware
of itself as the New Israel, for the essential fact of its
self-consciousness here is its sense of belonging to Israel,
with an urgent mission to Israel, but with no thought
of being apart from Israel.   The difficulty of the " New
Israel " theory [1] is that it does not allow to the full
for the vital sense of oneness with Israel which the
primitive Church possessed.   Even Paul never got any
further than the possibility of God's rejection of Israel.
The primitive Church experience continues the older
faith in its truer form.   Jesus did not criticize the
Pharisees because they were Jews, but because of their
failure to live up to what was the best in the Jewish
faith and experience.   " The disciples " likewise did not
condemn Israel, nor did they detract from the prized
privilege of solidarity with the ancient People of God.

[1] As stated by Harnack, *op. cit.* pp. 240 f., and H. F. Hamilton,
The People of God, 1912, vol. ii. pp. 24–39.

As a community of the Spirit, however, they were concerned with the fact that Israel was not living up to what it knew to be the highest and best in their own faith, and that the nation was in need of repentance unto salvation in the divine Kingdom.[1] The primitive Church directed its message of Jesus to influence Israel to become what was felt to be the purpose of God as Jesus had revealed it.

The aim of Jesus had been to win Israel to redemption in view of the imminence of the Kingdom (Mark i. 15). He reiterated His gospel of repentance in the synagogues (Mark vi. 1–6) ; this was the motive behind His desire to preach in the villages of Galilee (Mark i. 38 f.). His wonderful works, especially in the casting out of demons, were signs that the great deliverance was at hand. In His words, especially in the parables, Jesus sought to awaken Israel from its purely nationalistic conceptions of God, and so to liberate its faith for its God-intended mission to the Gentiles. There was urgency in the matter, for the Kingdom was imminent. Only an Israel redeemed could be "a light to lighten the Gentiles." Jesus sought to convert His nation to a higher acceptance of the will of God. In the light of this consideration we are able to approach the apparently insoluble problem of the so-called particularistic and universalistic passages in the Gospel of Matthew. On the one hand we have exclusive passages such as " I was not sent but unto the lost sheep of the house of Israel " (xv. 24), " go not into any way of the Gentiles, and enter not into any city of the Samaritans " (x. 5), or again, " ye shall not have gone through the cities of Israel until the Son of Man be come " (x. 23). These

[1] The prophets had often pointed out the faithlessness of Israel to its true ideals ; cf. the rebukes of Amos (iv. 4 ff.), the pleading of Hosea (ii. 10 f.), the despair of Jeremiah (xliv. 1 ff.).

passages imply the restriction of the mission of Jesus
and His disciples to Israel only. On the other hand,
there are sayings of an opposite character, such as,
" this gospel of the kingdom shall be preached in all the
world for a witness to all the Gentiles " (xxiv. 14),
freedom from Jewish legality in the discussion on the
Sabbath, especially in the words, " if ye had known
what this meaneth, I desire mercy, and not sacrifice,
ye would not have condemned the guiltless " (xii. 7),
and in the closing charge to the disciples, " Go ye
therefore and make disciples of all the nations (Gentiles) "
(xxviii. 19). The solution to these inconsistent presentations does not lie along the lines of a Jewish
recension,[1] nor in the personal idiosyncrasies of the
author rather than in the literary strata of the gospel,[2]
but in the sensitive insight of a writer—or the tradition
he has carefully preserved—who has discerned that
before Israel could redeem the Gentiles, it must first be
redeemed itself. The appeal, therefore, is first to Israel,
and the disciples are to preach at the outset to their
fellow-Israelites. The wider field of conquest awaited
them, but Israel must first be won for its mission.

In this spirit the primitive Church, aware of its
oneness with Israel, sought to rouse the nation to its
opportunity in the Kingdom of God. Not at once did
the disciples realize the wider universal implications.

It is in the light of ideas of an Israel to be redeemed
prior to its mission to redeem the Gentiles that we have
to view the two passages in the First Gospel where
Jesus is represented as using the word *ecclesia*, or its
Aramaic equivalent. The one reference is no more than
a hint of Jewish procedure in respect of offenders who
may be excommunicated from the congregation of

[1] As Schmiedel thinks, *Enc. Bi.* vol. ii. cols. 1842 f., 1870.
[2] J. Moffatt, *Intro. to Literature of the New Testament*, p. 255.

Yahweh (xviii. 17 ; Deut. xxiii. 2-4, 9) ; to refer this
to the Christian Church is to read back into the gospel
tradition the practice of later ecclesiastical theory. But
ecclesia occurs in the Matthæan story of Peter's confession, following which Jesus commends His disciple
and says, " on this rock I will build my *ecclesia* "
(xvi. 18). Jesus probably spoke Aramaic, and we do
not know the Aramaic word which *ecclesia* translates, or
if we may infer it, we are ignorant of its linguistic history
and meaning, we do not know what Jesus actually
said. Yet Hort's suggestion cannot be very far from
the truth, that, if we substitute " Israel " for *ecclesia*
here, we have an approximate impression of what the
sentence probably indicated to the listening disciples.[1]

It is sometimes supposed that at this point Jesus
broke off from Judaism and authorized the emergence
of His own *ecclesia* or Israel. Jesus " had just ended
His public ministry in Galilee, had taken the disciples
a long journey alone, and was about to go to Jerusalem
with the avowed intention of being killed ; no moment
was more suitable for preparing His followers to become
a new body, isolated both from the masses and from
the civil and religious authorities." [2] Such a judgment,
however, assumes a breach between Israel and the
disciples which was absent not only on the occasion
when Jesus spoke the words, but also from the self-
consciousness of the primitive Church, and such breach
would be all the more remarkable if the disciples had
received any such idea from Jesus. Why did they only
slowly awaken to the world-wide mission as a new and
distinct organization if this direct inauguration of a
community distinct from Israel by Jesus were the
historical and empirical probabilities of the case ? If
Jesus had intended to set up a new and distinct com-

[1] *Op. cit.* pp. 10 f.   [2] A. H. McNeile, *St. Matthew*, p. 242.

munity in the " my Israel," it is remarkable that the primitive Church knew nothing of it. This difficulty lends force to the suggestion that even in this reference we have later Church theory influencing the gospel tradition, especially when taken with the apparent heightening of Peter's authority. It is true, as Goguel reminds us, that " the text of Matthew is certainly secondary to that of Mark." [1]

At the same time, the reference to " my Israel " may be looked at from the angle of Jesus' mission to redeem Israel in order that Israel may be " a light to lighten the Gentiles." Jesus had decided to go to the central shrine of Israel's faith and there challenge the whole nation in the person of its accredited representatives. The challenge which His own crucifixion would provide might prove just the very thing needed to arouse the nation. Already He had gathered around Himself a band of disciples on whom, after His decease, the mission to Israel must devolve. Reinforced by His resurrection, they would go on to achieve the " my Israel " when the nation had awakened to its redemption to enter upon its mission to the whole world. Through Peter and his fellow-disciples the true Israel would emerge, not as a distinct entity from the nation, but Israel itself redeemed for the highest purposes of the divine Kingdom. This is the " my Israel," the " my *ecclesia* " as Jesus views it. Only in a very limited sense, however, were the disciples yet prepared for their witness. The thought of His death confused them, and a new change, a new alignment of their lives to His creative purpose, had yet to be made in them. Almost all that Jesus could do at this stage was to prepare them so that they might not ultimately miss the redemptive aspects of His mission. When the crisis came it would bring its own dynamic

[1] *The Life of Jesus*, Eng. Tr., 1933, p. 379.

light on the practical problems that would arise as the
disciples went forward with their gospel to Israel. Had
Jesus indeed forecast these problems for their minds,
their confusion would have been overwhelming ; thus
Jesus had to leave much to subsequent initiative and
discovery. That He did so shows His own confidence
in the effectiveness of the salvation which He was
bringing through them to the world of men.

As events turned out the new community arose
through these very eye-witnesses, as did also the work
of summoning Israel to repentance in the Kingdom of
God. In this sense Peter and his colleagues may be
viewed as experientially founding the *ecclesia*. At a
later stage it began to be seen that Israel was persistently
apostate from the salvation offered it, and through it,
to the world by Jesus, and through Him, by the community that arose from His creative influence. The
ecclesia then began to pursue its own distinctive course,
and Israel was sundered from the *ecclesia* of Christ,
going on its own way while the Church went forward
to be the light unto the Gentiles.

By contrast with the synagogue, the normal local
centre of worship for the Jews, the *ecclesia* was the
community being prepared to receive the Kingdom of
God. While the name marked the sense of continuity
with Israel, it also indicated that the community was
conscious of itself as the nucleus of the divine Kingdom,
entrusted with the salvation pertaining thereto. This
awareness gave the believers a distinctiveness among
themselves ; they organized their own life, and began
to frame their own teaching ; they engaged in specific
acts such as the " breaking of bread," and worked out
their ideas accordingly. They were their own executive
under the guidance of the Spirit. The *ecclesia* appointed
special officers to deal with the daily ministrations

(Acts vi. 5) ; one *ecclesia* set apart Barnabas and Saul for the mission to the Gentiles (Acts xiii. 1–3). Each *ecclesia* planned its life and witness accordingly and was led by the Spirit to make its decisions. Representatives were sent from Jerusalem to confirm what was being done (Acts viii. 14–17), and these were not always official apostles (Acts xi. 22–24). The local *ecclesia* did not always treat as authoritative what the emissaries from the mother Church laid down ; it was not afraid of standing out in opposition and going on its own way (Acts xv. 1 f.). With the advance of the Gentile mission the mother Church's authority diminishes into a mere respectful concern on the part of the *ecclesiai* in her need during times of famine (Acts xi. 29 f.).

The primitive Church began to develop its own distinctive " Way " of life, and at a fairly early date came to be known as " the Way " (Acts ix. 2, etc.). It may have included what was embraced in " the apostles' teaching " (Acts ii. 42), the " Way " being rooted in what the eye-witnesses had seen and heard in their personal contact with Jesus. We must not, however, assume that this teaching was a definite body of doctrine ; the variants of the " Lord's Prayer " (Matt. vi. 9–13 ; Luke xi. 2–4), the divergences in the setting and words of the farewell supper (Mark xiv. 22–25 ; Matt. xxvi. 26–29 ; Luke xxii. 14–20 ; 1 Cor. xi. 23–26), the fluidity of the teaching indicated by the different recensions of the Beatitudes (Matt. v. 1–12 ; Luke vi. 20–23), and the teaching of the Sermon on the Mount generally, reveal an absence of anything like fixity or definiteness in the teaching. We are in the presence of religious experience with its eager, spontaneous faith and expectation in Christ, and the very vagueness in the teaching is due to the nature of the new movement in its untried and unformulated condition of new life, a condition which had not yet given way to the more reflective mood necessary for precise formulation of belief.

This general consideration makes it almost impossible to accept either the Epistle of James or the *Didache* as a description of the new " Way " characteristic of the primitive Church. James's Epistle reflects the later atmosphere of the apostolic age, and is too formal in character ; as for the *Didache*, while it may be urged that the apostles drew up some formal catechism which may be the source of the " Two ways " section (i.–vi.), yet the Jewish tone may be accounted for equally from Jewish religious experience or by reference to Jewish-Christian religion. The apostles' teaching would have a more direct character as befitting their personal contact with Jesus than appears here.

There was teaching based on the recollections which came forward from time to time, as the words of Jesus were transmitted. Moral instruction was already given in the synagogues where the converts did not cease attendance, yet what they learned there would receive a new interpretation in the light of what they were gleaning of Jesus through the apostles' teaching. This instruction centred around Jesus as the the eye-witnesses shared their impressions and contacts with the converts ; the death of Jesus would be taught, as necessary to Messiah's purpose, by reference to Scripture. The resurrection experiences would be carefully passed on, together with what was meant in the coming of the Spirit as related to the Kingdom of God. Maxims of Jesus such as we have in the Sermon on the Mount, His parables, particularly as these had reference to the imminent crisis—here we have to reckon with the experiential limitations of the apostolic teachers who were able to reveal the inner meanings of what Jesus

said and did, as these came to be apprehended.   Sometimes the wrong constructions were placed on His
words,[1] or misleading interpretations given of parables.[2]

At this point we begin to touch the experiential
basis of the gospel tradition which grew into the Synoptic
Gospels.   Some of the recollections came at last to be
embodied in Q, the hypothetical corpus of sayings
generally admitted to be older than Mark's Gospel.   The
contents of Q probably represent the sort of teaching
that was being given with regard to the way of Jesus,
and help us to discern something of the nature of the
" Way," as impressed on the mind and life of the believers.   The " Way " is a condition of blessing resulting
from the exhibition of personal characteristics such as
being poor, or mourning, or being hungry, or enduring
reproach for Christ's sake ;   these passed into the more
specific spiritual characteristics such as being poor in
spirit, hungry and thirsty for righteousness ; [3]   the
Beatitudes reveal the personal qualities expected in
those about to inherit the Kingdom.   The spirit of the
" golden rule " (Matt. vii. 12 ;   Luke vi. 31),[4] love for
others to include even the hostile (Matt. v. 44 ff. ;
Luke vi. 27 f.), counsels as to charitable impressions of
others (Matt. vii. 1–5 ;   Luke vi. 37 f., 41 f.), the recognizing of the quality of the life by its fruits (Matt. vii.
16–18 ;   Luke vi. 43 f.), all pointed to the distinctive
qualification for being saved to the divine Kingdom in
the doing of the will of the Father (Matt. vii. 21, 24–27 ;
Luke vi. 46–49).   Labourers are required to work in
the divine vineyard, and the call to service was a feature

[1] As in the reason for speaking in parables (Mark iv. 12).

[2] Cf. the interpretation of the Parable of the Tares (Matt. xiii. 37–43).

[3] Matt. v. 1–4, 6, 11 f. ;   cf. Luke vi. 17, 20–23.   Matthew's
spiritualizing may be the more original, for Luke's " social " emphasis
has to be taken into account (p. 216).

[4] Cf. its negative form in the *Didache* (i.).

of the " Way " (Matt. ix. 37 f. ; Luke x. 2) ; instances
would be cited from Jesus' own way of life of his " doing
good " (Matt. viii. 5–10 ; Luke vii. 1–10 ; Acts x. 38).
There were injunctions to be simple and bold in approaching the mercy and love of God revealed as the Father
(Matt. vii. 7–11 ; Luke xi. 9–13), with illustrations of
the spirit in which believers were to pray (Matt. vi.
9–13 ; Luke xi. 2–4). The believer's life was to be
as the lamp that illuminated the house at night-time,
but the lamp must burn true—that is, the inner life of
the believer must be single-minded and trustworthy
(Matt. v. 15 ; Luke xi. 33 ; Matt. vi. 22 f. ; Luke xi. 34).

Many references were made to the imminent crisis of
judgment and the advent of the Kingdom. Everything
was to be uncovered and brought out into the open
(Matt. x. 26 f. ; Luke xii. 2 f.) ; the believers were to
be unafraid, for the divine care would be over them
(Matt. x. 28–31 ; Luke xii. 4–7) ; let them be faithful
before men, and Messiah would acknowledge them in the
great day before the Father (Matt. x. 32 ; Luke xii. 8).
Believers are not to be led astray by false Messianic
claimants ; when Jesus came there would be no doubt
about it, so sudden would His advent be (Matt, xxiv.
26–28, 37–41 ; Luke xvii. 23 f., 26 f., 34 f.).   The
converts were thus taught the duty of watchfulness
for Him (Matt. xxiv. 43–51 ; Luke xii. 39 f., 42–46).
Parables had their place in such teaching (Matt. xiii.
31–33 ; Luke xiii. 18–21). The believers learned that
the family of the Kingdom had paramount claims which
superseded even those of the ordinary family life (Matt. x.
37, 34–36 ; Luke xiv. 26, xii. 51, 53) ; they learned not
to be over-anxious about temporal needs, since their
treasure was not in earthly goods, but in the riches of
the coming Kingdom of heaven (Matt. vi. 25–33, 19–21 ;
Luke xii. 22–31, 33 f.).

As they were apprehending the words of their Master
the believers received the illumination which came
through their eyes seeing what they were being taught
to see, and their ears hearing what was imparted to
them. Hence they were seeing and hearing things
which even prophets and great ones of the earth never
saw nor heard (Matt. xiii. 16 f. ; Luke x. 23 f.), and
shared in the experience of being blessed as they awaited
the return of their Lord, or were encouraged to carry
their cross and follow Him who had carried His before
them (Matt. x. 38 ; Luke xiv. 27), or as they sought the
wanderer as Jesus had done (Matt. xviii. 12 f. ; Luke xv.
4–7), or discovered that they could not serve two masters
and so declared for their loyalty to God over against the
mammon worship so soon to perish (Matt. vi. 24 ;
Luke xvi. 13). They learned to count their life as
nothing so that they could serve their Master, and in so
doing, discovered a fuller and more vital life that they
had not hitherto conceived to be possible for them
(Matt. x. 39 ; Luke xvii. 33) ; they knew that though
heaven and earth should pass away in the imminent
consummation, their Master's words would not pass
away (Matt. v. 18 ; Luke xvi. 17). They came to understand that the divine promises to Israel were for them,
in their new status of being redeemed to the coming
Kingdom, but that many of the leaders of Judaism were
running the risk of being left outside, salvation being
missed at the last through being unready (Matt. viii. 11 f. ;
Luke xiii. 28 f.).

These were some of the distinctive principles of life
as reflected in the " Way " of Christ followed by the
primitive Church. These principles were taught first
by Jesus to His disciples, who in their turn imparted
them to the converts. The essential motive of the
teaching was to shape the outlook of the believers after

16

the pattern of the coming inheritance in the new order soon to be inaugurated, to conform inwardly their lives to the life and spirit of the divine order of which the primitive Church was the embryo community. This approach seems to fit the religious experience of the earliest believers in its growth and expression as a " Way " better than the later idea which viewed Christianity as a new " law " and made Jesus a greater Moses and the legislator for the new Church. According to such a theory, the teaching of Jesus formed a series of binding enactments on a different scale from that of the Mosaic code, yet none the less a code. This view is encouraged by the grouping of the sayings of Jesus into a Sermon on the Mount (Matt. v.–vii.), and supported by the semi-systematic moral teaching in the Epistle of James and in the *Didache*. But contrasted with the direct, vivid sayings of Q or its precursors, the commonplace moralities of James or the conventional Jewish precepts of the *Didache* lack life and vitality, and do not express in any spontaneous way the vital power and spirit animating the new community of Christ. This empirical difference is the reason why, in the last resort, we feel little confidence in using these two documents to interpret the religious life of the primitive Church ; that vital religious experience is one thing, but it becomes a pale shadow when reduced to a sort of code analogous to that of Judaism. This is not to assert that what we have in James or in the *Didache* is in any way contradictory to the discoveries of the primitive Church. The very experience of the Church, however, rested on an intimate, vital connection with Jesus through the impressions and contacts of the eye-witnesses ; over against this living, vital, and personal religious connection, the secondary and even tertiary atmosphere of the later moralistic writings stands out in sufficient contrast to afford but little confidence in their authority for the life of the primitive Church.

The new religious experience was no law, but a " Way," the " Way " of citizenship in the new order of the Kingdom. It was rooted in an ethical discipline which went directly back to Jesus; as far as they had already apprehended the " Way " marked out by Jesus, strait and narrow as it was (Matt. vii. 14), the believers endeavoured to obey the will of God, conforming their lives inwardly and outwardly to what God required of them. It was this growth in religious and ethical realities that saved the primitive Church from being no more than a band of apocalyptic visionaries, and, going back as these did to Jesus, saved the new experience from vanishing as the eschatological expectations proved to be unfulfilled.

We see the central place of the spiritual and ethical emphasis in the First Epistle of Peter. Through the apocalyptic hopes begotten of the resurrection of Jesus, and the expectation of the inheritance incorruptible and undefiled, reserved in heaven, to be revealed in the last days, the believers are seen to be " children of obedience," conforming to the holy " way," loving one another as fellow-sharers in the divine re-creation of their lives (i. 3-5, 14-16, 22 f.). The new community is " an elect race, a royal priesthood, a holy nation, a people of God's own possession," and they follow the " Way," which reveals " the excellencies " of Him who had called them " out of darkness into his marvellous light " (ii. 9). Allowing for the influence of later ideas, we are carried back to the experiential atmosphere of the primitive Church where the enthusiasm for the apocalyptic consummation was controlled by a deepening moral discipline which enabled the believers to discover the higher righteousness received from Jesus when the literal eschatological hopes had begun to fail. Finally, the goal came to be seen less in an external consummation, and more in a life of perfect fellowship with God.

The primitive Church was cradled within a vivid atmosphere of apocalyptic expectation. The tendency to literalize both Messiah and Kingdom, which had been responsible for the "Great Misunderstanding" of the suffering and death of Jesus (pp. 113 ff.), was carried forward into the new community by the eye-witnesses. For the moment the death of Jesus was interpreted within the apocalyptic scheme as the necessary prelude to Messiah's exaltation (Acts ii. 23, 33). The believers gathered within the temple from time to time expecting to welcome the returning Messiah as He descended the pinnacle. The experience of Pentecost is explained in apocalyptic categories, being connected with the "last days" by a prophecy of Joel (Acts ii. 17 ff.), the Spirit's descent being an "earnest" of the forthcoming climax. Paul was doing no more than handing on this primitive Church eschatology when he preached the end of all things through Jesus of Nazareth who was none other than Israel's exalted Messiah (1 Thess. i. 10, ii. 12). Another writer akin to the primitive community refers to the living hope of "an inheritance incorruptible and undefiled, and that fadeth not away, reserved in heaven. . . ." (1 Pet. i. 3 f.), an undoubted reference to the advent of the Messianic Kingdom. A salvation was prepared, to be revealed in the day of crisis (1 Pet. i. 5); believers are urged to be patient; the end of all things is at hand (1 Pet. i. 7, 10 f., iv. 7).

The primitive Church was therefore aware of itself as the heir to the new order about to be inaugurated, the Spirit-possessed community being prepared to receive the Messianic glory. The believers looked for the crisis

to come any day, and pictured it more or less imagina-
tively as they subconsciously drew their ideas from an
apocalyptic environment. It was the " sensuous " conception of the Kingdom that was uppermost, but the
spiritually and ethically educative processes were already
at work to mellow the crudity and the literalness into
conceptions more akin to the mind of the Jesus who had
inspired the deeper levels of apprehension.

Along with the imminent and future aspects, Jesus
had revealed the divine Kingdom as an experience
actually present among men ; like the leaven in the meal,
so even now the Kingdom is fermenting the life of men ;
the seed is growing secretly here and now ; already,
as the mustard seed, the Kingdom is present in
its minute beginnings (Matt. xiii. 33 ; Mark iv. 26–29,
30–32). The Kingdom was even now " among you "
(Luke xvii. 21). It was difficult, however, for the primitive Church to grasp this fact, for it involved a discipline
of understanding and insight that was harder to achieve
than the mere indulging in eschatological extravaganza.
But the spiritually educative processes were at work,
almost unknowingly to the believers ; even now they
were breaking away from the old order and taking
their stand on the new, claiming their heavenly citizenship.

The experiential synthesis of these future and
present aspects of the Kingdom was reached by the
primitive Church in due course. The apocalyptic hope
failed in the non-fulfilment of the desired consummation ;
inasmuch as the failure became apparent, so the experience
of the Kingdom as a present possession came to the fore ;
the apocalyptic hope itself was transmuted into the
expectation of life in " the kingdom not of this world,"
as the " sensuous " idea faded and revealed the vision
of the Hereafter more clearly. At the one end of the

scale is the literal apocalyptic hope ; at the other there is the consciousness of citizenship in the divine Kingdom as experience of eternal life in the midst of time, the Johannine substitute for the eschatological Kingdom (John iii. 15 f. v. 24, vi. 40, 47, 54). Within this empirical development the primitive Church has its definite contribution in that, as the consummation was more and more delayed, the community became all the more aware of the Kingdom as being possessed here and now in the world. We proceed to discuss more fully what we here state in a summary form.

(*a*) The primitive Church came into being out of the experience of a grand failure, namely, the non-fulfilment of the apocalyptic hope of the return of Christ in the Kingdom. Far from the community crumbling away, however, the fading of the literal expectations made it all the more possible for the deeper significance of Jesus to come to the forefront, with the inner aspects of the Kingdom, the deeper understanding of the creative personality of Jesus in His more specifically spiritual and ethical worth.

(*b*) The fading of the eschatological hope influenced the Messianic community of the future Kingdom to develop into the *ecclesia* conscious of itself as entering into possession of the Kingdom as a present experience. The Church came to be aware of its calling as the divinely appointed body of Christ existing in the world for the redemption of the world, as it apprehended the Kingdom as the spiritual, suprahuman order already in the midst, creating a religious experience which the believers wished to share with all men, as its dynamic moved the Church's message far beyond the racial and religious limits of Israel. Along with this growth there went the wider experience of salvation, which, emphasized in the first place as eschatological, that is, salvation to the imminent

Kingdom, came to be known as the higher salvation inherent in the new life and the new righteousness which Jesus revealed, as the believers entered upon the moral and spiritual redemption mediated by Jesus in virtue of His " Way."

(c) These spiritually educative processes, inherent from the first in Jesus, influenced the transmutation of the idea of the imminent eschatological Kingdom into a consummation of a more definitely spiritual character. The more spiritual became the apprehension of the divine Kingdom, the more spiritual did the believers conceive its consummation to be, until it was desired as eternal life in the heavens. On the one hand, there was the growing awareness of the divine Kingdom as already present in the world, destined through the Church to change mankind through the potency of present redemption in Jesus Christ. On the other hand, there was the Kingdom not of this world, having its centre of gravity in the unseen and the eternal order. In so far as the Kingdom was present in the world it was representative of the Kingdom in the unseen order, being experienced as eternal life amidst the time series of earthly living. As the literal eschatological expectations faded away, the hope of life in the Hereafter came forward in fuller strength. The development had been prepared to some extent by current transitions of thought from the " sensuous " to the higher spiritual conception of the Kingdom, but whereas current apocalyptic viewed the world as hopeless, and in the despair of pessimism transferred the desired consummation to eternal life in the heavens, the world came to be the scene for the redemptive activity of Christ working through his witnesses. The influx of Gentiles into the Church helped on this transmutation, although in the main its roots go back to Jesus and the personal contacts

the disciples had with Him, especially in their experience
of Him as risen from the dead.   The Gentiles, however,
were not unacquainted with hopes of immortality,
and they were less concerned with apocalyptic crises ;
indeed, the Gentiles moved the primitive Church away
from its preoccupation with apocalyptic enthusiasms
to the more spiritual apprehension of eternal life.
Stephen, in his death, prayed that the Lord Jesus would
receive his spirit (Acts vii. 59) ; if this is to be understood
in terms of Jewish religion, it is also possible that the
Gentile outlook of the martyr breathed a desire for
eternal life with Jesus who had gone before him.   Paul
was greatly influential in the change of emphasis which
turned the apocalyptic hope into an ardent expectation
of eternal life as the crown of the believer's pilgrimage
(1 Cor. xv. 35 ff.).   At last the literal Kingdom fades
away into the background as it comes to be seen
more clearly in " the Ecclesia triumphant and
glorified and in manifest communion with the saints
in heaven." [1]

(d) The whole series of the eschatological concepts,
Kingdom, Messiah, Last Days, signs and portents, the
Judgment apparatus, angels, archangels, demons,
Messianic woes, etc., is seen to be of the experiential
framework of the religious experience of the primitive
Church, the thought-forms in which the vital movement
centred in Jesus clothed itself, accidental to the people
among whom the new life came to birth.   While it is
true that terms such as " Messiah " and " Kingdom "
had historical and spiritual significance which lifted
them above their purely catastrophic and literal character
for popular expectation, the aspect which was uppermost in the mind of the disciples, and through them the
expression of salvation for the Church at the first, the

---

[1] *The World to Come and Final Destiny*, J. H. Leckie, 1918, p. 64.

essential spiritual convictions they enshrined are the vital matters. As the catastrophic forms fell away, the Church was set free from the literal framework within the apocalyptic scheme, and there were revealed more potently the permanent aspirations of the human spirit as fed by the mind and spirit of Jesus, as symbolic of the eternal realities that lie at the heart of Christian experience of the Living Christ. The Church thus came to offer the new life which, in believing Jesus, men came to have in His name.

(*e*) From another angle, the literalness of the eschatology exercised a distinctively positive influence on the primitive Church. It provided an immediate freedom from common-sense considerations that might otherwise have proved an effective hindrance to the operation of the new experience. The confident expectation that the end of all things was at hand allowed no room for any safeguards such as prudence, common-sense provision for practical needs, or compromise in order to live the life of the world while cherishing in the heart the call of the higher experience. If there were eschatological exaggerations, such at least gave inspired courage and determination to follow where the call of the exalted Messiah led.

The Christian Church emerged from the primitive Messianic community as a " throw-back " from the failure of apocalyptic expectation. This " throw-back " was into the world of men and affairs, into the world of human sin and suffering, to concentrate on the divine mission of salvation offered as a present blessing in the very existence here and now of the divine Kingdom as an experience to be shared. The increasing awareness of present salvation brought quickened life in Christ's name, opened up new avenues of approach to the heart of God, and operated as a spiritual resurrection in a world religiously bankrupt and longing for vital redemption.

The whole apocalyptic movement was founded upon the conviction that good was powerless in the world. The primitive Church shared a similar view, but although the believers did not realize it at first, the apocalyptic pessimism concerning the powerlessness of goodness in the world had been literally exploded by the spirit and presence of Christ. As the truth of this came to the conscious forefront of their minds, it weakened the pessimism underlying their apocalyptic ideas, and gave an added present experience of joy and power and abounding life that made the postponement of the parousia more than tolerable. It is significant that there is little, if any, evidence of disappointment because of the non-fulfilment of the apocalyptic hopes. The primitive community came to be ultimately preoccupied with its present blessing and opportunity in spreading the divine Kingdom among men in the wonder of immediate possession.

The chronological aspects of this development cannot be traced ; this is due not only to the paucity of the records, but also to the nature of evolution in religious experience. The whole process was one of spiritual growth motived by the dynamic personality and power of Jesus of Nazareth in the first place, and thereafter by the vital contact with His living presence as the Christ who was with the believers always. And growth knows no specific dates. Here and there the old and the new run together in equal strength, but the tendency was for the new to encroach on the old until it finally gained the victory. First, the Messianic community with its ardent eschatological hope ; then, the primitive Church emerging from the failure of the hopes, and rising to a more vital experience of the living Christ.

CHAPTER IX

The Consciousness of Salvation

THERE was an overwhelming awareness of salvation within the religious experience of the primitive Church. The "last days" had arrived (Acts ii. 17), the great deliverance for which prophets and apocalyptists had looked was on the eve of fulfilment. The eagerness with which it was awaited, and the character it had for the disciples, are seen in the question whether Jesus was going to restore the Kingdom to Israel at this time (Acts i. 6). The salvation experience was therefore of an eschatological kind. On its positive side the believers were being prepared for the life of the new order ; on its negative side, it signified deliverance and acquittal in the Judgment about to come upon the world as the prelude to the establishing of the divine Kingdom. Both these aspects are stressed in the early Christian preaching as the hearers are urged to share in the blessings, and to save themselves from the generation about to be judged by a true repentance to result in remission of sins (Acts ii. 38 ff.).

As the divinely appointed Messiah the exalted Jesus will be the medium of this consummation with its accompanying salvation (Acts ii. 36, iii. 20 f.). He is the "Author" of the life offered in the Kingdom, and the Saviour to the Kingdom of all who repent (Acts iii. 15, v. 31). He saves from the Judgment, and through Him alone can deliverance come (Acts x. 42, iv. 12). Faith is therefore an indispensable element in the saving activity of Jesus, as the believers trusted Him to save

251

them from the imminent Judgment and to bring them to the new life (Acts ii. 41, iv. 4, v. 20).

Following the traditional conceptions of Israel's oneness as a people before God, the unit of salvation is the new community which individuals are urged to join and so enter the Kingdom in virtue of their identification with the community. At the same time the apocalyptic development has brought forward the moral responsibility of the individual, and in the primitive Church a distinctive place must be left for the greater significance of the individual believer than the customary outlook of Israel allowed. Individuals were urged to conversion by the fear of unpleasant consequences in facing the imminent Judgment. Had Jesus come in the first place in power and great glory to save the People of Israel after the manner of the conventional expectation of Messiah, He might have won the whole nation to an acceptance of Himself as Israel's Messianic Redeemer, yet such loyalty and acceptance would have had no basis in moral and spiritual values. Only those individuals whose hearts were ready by moral and spiritual insight were able to discern the true divine glory in Jesus as He fulfilled the divine purpose. In this way individual and personal religious experience came to the fore, inasmuch as each believer had to make a definite moral choice in accepting Jesus, the Messiah so unlike the conventional national ideas of His nature and function. The recognition that Jesus had reached this dignity through His suffering was a fact that had to be ethically and spiritually apprehended in personal choice. The appeal to conscience aimed at arousing the moral and spiritual sensibilities of the individual to an act of choice in accepting the Messianic status of Jesus who had been rejected by the nation, and through Him to attain to the salvation of the Kingdom which He was to inaugurate (Acts ii. 32 f., 37 f.).

The conversion process awakened the sense that the individual Jew was deeply implicated in the national rejection of Jesus, and as this was realized, remorse of an intense character resulted (Acts ii. 37).   Then followed repentance for the state of heart which reflected the pride and stubbornness of Israel in rejecting the way of God and resisting the influence of the Spirit (Acts ii. 38). This repentance carried with it an entire change of mind with regard to Jesus ; where He had been rejected, now He was recognized and accepted by the individual adherents of the community, who refused to be associated any longer with the national sin and apostasy.

This salvation included the moral experience of submission to Jesus the Messiah.   A personal relationship to Jesus resulted from such obedience, and those who confessed Him were His " disciples."   In turn they came to experience the power of the Spirit in their personal lives as the individual convert realized himself as being numbered within the community of salvation. Such moral and spiritual elements began the transition from the experience of salvation eschatologically conditioned to that of salvation in its own spiritual right as centred in Jesus Christ.   The fading of the eschatological hope as such encouraged the awareness of salvation as a present experience just as the blessing of the Kingdom came to be received as a possession here and now.   The enjoyment of salvation through the present Kingdom, with its consummation in the receiving of eternal life in the Kingdom not of this world, reacted vitally upon the ethical responsibility of living for the present life in a manner worthy of one who confessed loyalty to Jesus.

The connection of the death of Jesus with the salvation experience was somewhat obscure, for as yet the believers had not reached any definite conception with

regard to it. At the same time, since for them the
death of Jesus was the necessary prelude to His Messianic
glory, it came to be intimately connected with the hope
of redemption to the Kingdom to be ushered in by
Jesus as He returned in His glory. Because of the
sufferings of Jesus, the Kingdom was brought within
reach of the believers. As, however, salvation came to
be experienced as a present blessing, so the more redemptive aspects of the death of Jesus came forward.

There seems little doubt that Jesus regarded His
coming death as having redemptive significance, and
that this has been apprehended by the eye-witnesses
whose impressions are preserved in the Gospels. His
Temptation makes it clear that Jesus chose to fulfil His
vocation entirely in terms of what God willed, whatever
this would lead to. W. Wrede's insistence that the
saying about the bridegroom being taken away
(Mark ii. 20) is a prophecy of Jesus' suffering and death,
and not merely a foreboding of such,[1] is probably the
right interpretation. After Peter's confession of Jesus
as Messiah, Jesus openly declared that His death was
necessary (Mark viii. 31), and went on to insist on the
need of losing one's life to save it (vv. 35–37). He had
a baptism with which to be baptized (Luke xii. 49–53).
The famous words about the Son of Man giving His life
a ransom for many (Mark x. 45) are spoken to draw a contrast between the self-seeking glory of James and John
at the expense of others (vv. 35–45) and the self-sacrifice
of Jesus who, unlike them, gave His life for others.
Indeed, " the death of Jesus did for His followers what He
had hoped it would do for His people—it freed them from
the binding prestige of the religious authorities which was
holding them back from His truth, and their hearts
were reborn by the power of love known and felt in His

[1] *Das Messiasgeheimnis in den Evangelien*, 1901, p. 19.

death." [1]   Further, if Jesus' death was conceived in His mind to be the divinely willed prelude to the advent of the Kingdom, then by dying Jesus was giving Himself on behalf of the many who would be won to the Kingdom ; in this sense there is redemptive significance in the " ransom for many." In the Farewell Supper the cup is passed round as the pledge of the Kingdom (Luke xxii. 17 f.), followed by the broken bread foreshadowing the death of Jesus as necessary to fulfilling the pledge made in the cup (ver. 19). The " ransom " passage does not carry with it here the later thought about Christ's death such as, for example, we meet with in Paul. It simply means, in the Gospel, and in the primitive Church, that the death of Jesus is a means of liberating many, and leaves it at that. His whole life was one of saving activity, and the death is the culmination of this life of self-giving on behalf of the many.

The primitive Church felt Jesus' death to be redemptive in so far as it was the means of winning to the Kingdom of God the believers who responded to the summons to repent. The sin in view is the apostasy which rejected and crucified Jesus as Messiah. This is strictly an eschatological view of the suffering and death of Jesus, yet there were deeper aspects involved even if not clearly discerned. For Paul the death of Jesus is connected with the forgiveness of sins in the tradition he received from the primitive Church (1 Cor. xv. 3). The recognition that it was due to the divine purpose caused the death to be viewed in a deeper light than as the mere result of human wickedness (Acts iv. 27 f.). The suffering was also interpreted in the light of the Suffering Servant, and the efficacy of suffering set out in the " Servant " poems of Isaiah (pp. 45 f.) was

[1] A. T. Cadoux, A New Orthodoxy of Jesus and Personality, 1934, p. 151.

applied to the case of Jesus, whose death came to be viewed as an offering for guilt as Jesus bore the sins of many (Acts viii. 32–35 ; cf. iii. 13–16). But the fact that the sacrificial suffering is viewed in the first place through prophetic eyes makes it highly probable that the offering for sin is of a moral, rather than of a penal, character, and this in turn would attach to Jesus' sacrifice.

It is difficult, however, to estimate how far the primitive Church used the prophetic conception of the suffering as having moral character when applied to Jesus. We have so little information to guide us. Yet the eschatological approach to the death of Jesus implied inner moral significance, since at least the purpose of God in the divine Kingdom was being fulfilled. There are no grounds for concluding that the primitive Church looked on the suffering of Christ as in any way penal ; the point that is made clear is that the endurance and innocence of the Servant are proved, and his final vindication made manifest.[1] Such moral aspects may well have been ascribed to the suffering and death of Jesus ; it would involve too great a strain upon their religious outlook to suppose that the believers in the Church applied ideas of atonement to Messiah, for what was it Messiah was to atone for ? The believers were thoroughgoing Jews, faithful to the law which prescribed the atoning offerings for sin ; to view Jesus as atoning for sin in his death is as yet too violent a departure from the Jewish loyalty and outlook characteristic of the primitive Church. Suffering was known to have

---

[1] As W. Beyschlag, *New Testament Theology*, Eng. Tr., 1896, vol. i. pp. 312 ff.   J. K. Mozley thinks that there was not more than this in Philip's talk with the eunuch " is really beyond the power of Beyschlag or any one else to prove " (*Doctrine of the Atonement*, 1915, p. 63), but that there was anything else other than such allusions is beyond Mozley's or any one else's power to prove. Unfortunately, Mozley's line is too double-edged to be of service here.

atoning value, but it was another thing altogether to add
to the prescribed ritual of the law the death of Jesus as a
further means of atonement for sin.   Only as the Church
broke away from its Jewish environment did atoning
ideas attach themselves to Christ's death on the cross.

The believers were therefore aware that in some way
the death of Jesus was associated with forgiveness of
sin.   The experience of divine forgiveness resulted from
repentance for being implicated in the national guilt
of rejecting Jesus as Messiah, and this experience
went along with an act of faith and submission to the
Messiah they now accepted as Redeemer.   It was seen
that Jesus had offered Himself up that the fulfilment of
the Kingdom might be assured for the blessing of the
many, and thus far a vicarious element in His death
was discerned by the primitive Church.   All through
the controversy with the Judaizers Paul assumes a
belief which is held by him and them in common, namely,
there is a redemptive significance in Christ's death.   He
does not charge his opponents with denying the saving
elements in the crucifixion, but with their insistence on
secondary matters such as circumcision, making the cross
of none effect in that salvation could not be experienced
apart from circumcision.   How far the redemptive significance was discerned by the primitive Church we have no
means of concluding ;   there are the definitely eschatological aspects of salvation to the fore, but, as these
faded, the more moral and spiritual meaning and worth
of the cross came to be more clearly seen.   We are amidst
a vital religious experience expressing itself in countless
ways ; there had not yet been time nor inclination to reflect
more theoretically on the connection of Jesus' death with
forgiveness.   The Church was meanwhile rejoicing that
through that divinely purposed death the Kingdom with
its salvation was brought nigh unto them that believed.

17

We have now to discuss the scope of the salvation experience as the Church struggled forward to widening horizons and was compelled to face the crucial question of the capacity of the Gentiles to benefit by the salvation offered in Jesus Christ. From the outset there were powerful influences which safely anchored the new community within the haven of Jewish religion. There was the consciousness that the new community was one with Israel, and that its salvation was for Israel. Again, the disciples carried into their new experience their traditional Jewish conceptions, preconceptions, and ideas. The new experience was cradled within Jewish faith and religious experience. Racially, psychologically, and religiously, the disciples were Jewish to the core. Once more, the religious environment from which the primitive Church emerged ensured that the new faith would be shot through and through with the religious ideas of Judaism; there could be no real salvation apart from circumcision and incorporation within the agelong People of God; fidelity to the law was axiomatic, the sense of privilege in belonging to the chosen race over against the Gentiles—all this was active in the outlook of the primitive community of Christ. The apocalyptic beliefs in which the Church was cradled held out nothing but judgment for the Gentiles.[1]

The door for the non-Jews, however, was not irrevocably closed. The intercourse between Jesus and Gentile elements such as the publicans and sinners would help towards a sympathetic approach to the Gentile position. The disciples caught the new accents in Jesus which fain would arouse Israel to be a light unto

[1] Even the nobler universalism of " The Testaments of the Twelve Patriarchs " was subject to the same limiting influence as operated even in the case of Jeremiah's broad outlook ; there was to be salvation for Gentiles, but only by the royal way of submission to Israel.

the Gentiles. During one of the resurrection experiences the disciples apprehended in vision that the gospel was for the whole world. Further, among the new converts there would be many who were numbered among the outcast elements, publicans, sinners, and the like, for whom the question of incorporation within Israel did not count for very much ; such would be among the more liberalizing section of the new community. There is no reason for supposing that in the enthusiasm of the earliest period of the Church questions were asked as to whether the disciples were Jew or Gentile. A further factor is the presence of Hellenistic Jews in the Church, who were conversant with the wider outlook of the world of the Diaspora ; there was no conscious loosening of their devotion to Judaism, but subconsciously the more liberal influences would operate through them. We have also the Hellenists, who were proselytes to the Jewish faith by circumcision, who by no means shed their Gentile psychology ; this type was bound to be influential in the primitive Church towards a more sympathetic approach to non-Jews. Finally, there were the God-fearers who, while admiring the spiritual worth of Israel's piety, refused to be circumcised and were therefore not incorporated within the People of God. Such were able to accept all that was truly spiritual in Israel's religion without feeling too scrupulous about their devotion to the parts of the law that made no appeal.[1] This fringe of non-Jews, of whom there would be many in Jerusalem, provided splendid material for converts to the primitive Church.

Then the discovery was made that non-Jews were capable of receiving the new experience of the Spirit without being admitted into the Jewish theocracy by circumcision (Acts x. 44 f.). This testimony of spiritual

[1] Cf. G. F. Moore, *op. cit.* vol. i. pp. 323 f.

experience was ultimately to prove inexorable in its logic in the admittance of the Gentiles to the Church of Christ.

The stage was therefore being set for the working out of the struggle between the exclusive and the extensive conceptions of the scope of salvation. The primitive Church was slow to accept its mission to the wider field, and this is incredible if the original eye-witnesses had received a direct charge from Jesus to go out into all the world and make disciples of the Gentiles. There is the further difficulty that the religious discoveries of a later period of the Church were read back to the first beginnings. The author of the twofold work " Luke-Acts " sets forward his narrative as if the Gospel were destined for the whole world right from the inception of the Church, beginning at Jerusalem, on to Samaria, and to the uttermost parts of the earth, until it became a power in Rome itself (Acts i. 8 ; cf. Luke xxiv. 47). While in actual history this was the course of events, it is by no means certain that the conscious missionary motive was there at the outset, and the charge of Jesus to world evangelization may be no more than making Him the mouthpiece of the later discovery, as the implications of the gospel were more clearly unfolded and acted upon.

On the other hand, the universal scope of the gospel and the call to go out into the world and preach it may have been apprehended by the disciples in an experience of the resurrection of Jesus, that is, in a vision of the risen Jesus. Their conscious mind rested upon the narrower basis of apocalyptic hopes heightened beyond measure by the experienced triumph of Jesus ; yet it may be that just as subconsciously they had grasped the significance of Jesus' uniqueness, so they were growing in the spiritual quality of the Kingdom, with a corresponding apprehension of the more exalted purpose of

Christ with His Kingdom and its universal range over men, Jew or Gentile. The preservation of so many parables reflecting the supernational content of the Kingdom shows that the primitive Church had some sense of this side of the truth. There were therefore psychological elements in the experience of the eye-witnesses which predisposed them to receive a revelation of the ultimate world purpose of Jesus, even if it was to be long before they consciously grasped the truth and translated it into practice (Matt. xxviii. 16–20).

The more liberal elements come to the surface in what seems to be a sudden emergence of a Hellenist section in the Church, including, no doubt, Hellenistic Jews, Gentile proselytes, God-fearers, and outcast elements such as publicans and sinners. As a result of some complaint of neglect of its side of the Church's needs, seven men are appointed to attend to it (Acts vi. 1–6). This dissension has deeper roots than is here implied. The Seven were appointed to serve the Hellenist widows, while the Twelve were probably still to concern themselves with the ministration to the Jewish section of the community. When the Twelve declared that it was not right that they should imperil the preaching of the Word by preoccupation with the more practical duties (Acts vi. 2), what they probably meant was, that as matters stood, the duty of caring for the practical ministrations for both sides of the Church was too much to carry out, except at the cost of their preaching witness. The Hellenist side had not been cared for as it ought to have been, hence the complaint. The appointment of the Seven saved the situation ; the Twelve were able to go on with their preaching, and to overlook the practical needs of the Jewish section.

It does not follow, further, that the Seven were confined to the daily ministrations. We find that

Stephen works signs and wonders among the people, and that he, too, preaches in the Jewish synagogues (Acts vi. 8 f.).   What seems to have taken place is a division of spheres of activity rather than one of duties. The Twelve attended to the Palestinian side ; the Seven took charge of the Hellenistic section.   The Twelve were nominally at the head of the whole community, but in actual practice the task was too large for them to carry out.   The Twelve witnessed and served amid the Jewish section ; the Seven preached and attended to the needs of the Hellenistic side.

We may therefore discern two distinctive types of religious outlook within the primitive community, the characteristic Jewish, and the freer, semi-Gentile types. The nature of the more liberal interpretation of Judaism promoted by the Hellenist religious experience in the Church may be gleaned to some extent from Stephen's speech before the Sanhedrin (Acts vii. 1–53).   The narrative, however, is not free from confusion ; there is the formal trial (Acts vi. 15, vii. 1), yet Stephen was the victim of a mob's fury (Acts vii. 54, 57–59).   Again, while the council could pass the sentence of death, the decision had to be ratified by the Roman civil power ; no such sentence, still less any ratification of it, is mentioned.   It looks as if the council had set in motion an investigation of charges against Stephen, and that during it a popular tumult arose in which Stephen was stoned to death, the council having no difficulty in conniving at it.   Further, the charge formulated is not clearly stated.   False witnesses attempt to testify that Stephen had uttered blasphemy (Acts vi. 11) against Moses and against God, yet once more the charge is stated to be that he frequently spoke blasphemy against " this holy place and the law " (ver. 13), the blasphemy being defined as " we have heard him say that this

Jesus of Nazareth shall destroy this place, and shall
change the customs which Moses delivered to us"
(ver. 14). The martyr seems therefore to have been
brought to trial for blasphemy against the temple and the
law. In his speech he asserts his loyalty to the law,
and reverence for the traditional history of his nation,
while the accredited leaders are sternly rebuked for not
living up to that law and the faith contained in the
history (Acts vii. 51 f.). It was his accusers who were
blaspheming the law by their own failure to live up to
its best spirit and ideal. As for the charge of blasphemy
against the temple, neither the ark nor the tabernacle,
nor later, the temple, was any guarantee that God was
present with His favour and blessing, since the heaven
was His real throne and dwelling-place (Acts vii. 49).
The externals of worship are useless without the contrite
heart which is God's true abode. There was no temple
cultus during the sojourn in the wilderness (Acts vii. 42 f.).
Stephen's accusers were the real culprits in their dis-
obedience to God, in their crucifixion of God's own
Messiah ; in view of such a perverse spirit the temple
was no guarantee of the divine presence.

It is a strange speech for a man on trial before the
Sanhedrin, and the possibility is that there was no
formal trial, but that Stephen was hounded to death
by an infuriated mob. This fate once almost befell
Jesus (Luke iv. 28 f.). The speech may be no more than
a specimen of the sort of argument he used when disputing with the Jews in the synagogues. From this
angle it becomes very suggestive for the freer attitude
of the semi-Gentile outlook within the primitive Church.
It is in the old prophetic style, a sort of religious philosophy of Israel's history. Stephen carries the case for
the divine claims further back than Moses, the historical
limit for the authority of the law, to Abraham (Acts

vii. 1b–8, 17), in the style of Paul (Rom. iv. 1 ff.), and as does the author of the Epistle to the Hebrews (v. 1–6, vii. 1–9, xi. 8–19). The Pauline approach to the Christian experience through Abraham is thus seen to be anticipated in the primitive Church, in the widening approach to the law on the part of the Hellenistic section. Even Moses, the revered authority for the law, was treated evilly by the people (Acts vii. 7, 24–29) ; they even refused to obey the law he gave them (Acts vii. 38 f.). The prophets were continually taking the people to task for seeking refuge from obeying the weightier matters of the law in meticulous observance of the prescribed ritual (ver. 42 f.).

Among the Hellenistic wing of the primitive Church there seems to be taking place a reaction from traditional Jewish observances, which suggests the spirit in which Jesus Himself approached the same tradition. Stephen was its powerful exponent, and his speech rings with the tones of " the aggressive critic of the perverse religious spirit of his race, which lives in his persecutors." [1] Stephen has a more spiritual understanding and experience of the law, and his freer attitude which this encouraged was not only in the spirit of the great prophets, but suggests that the new faith in Jesus was producing its own distinctive approach after the manner of Jesus Himself. It is true that, as McGiffert points out,[2] there is no reference in the speech to the calling of the Gentiles any more than to the setting aside of the law. But with the more spiritual emphasis, the more spiritual character of the faith centred in Jesus would become increasingly discerned, the inner meanings of what Jesus said would be uncovered. As this process gathered momentum it reacted against the more formal Judaism just as

[1] J. Mackinnon, op. cit. p. 29.
[2] History of Christianity in the Apostolic Age, 1897, pp. 85 f.

Judaism was beginning to react against the new community. Minds given to reflection and speculation,
with no thought of disloyalty to Israel's faith, began
to perceive in the words and ethic of Jesus a leavening
quality the germs of which they found in the great
prophets. The Twelve were making no move towards
any freer attitude as far as their duty to the Gentiles
was concerned. Even the one exception to this, Peter's
admittance of Cornelius into the community of the
Spirit, evoked strong protest from his fellow-apostles
(Acts xi. 1–3).

The movement towards the larger duty began with
Stephen and the religious ferment that arose around his
name, and represented a reaction towards the deeper
spirit of the ethic of Jesus with its more spiritual approach
to the traditional faith of Israel. The beginnings here
outlined, if the inspiring ferment took its course, could
have no other ultimate result than the emancipation of
the Church from the secondary fetters which chained it to
the older ways, leading to the admission of the Gentiles
to the Church with equal status and privilege with the
Jew in the Messianic Kingdom. This is the empirical
significance of the religious ferment that gathered around
Stephen. That something inimical to the traditional
faith was implied is seen in the persecution that followed
his death. The subsequent dispersion of the preachers
seems only to have affected the Hellenistic side of the
Church, for the Twelve seem to have remained un-
molested in Jerusalem. The scattering of the Hellenists,
however, proved unwittingly to be the very means of
initiating the inclusion of the Gentiles within the Church.
They preached the gospel wherever they went, but took
care to avoid the reproach implied by the persecution,
namely, disloyalty to the law, by preaching only to
Jews (Acts xi. 19). The inevitable happened. Converts

made at Cyprus and Cyrene overleapt the barriers and
preached the gospel direct to Gentiles in Antioch,[1] and
there is no reason to suppose that this was an isolated
instance.   The response of the Gentiles justified the
action of the preachers who courageously took the
message to them (Acts xi. 21).

Was it Stephen's preaching in the synagogue that
started the sequence of doubts and fears in the mind of
Paul as touching the law ?   He seems to have been among
the instigators of the charge against him, and certainly
led the subsequent persecution.   The conversion of Paul
occurred as he was making a journey intent on apprehending believers.   The Stephenite ferment may well have
subconsciously quickened the coming of Paul's inner crisis.

The story of the conversion of Cornelius has been
subject to much critical investigation,[2] but it is clear
enough that it sets forth a Gentile as being capable of receiving the new life and spirit of the Messianic community,
and to show in his actions that the Spirit had descended
upon him (Acts x. 1, 44 ff.).   Peter's recent growth in his
conviction that the gospel was for Gentiles, due to the
vision on the housetop in Joppa (pp. 170 ff.), enabled him
to receive the new convert, although he was not a Jew,
directly as a member of the Church.   His action was afterwards challenged by the Church leaders, the basis of
their criticism being that Peter had gone in to men uncircumcised and had had table fellowship with them (Acts
xi. 2 f.).   In defending himself, however, the apostle
says nothing about eating with the uncircumcised,
but confines his reply to relating the circumstances
which led him to receive the Gentiles into membership

---

[1] Acts xi. 20, where *Hellenas* is the right reading ; cf. Appendix VI.,
pp. 361 f.

[2] For a comprehensive discussion of the critical problems raised
by this narrative, cf. McGiffert, *op. cit.* pp. 101–106.

of the community, as if this were the gravamen of the charge. Has Luke here telescoped together two charges, the eating with the uncircumcised, and the admission of Gentiles into the Church fellowship? Were there two principles to be established, two controversies settled, before the horizons were widened into universalism? Was the admission of the Gentiles one thing, and the terms of social and religious fellowship with them a matter to be further settled?

The Jerusalem leaders reacted to Peter's account of the Spirit's attestation in Cornelius (Acts x. 44, 46) by a mood of astonished gladness that God could give repentance unto life to the Gentiles (xi. 18). That such was possible had evidently not come within the ambit of their outlook, or the example of Jesus and His fellowship with Gentile elements among the publicans and sinners had been lost sight of. They accepted the *fait accompli* without further question. It seems to have been no more than an isolated instance at the moment; there was no thought of sponsoring missionary activity among the Gentiles as a result of this incident. It was no more than a hint of what was to come when the issue was fully joined.

The rapid spread of the *ecclesiai* which followed the scattering of the preachers after Stephen's death was the first really effective widening of the horizons of the primitive Church. At Antioch there arose a Church through direct preaching to the Gentiles there (Acts xi. 20), a Church distinctively Gentile in character, bringing to bear upon the new experience a new set of thought-forms and ideas. Circumcision was unnecessary for salvation, for the new religious experience in Christ came into its own right, unhampered by Jewish swaddling clothes. The rise of the new term, " Christian," to describe the believers at Antioch was, as Harnack points out, "itself a proof that the community in Antioch stood out in bold relief from Judaism."[1] The new experience could now be referred to as the "Christian" experience, irrespective of its Judaistic origins. It took root and brought forth fruit in virtue of its own creative power as derived directly from the life and activity of Jesus Christ, and all without reference to Jewish religion save in its use of the categories wherein Jesus Himself had taught, and in which His disciples had preserved and interpreted their impressions and contacts. The religious experience of the primitive Church, by a fortuitous chain of circumstances going back to the religious ferment that arose around Stephen, was uprooted from its Judaistic soil, and began to grow in a healthy manner within the soil of purely Gentile religious experience.

Not the Twelve nor their successors in Jerusalem were responsible for such a widening of the scope of salvation. Despite their personal proximity to Jesus, they seemed unable to take any lead in the wider mission. They played their part nobly in the more restricted circle of their magnificent appeal to Israel; through their fervent courage and faith the primitive Church came into being, but their traditional Jewish inheritance proved to be an effective hindrance to any suggestion that the Gentiles might be won for the divine Kingdom. Barnabas was sent to investigate events at Antioch, and once more the apostolic leaders were forced to consent to the spiritual logic of the *fait accompli*. "Christianity had an expansive power which was too strong for the bonds that they had put upon it, and it burst those bonds, we may say, of itself."[2] The new experience was not deliberately sent out to the Gentiles; it just went out to them and proved its spiritual validity among

---

[1] *Op. cit.* vol. i. p. 54.   [2] McGiffert, *op. cit.* p. 112.

its new adherents, apart from any Jewish sanctions or
Jewish authority of any kind.   The Gentiles came to
feel their incorporation within the People of God, but
they had no Judaic authority for it.   Nor was any such
authority necessary, for of its own creative vitality the
new faith centred in Jesus set them firmly within the
redemption of the Kingdom of God.

Among the sayings of Jesus we have one significant
for this advance, " The earth bringeth forth fruit of
itself " (Mark iv. 26–29).   Jesus recognizes the way in
which the fruits of the earth came, and deduces the
principle of spiritual development therefrom.   What He
found resulting from the work of others He looked for
as the result of His own.   He devised no programme,
nor planned any progress for the Church: He sowed
the seed and left it to bring forth its own fruit in due
season.   Did Jesus realize that persecution would be
an effective aid to the growth ?   He knew that His
own disciples would fare little better than their Lord
(Matt. x. 24 f.).   Evangelism in Israel would lead to
persecution, and this again would result in the spreading
of the gospel everywhere and the repudiation of nationalistic limits, since it was the nationalistic spirit of Israel
that would inspire any such persecution.   It looks as if
Jesus meant His followers to feel their way by learning
from their mistakes, their experience and guidance of
the Spirit, and that no other way than the way of
religious experience in its growth by acceptance and
rejection was possible.

The development among the Gentiles illustrates
these guiding principles of Jesus' method and expectation.   It was taking place even while the original
disciples were content with pouring the new wine into
the old traditional wineskins, with sewing on the new
cloth to the threadbare garments of Jewish prejudices

and observances, still unable to realize that the new experience could be anything else than a facet of their Jewish faith.

Events at Antioch, with its own missionary call and success, seem at last to have aroused alarm in the Jerusalem community. It is true that the apostles had formally approved the Church there, and that Cornelius the Gentile had been received into the Church apart from circumcision. But there is no reason for supposing that the Jerusalem community was all of one mind, or that Jewish-Christians as a whole endorsed the Cornelius incident. Further, the phenomenal growth in Gentile accessions in Antioch and elsewhere was taking no account of Jewish requirements such as the necessity of circumcision to salvation. On the other hand, the Jews attracted to the new faith would also increase in number in the wider Diaspora, and such could not view the spread among the Gentiles with any easiness. Much pressure could thus be brought to bear upon the Jerusalem Church, as indeed on the Gentile churches, to refuse the Gentiles the religious privileges associated with Israel unless they first submitted to become proselytes to Judaism. We have to remember that a Jewish-Christian's attitude to the Gentile expansion reflected, by implication, his fidelity or infidelity to the law of Moses ; the greater the zest with which the law was observed, the greater the alarm at the growth of the Gentile communities. Further, in this period there were varied strata of conviction as seen in attitudes "reaching from Peter, through James, down to the Judaizers who came to say, 'Except ye be circumcised after the Mosaic usage, ye cannot inherit salvation at all.' " [1] It is not difficult, therefore, to foreshadow the rise of an influential body within the primitive Church,

[1] J. V. Bartlet, *Apostolic Age*, p. 63.

inspired with the sincere conviction that a halt must be called to the admission of the Gentiles, that there should be a return to the true Jewish basis of the faith. Hence the arrival of emissaries at Antioch claiming to be sent by the Jerusalem Church, and demanding the enforcement of circumcision as the condition of membership within the " ecclesia." The consternation that ensued may be imagined (Acts xv. 1 f.) ; after some discussion Paul was requested to go to Jerusalem and arrange the matter with the apostles there. This request (Acts xv. 2) is not inconsistent with Paul's own conviction that he went up by " revelation " (Gal. ii. 2), since the inner decision of Paul coincided with the Church's request, or it may well be Paul's way of referring to a Church decision of the sort described in Acts xiii. 2. In either case it does not at all invalidate the Church's appointment, as McGiffert supposes.[1]

The Council ot Jerusalem followed, and the discussion still remains unsettled as to the historicity of such a council. Bishop Lightfoot's statement is still the best for the view that Acts xv.= Gal. ii.[2] F. C. Burkitt is a recent exponent of the view that Acts xi. 30= Gal. ii. 1-10.[3] The third possibility, that Acts xi. 30 and xv. both describe the visit to which Gal. ii. refers, and have come from two different sources, is the present position of Kirsopp Lake,[4] who has abandoned his former view that the second alternative is to be preferred.[5] A fourth alternative has met with scanty acceptance ; it places Acts xv. after Gal. ii., the latter being based on a private discussion which Paul had with the Church

---

[1] *Op. cit.* p. 194, n. 1.
[2] *Galatians*, 7th edn. 1881, pp. 123–128.
[3] *Christian Beginnings*, pp. 116 ff.
[4] In *BC.*, ed. FJ. and L., vol. v. p. 202.
[5] *Earlier Epistles of St. Paul*, pp. 48–60.

leaders in Jerusalem, and on the result of which is based his rebuke of Peter (Gal. ii. 11 f.).[1]

Our standpoint is the third of these alternatives, namely, that Acts xi. 30 and xv. are independent accounts of the same visit of Paul to Jerusalem, and that this visit is the one to which Paul refers in Gal. ii. 1–10. This hypothesis best accounts for the facts and is the most free from difficulty. Luke came across two independent accounts which, presenting diverse settings, may well have caused him to interpret them as two distinct visits to Jerusalem ; Gal. ii. by no means precludes a twofold purpose in the visit, for Paul mentions how he was requested to remember the poor, and adds, " which very thing I was zealous to do " (Gal. ii. 10). This did not refer to the great collection which he took with him on his final visit to the holy city (Acts xxiv. 17), but is a reference back to the offering he took when he went to Jerusalem over the Gentile question, and which Luke has recorded in a separate account.

Amidst the obscurity of the whole question the general issue is fairly clear both in Acts and Galatians. The admission of the non-Jews was conceded to be legitimate by the apostles, elders, and indeed by the whole council save for the stricter Pharisaic element, which seems to have been overruled (Acts xv. 4, 6, 22–26 ; Gal. ii. 6–9). The recognition that Paul and Barnabas are entrusted by God with the mission to the Gentiles is sealed by giving them the right hand of fellowship (Gal. ii. 9). This, of course, did not commit the Jerusalem Church to any mission to the Gentiles ; it implied no abrogation of the law for Jewish-Christians. The decision was the recognition of a distinct field, that of the Gentile mission ; the gospel witness was once more divided up into two spheres of activity, the circum-

[1] Bartlet, op. cit. pp. 59 f.

THE CONSCIOUSNESS OF SALVATION

cised and the uncircumcised, as we have foreshadowed
in the appointment of the Seven.   There was a distinct
message for the Gentiles ; there was the original, superior
gospel for the true heirs of salvation, the Jewish
Christians, with their observance of the law and their
racial privilege as sons of Abraham.   The "uncircumcised" were proved capable of receiving the Spirit, but
the Gentile type of religious experience would be recognized as of a distinctly inferior and less perfect order.
While the Jerusalem Church would not interfere with the
Gentiles as they accepted Christ, they did not give the
right to Paul to go to Jews and proclaim liberty from
the bondage of the law in the name of Christ, and Paul
seems to have faithfully recognized this.

The problem of intercommunion between the two
sections of the Church does not really seem to have
been settled at the Council.   As good Jews, the Jewish-
Christians were prohibited by the law from eating with
Gentiles or having fellowship with them.   Though the
admission of Cornelius was ratified, Peter was taken to
task for eating with the uncircumcised (Acts xi. 3), and
later, at the behest of the Judaizers, he withdrew from
table fellowship with the Gentile Christians at Antioch
(Gal. ii. 11 f.), thereby influencing others who had been
liberally inclined to withdraw also (vv. 13 f.).   There
was no intercommunion, therefore, between the Jewish
and Gentile wings of the primitive Church.   At Antioch
some Jews had thrown off their over-scrupulousness
and were fraternizing on an equal footing with non-Jew
members of the Church.   This did not signify that they
abrogated the law as such, but they were definitely dis-
regarding the particular precept which forbade fellowship with uncircumcised people.   Along with Peter, even
these withdrew when strong protest was made, and
Paul's strong criticism of Peter was dictated not by the
18

apostle's inconsistency, but by the deeper reason that Peter, in so withdrawing, had thereby signified to the Gentile Christians that, if they desired fellowship with him and the Jewish-Christian Church, *i.e.* the original Church based on Christ, but also on racial kinship with Abraham, they must conform to the Jewish faith in circumcision. By his own action Peter was preaching the gospel of the circumcision to those of the uncircumcision, and thereby violating the agreement reached at the Council of Jerusalem. If Paul was entrusted with the mission to the Gentiles, and in honour refrained from influencing Jewish believers to depart from their loyalty to the law, here was Peter invading Antioch and by an eloquent action plainly indicating that the Gentile Christians must conform to Judaism if they were to attain to the highest fellowship in the Church.

The issue here raised for religious experience is of great significance, namely, the practical issue of the intercommunion of Jewish and Gentile Christians. It became crucial when the two sections existed side by side in one Church such as that of Antioch. Had the Judaizers from Jerusalem not interfered, the believers would probably have felt their way, in the spirit of their Lord, to the solution of their own intercommunion in liberty of conscience. But it was the distinction of these worthy representatives from the mother Church, now under the rule of James, the Lord's brother, to insist on the rigid observance of legal requirements if the Gentiles desired the fullest fellowship with the Jewish-Christian Church. Paul recognized the real nature of the issue when he declared that the Judaizers made the Jewish law, rather than Christ, the basis of the fellowship for the Church, thus making the death of Jesus a vain thing, because, on the Judaizers' own principles, it was not necessary (Gal. ii. 21).

The decision to recognize the validity of the Gentile mission, taken at the Council of Jerusalem, was forwarded to the Church at Antioch by an epistle, which also contained a list of " abstinences " required from Gentile Christians (Acts xv. 23–29).[1] Was this a food law, or a moral code ? Variant readings reveal the perplexity of a subsequent age in understanding the decree. The item " strangled things " is omitted by as good textual authority as inserts it,[2] and the manuscripts that omit it add after " fornication " the Golden Rule in its negative form, just as the *Didache* (i). The effect of this is to turn what probably was in the first place a food law into a moral code, in which case " idolatry " connotes " idolatry in general," instead of its ritualistic " things offered to idols," the " blood " becomes " murder " instead of " blood " in the ritual sense, and " fornication " denotes " all breaches of the seventh commandment " instead of intercourse with idolatrous rites.

Since the difficulty about the Gentiles was not their moral response but their ceremonial status, it seems probable that the decree would be concerned with such a status in their uncircumcision. Originally, therefore, the decree would be of a ritual character as suggested by a food law to be observed by Gentile Christians. This food law is not to be regarded as the minimum conditions laid down as a basis of intercommunion between

[1] We take the view that the decree belongs to one and the same council at Jerusalem (Acts xv.=Gal. ii.), as a more natural interpretation of the facts than the assumption of a second council meeting ; for the latter view, cf. Harnack, *op. cit.* p. 60; McGiffert, *op. cit.* pp. 211–216. Burkitt thinks that the existence of such a decree is confirmed by Rev. ii. 24 which says, " I put upon you no other burden "; ver. 20 mentions the false teaching which encourages the Christians " to commit fornication and eat things offered to idols "; cf. Acts xv. 28 f. (*op. cit.* pp. 113 f.).

[2] Aleph* A* BC 81 614 insert it;   D (lat.) Iren. (lat.) Cypr., *i.e.* the Western Text in general, omit.

Jew and Gentile Christians, for there was little thought of this as far as the Jewish side was concerned. The Church was prepared to recognize the *fait accompli* of the Gentile expansion, but not to fraternize on a basis of religious equality and fellowship with the Gentile communities. It wished them well, but was not going to give up its own consciousness of possessing the superior faith. The food law or ritual decrees signified that certain ritual requirements were to be made of the Gentiles in order that they might not offend the Jews or cause any Jewish Christian to stumble if haply he found himself in table fellowship with them. At the same time the decree was an implicit assertion that the Jewish-Christian faith was the higher, and had greater authority than that of the Gentiles which rested only in Jesus Christ.

Here we must leave the question. Nothing is really settled, for the primitive Church never came to any real conclusions about the matter. Although the Gentile mission was confirmed at Jerusalem, a long struggle was to take place before, at last, the Gentiles became the predominant power in the Church, when the idea of the Christian salvation as depending on Jewish requirements died a natural death. But this development, sponsored so forcefully by Paul, the apostle to the Gentiles, belongs to the second half of the Apostolic Age, and its working out lies beyond our purview. Finally, the Church universal, long emancipated from its Jewish limiting influences, began to regard the Jews as heretics, placing them upon her roll of heretics when in A.D. 180 " the heretics turned their former judges into heretics." [1]

[1] Harnack, *op. cit.* p. 63.

CHAPTER X

THE RELIGIOUS EXPERIENCE OF THE PRIMITIVE CHURCH AS EXPRESSED IN THE ORDINANCES

THERE were three aspects in which the primitive Church viewed the ordinance of baptism, if we may assume for the moment that we can speak of the rite as a definitely required ordinance of the Church. First, there was the baptism in water in the name of the Lord Jesus which did not in itself confer the gift of the Spirit, this being given only after the apostles, or in later times, their successors duly appointed and ordained, had laid their hands on the recipient. This was the view which finally was to prevail in the Ancient Catholic Church. For example, the converts in Samaria had been baptized in the name of the Lord Jesus, but did not receive the Spirit until two visiting apostles prayed and laid their hands upon them (Acts viii. 4-8, 12-17). Here the baptism and the receiving of the Spirit are two distinct experiences. Second, we have the baptism in water which resulted in the possession of the Spirit only if the baptism was in the name of the Lord Jesus. The believers in Ephesus had been baptized in the name of John, hence they had not received the Spirit. Paul baptized them in the name of the Lord Jesus, and they received the Spirit as he laid his hands on them (Acts xix. 1-6). This laying on of hands is here regarded as no more than a part of the ceremony of baptism, a sort of fitting climax, being not the apostolic mediation of the Spirit since Paul was not a member of the official collegium. Three experiences are here combined together ; the baptism in water, baptism in water in the name of the Lord Jesus, and receiving the Spirit as a result of this baptism. Third, we meet with the baptism of the Spirit bestowed on members of the new community in contrast with the mere baptism in water associated with the name of John the Baptist. The risen Jesus declares that John baptized with water, but the disciples were to be baptized soon with the Holy Spirit (Acts i. 5 ; cf. Mark i. 8). Peter's defence of his action in receiving Cornelius into the Church turned on the idea of the Spirit baptism which fell upon the centurion and his friends, after which attestation, no one could reasonably withhold the baptism of water, the water rite of John the Baptist (Acts xi. 15 f.). This baptism with water was the formal admittance of the Spirit-possessed Gentiles to the new community of the Spirit.

In the first view, the Spirit is conferred after laying on of hands by apostles ; we are amid conceptions which bring us to the frontiers of the Catholic thought and practice of the following century, when the idea of the apostolic collegium was taking shape and influencing the primitive tradition. In the second view, there is an intrinsic connection between the experience of baptism and the experience of the Spirit probably due to the association between the two, since possessing the Spirit often led on to the formal step of joining the Messianic community by an act of baptism. This developed into the working theory of the second half of the Apostolic Age ; Paul brings the gift of the Spirit and its results in human life into intimate relation with the experience of baptism (1 Cor. vi. 11, xii. 13) ; the Fourth Gospel indicates that " water " and the " Spirit " are in close conjunction (iii. 5). In the third view, there was originally no intrinsic connection between the experience of baptism and the experience of the Spirit ; to receive the Spirit was in itself a baptism in contrast with the baptism in water characteristic of John the Baptist.

The teaching of the Catholic Church is that baptism belongs to the very beginnings in that it was instituted by Jesus, but the influence of the Mystery Religions which ascribes a sacrament to the direct institution by the central figure of the cult is at work in such a judgment. If any attention is to be paid to the Synoptic Gospels, it is obvious that we cannot regard Jesus as the founder of the baptismal rite for the Church. There is no mention of the rite in Mark, in *Q*, nor in Luke. The Matthæan reference to baptizing the nations as commanded by Jesus (xxviii. 19) is exposed to textual uncertainties which raise the question whether the verse as it stands belongs to the true text at all.[1] Further, the remarkable fact is that if Jesus gave such a command the Twelve made no attempt to obey it. There is no word of Jesus baptizing His disciples ; on this point the Fourth Gospel cancels itself out in two inconsistent references (iii. 22, iv. 1 f.). What Jesus has to say about the Spirit is not connected with baptism. It may be accepted as certain that Jesus did not institute the rite ; had this been the case something would have been said about it in the gospel story in view of the importance that was attached to baptism at a later time.

Jesus, however, received baptism from the hands of John, which was the outstanding fact in the Baptist's message. The only thing we can ascertain about the rite in Judaic usage was that over and above circumcision, it was the specific rite for admitting Gentile proselytes into Judaism.[2] John was therefore using for

---

[1] Cf. *BC.*, ed. FJ. and L., vol. i. 1920, pp. 335 f., and Allen's *Matthew*, ad. loc.
[2] Cf. *BC.*, ed. FJ. and L., vol. i. pp. 342 f., and vol. v. art. xi. by Silva New, pp. 123 ff.

Jews who responded to his message a rite that was
usually reserved by Jews for Gentiles, thus suggesting
that the national privilege was insufficient for the
imminent crisis of the Kingdom which John was announcing (Mark i. 4, 7 f.) : " Think not to say within
yourselves, We have Abraham for our father " (Matt.
iii. 9), since the racial connection was useless without
a change of heart and life.   And as John's message
centred on apocalyptic expectation and its urgency
(Matt. iii. 2, 7, 12), the baptism of John would be the
admission from Israel as it was to the Israel as it was
to be in the imminent Kingdom.   If this is so, John's
baptism would be a very bold gesture ; we can understand the willingness of Jesus to be baptized.   No
wonder Jesus appreciated John, if our interpretation
be adequate.   Possibly the connection of John's baptism
with apocalyptic urgency suggested and endeared the
rite to the primitive community which summoned the
Jews to repentance and baptized those who responded
into the new Messianic community.

If apocalyptic expectation influenced the use of
baptism as John practised it to admit converts into the
community of the Kingdom, and if this be taken with
the eschatological significance of the gift of the Spirit
in the primitive Church, we have a twofold series of
ideas which tended to draw together, so that two experiences originally separate came to be more and more
closely associated.   Further, the act of being baptized
often coincided with a very sacred religious experience
for the convert, whereby he had broken with his sinful
past and submitted to Christ.   Such a moment was an
inspired one ; it may be expressed in tongue-speech, a
vision, or the other ways in which the presence of the
Spirit was attested.   The coincidence of all such
phenomena with the baptismal experience brought it

alongside the receiving of the Spirit. As with their Master, the believers discovered that the very intensity of their baptismal experience led them to feel as if the heavens were opening and the Spirit of God descending upon them. The baptized convert passed into the Spirit-controlled community, and shared in the new life inspired by the Spirit. Baptism tended to become the open door to inspiration and thus became more closely associated with the receiving of the Spirit. In the course of time the two experiences came to be felt as being intrinsically connected ; in the primitive Church the baptism with water followed up the baptism in the Spirit, but these empirical links were forgotten and became ultimately formulated into the distinctive doctrine which taught that the gift of the Spirit was conditional upon baptism, to be later woven with the doctrine of the apostolic collegium which made the giving of the Spirit follow the laying on of hands by an apostle or one of the duly ordained successors to the apostles.

What is the experiential significance of being baptized " into the name of the Lord Jesus " ? [1] Explanation is sometimes sought in the light of analogies afforded by the papyri and inscriptions as these reflect the life of the ancient Græco-Roman world. For instance, an inscription of the beginning of the imperial period (CIG. ii. No. 2693e) has the significant statement, as Deissmann translates it : " after the sale of the aforementioned objects had been concluded with the purchasers into the name of God." [2] The purchasers represent the real purchaser who is the Deity. From this analogy, Deissmann concludes that " just as, in the inscription, ' to buy into the name of God ' means ' to buy so that the

[1] The Greek prepositions vary, but no stress can be laid on the alternatives, cf. J. H. Moulton, *Prolegomena to N.T. Greek*, p. 63.

[2] *Bible Studies*, Eng. Tr., 1909, p. 147.

article bought belongs to God,' so also the idea underlying . . . ' to baptize into the name of the Lord ' . . .
is that baptism . . . constitutes the belonging to God."[1]

The cumulative witness of the papyri shows that in
the ancient world generally, a name stood for the person
that bore it ; in the case of divine beings a mysterious
virtue was assigned to the god's name, so that he who
invoked it was brought into a personal relationship with
the god.[2] So the familiar argument develops that " in
the name " or " into the name " of Jesus is to be explained from magical ideas that have filtered into
Christianity from the ancient world and its beliefs.
Those who pronounce the name of Jesus over the person
receiving baptism are acting for the real purchaser,
Jesus Christ, whose name has a virtue able to possess
and protect the one over whom his name is pronounced.[3]
But the diffused ideas of the ancient world will not
account for the significance of " the name " as far as
the primitive Church is concerned ; its ideas are drawn
from a more confined area of thought and practice, and
from a far deeper source than the world at large yet
realized, than is implied in the wider life of the world.
The Church was expressing the vital religious experience
which centred in Jesus. The ancient world had no
knowledge of the deity walking the earth in human in-
carnation, making disciples, and inspiring the formation
of any community called by the name of such a deity.
The primitive Church, however, had the inspired remembrance of, and contact with, the personal Jesus into

[1] *Op. cit.* p. 147.
[2] " It is this assumption of the power of a name which must be
emphasized at the beginning of any intelligible treatment of its place
in the theory and practice of early Christianity," Silva New, *op. cit.*
p. 123.
[3] The typical exponent of this *ex opere operato* view is Heitmüller,
Taufe und Abendmahl bei Paulus, 1903, p. 14.

whose name they baptized the converts. The eye-witnesses had known him in person and in life. When the Church began to be divorced from the living Jesus and was thrown upon a transcendental Christ whose significance was construed in Greek philosophical categories, or tended to become an ancient world cultus with Christ as the central hero, ideas drawn from ancient magic and from the Mystery Religions began to filter into the original Christian facts as Christianity tended to become the dominant Mystery Religion. But it is another matter to transfer these later accretions to the primitive Church with its personal experience of a Jesus Christ known intimately in life, in His Cross, in His resurrection. The Church was reacting in its religious experience to no Christ myth, no mythical redeemer-hero in a mystical cult, nor to incantations and cabalistic signs, but to a personal creator in Jesus, to personal loyalty to a historic personality, in whose name the believers had come together in the Messianic community.

We need to keep clearly before us the fact that the vocabulary, ideas, and practices of the primitive Church were drawn, not from the religious eclecticism of the Græco-Roman world, but from the faith in which it was cradled, namely, Judaism and the Old Testament. Therefore magical papyri are not authoritative for the use of " the name " of Jesus in the real sense that the Old Testament is, and it is to this source we should turn to discover the empirical implications of " the name " for the primitive Church. Sometimes a man's name was taken to denote the sort of man he was (1 Sam. xxv. 25). The name was a token of ownership, as " Goliath, his name " (1 Sam. xvii. 4), *i.e.* the name which marked the giant out from every one else. Joab urges David to go out against a certain city, lest he himself capture it and it be called by his name instead of by David's

(2 Sam. xii. 28), *i.e.* belong to him ; in the same sense
seven women will petition a man that they may take his
name and avoid reproach (Isa. iv. 1), *i.e*, belong to him.
The Israelites call themselves by the name of the holy
city, *i.e.* they belong to that city (Isa. xlviii. 2).   When a
man represents another he speaks in the name of that
one (1 Sam. xxv. 5, 9) ;   Jezebel sends letters " in the
name of Ahab," and so represents him as she arranges
the murder of Naboth (1 Kings xxi. 8).   The ideas here
are that something is done or said in the name of some
one, so that it is as if that some one were actually doing
or saying the thing himself.

The "name" designates God Himself.   Men began
" to call on the name of the Lord " (Gen. iv. 26, etc.),
i.e. to call on the Lord.   Abram built an altar and called
"upon the name of the Lord" (Gen. xii. 8), *i.e.* he
worshipped the Lord Himself.   The place of worship is a
house "for My name" (2 Sam. vii. 13) ;   for the sake
of " the name " the stranger will come from far to the
temple (1 Kings viii. 41).   In these and other instances
" the name of the Lord " means " the Lord."   The
" name of the Lord " also denotes possession or ownership ;   the house called by His name is the house which
God owns (Jer. vii. 10).   When any one takes on himself
the divine name it means for that person that he belongs
to God, that God owns him (Jer. xv. 16) ;   Israel as a
nation is owned by the Lord by whose name it is called
(Deut. xxviii. 10) ;   the ark, the temple, and the holy
city are respectively known by the name of the Lord,
i.e. God possesses them for His own (2 Sam. vi. 2 ;
1 Kings viii. 43 ;   Jer. xxv. 29).   The " name of the
Lord " as representative of God is illustrated by Moses
who speaks to the Pharaoh " in Thy name " (Ex. v.
23) ;   David confronts Goliath as God's representative,
i.e. in God's name (1 Sam. xvii. 45).   It is as if the

Lord himself were speaking or acting what others are saying and doing " in His name." The idea grows until the " name " embodies the revealed character of the Lord (Ex. xxxiv. 14) and shows signs of becoming ineffable (Lev. xxiv. 11).

This was the empirical background of religious ideas in which we are compelled to interpret the significance of " in the name of Jesus " for the primitive Church baptism. First, " into (in) the name of Jesus " was another way of saying, " into Jesus," that is, Jesus Himself. The convert was conscious of being brought into a close personal relation with Jesus. The mystical " being-in-Christ " which characterized Paul's doctrine of baptism into Christ is not found in the primitive Church, yet an intimate association with Jesus was set up in the act of baptism. Second, he who administered the rite was regarded as the representative of the Christ into whose name he was baptizing the new convert. It was as if Messiah himself were admitting the believer into the community of salvation. Third, the convert was aware in his baptism of coming into possession of Messiah, and being owned by Messiah ; being baptized " into the name of Jesus " signified that henceforth Jesus owned his life ; the convert must needs submit and obey. Fourth, since the new community belonged to Jesus the Messiah, every one who came to be owned by Jesus in baptism came *ipso facto* within the ownership of the new community ; the convert knew that he had entered the redeemed community of Messiah, that he belonged to it, and shared in its life, its experience of the Spirit, its call, its claims to loyalty.

In this experience of ownership the Semitic and the Hellenistic viewpoints coincide, in that " the name " denoted possession by the owner of the name. The Gentile converts shared in much the same religious experience in baptism as did the Jewish Christians, but it should be made clear that the primitive Church received and interpreted its baptismal experience in the light of a religious background drawn from the Old Testament, in which the sense of being possessed by deity through His name was by no means strange. It did not need Hellenistic experience to bring into Christianity the idea of being taken possession of by the Lord ; it was already there in the native soil of Judaism.

We turn to the other great ordinance of the primitive Church, namely, the Lord's Supper. We meet with a rite known as the " breaking of bread," and this was celebrated " at home " (Acts ii. 42, 46). Was this an expression of the community on its " Christian " side in contrast to the previously mentioned gatherings in the temple which expressed the community on its Jewish side ? (ver. 46).[1] It is, however, doubtful whether the earliest believers were sufficiently self-conscious as a community to feel such a contrast ; the designation " Christian " is anachronistic at this stage. Whatever of " cultus " may be implied by the temple gatherings and the " breaking of bread " at home, we may be sure that there was *continuum* rather than *contrast* in respect of both. The temple pinnacle was a very likely place whence Messiah would appear, and the " breaking of bread " would continue the eschatological expectation in that Messiah's very footfall might be heard on the threshold at any moment. It is true that " there is nothing in the text here to suggest eschatological expectations," [2] but the whole *milieu* is strongly eschatological, whether the believers were in the temple, or " breaking the bread " at home. If the " cup " was passed round during the

[1] As Oesterley thinks, *op. cit.* p. 96.
[2] G. H. C. Macgregor, *Eucharistic Origins*, 1928, p. 121.

rite, the apocalyptic element is definitely introduced, but there is no mention in Acts of the cup. The distributive sense " in separate houses " is to be preferred ;[1] the whole body of believers gathered within the temple precincts for worship, hoping for Messiah to descend into their midst ; thereafter it breaks up into the smaller fellowship units in the various houses where the religious fellowship circles (Chabûrôth) were wont to assemble, reflecting the social and quasi-religious practice of the time in which Jesus and His disciples shared. Viewed from one angle the community of believers is a unified fellowship ; viewed from another angle it becomes a series of *chabûrôth*, and therefore more suited to " home " fellowship than to a place of worship. The farewell meal which Jesus had with His disciples was a special occasion of this Jewish social-religious custom, and its commemoration in the primitive Church first began in these home circles where the " breaking of bread " took place.

We have had occasion to refer to this Jewish practice of gathering in small groups for common meals which had a religious aim in view. In private houses, social, quasi-religious meals were of weekly occurrence, being arranged by " small groups or societies of friends."[2] This common meal was held prior to the commencement of the Sabbath and was interrupted as the Sabbath was about to begin. At this point the practice of " hallowing the Sabbath " occurred, the ceremony being known as the *Kiddûsh*.[3] The hallowing ceremony was known in the first place as the *Kedûshah*, and he who presided at it

[1] With Lietzmann, *H-C. zum N.T.*, *ad. loc.* Acts ii. 46. For a discussion on the exegetical alternatives offered for κατ' οἶκον cf. *BC.*, ed. FJ. and L., vol. iv. 1933, p. 29.

[2] Oesterley, *op. cit.* p. 167.

[3] Oesterley and Box, *The Religion and Worship of the Synagogue*, 2nd edn. 1911, pp. 374 ff.

uttered a benediction over it for the " sanctification
of the day " (*Kedûshath ha-yôm*). At a later stage,
in early post-Christian times, both meal and ceremony
were transferred to the synagogue, and the ceremony is
then known as *Kiddûsh*, an intensive form of the earlier
name.[1] The cup and the bread are now spoken of,
as well as the blessing over each, but there is no reason
to suppose that this was not done at the earlier hallowings
in the Jewish homes. The meal originally preceded the
sanctification ceremony for the Sabbath, although in
later times the ceremony came first.[2] The meal with the
Kiddûsh following took place on the eve of the great
festivals as well as on the Sabbath ; every special feast
had its hallowing ceremony, which also included the
remembrance for the Sabbath. The custom was therefore
familiar to Jesus, His disciples, and the primitive Church.

Was the " breaking of bread " rooted in this *Kiddûsh*
ceremony ? It is referred to as a daily custom (Acts ii.
46), but this may denote the ordinary family meals
which, in turn, may have taken on a " hallowing "
quality in expectation of the return of the Christ. At
least these meals provided occasion each week for the
Jewish duty of hallowing the Sabbath with the *Kiddûsh*
ceremony, at which all that was observed was shot
through and through with the remembrance of Jesus.

We turn to discuss the farewell meal which Jesus had
with His disciples in the Upper Room. The evidence for
it is fragmentary, and what we have is by no means
consistent. There are two sources of tradition, namely,
" Mark-Matthew," and " Luke-Paul." Mark's account
(xiv. 22–26) has the following : " And as they were

[1] Oesterley, *The Jewish Background of the Christian Liturgy*,
p. 170.

[2] Cf. Oesterley and Box, *op. cit.* pp. 374 f., and Israel Abrahams,
ERE., vol. x. p. 891.

eating He took bread ; having blessed it, he broke and gave it to them and said, Take, this is my body. And he took a cup, and having given thanks he gave it to them, and they all drank of it. And he said to them, This is my blood of the covenant which is shed for many ; verily I tell you, I will no more drink of the vine until that day when I drink it new in the Kingdom of God." Matthew's narrative (xxvi. 26–30) has slight variations only from that of Mark, whose " and they all drank of it " has now turned into a direct injunction, " drink ye all of it," and the phrase " unto forgiveness of sins " is added to define the purpose of the shedding of the blood under the new covenant (Matt. xxvi. 27 f.). This phrase is more likely to be added to than omitted from Mark. The Marcan " the Kingdom of God " becomes the " Kingdom of my Father," a personal detail which does not affect the general narrative. Thus Mark and Matthew stand together in a common tradition. In the course of the meal, Jesus took bread, blessed, and distributed it around, saying, " Take, eat, this is my body " ; then taking the cup, giving thanks, he passed it around desiring the disciples to drink, and all drank of it. Jesus then said that the cup was His blood of the covenant, shed for many, and declared that the next time He drank of the cup would be in the divine Kingdom.

The Luke-Paul tradition (Luke xxii. 15–20 ; 1 Cor. x. 16, 21, xi. 23–26) offers alternative ideas. According to Luke two cups are passed round, and in between them is offered the bread ; the Marcan saying about drinking the cup in the divine Kingdom follows the first cup, prior to the distribution of the bread. The second cup follows the dispensing of the bread, and Luke's words (xxii. 19) follow closely Paul's account (1 Cor. xi. 24 f.), the most noteworthy feature being the injunction to eat the bread in remembrance of Jesus ; Paul's narrative

19

supplies a similar injunction to commemorate Jesus in the cup (1 Cor. xi. 25). But there is very good authority for omitting the Lucan words, " which is given for you ; this do in my remembrance ; and the cup in like manner after supper, saying, This cup is the new covenant in my blood, which is shed for you," for the Codex Bezæ and the Old Latin texts omit them (Luke xxii. 19*b*, 20). On the other hand, the evidence for their retention is very strong, for nearly all the great Greek versions include them. Whether they be accepted or rejected as the insertion of some scribe who wished to harmonize Luke's account with that of Paul, we still have Luke's independent witness to the dispensing of the cup prior to the distribution of the bread. This feature places Luke over against the Mark-Matthæan tradition. If the words, " this do in my remembrance " are omitted, Luke does not testify to such an injunction from Jesus ; if we retain the words, then Luke joins Paul as a witness to the injunction, over against Mark-Matthew, which is silent on the matter.

Paul's account claims to be derived from the primitive Church (1 Cor. xi. 23), and in substance is very much as the Lucan story (xxii. 19 f.). Paul adds the injunction as to remembrance to the cup as well as to the bread, whereas Luke has it only for the bread. The first cup mentioned by Luke, and the eschatological reference to drinking the vine in the Kingdom of God which the three Synoptists contain, find no place in Paul's narrative here, but elsewhere he does mention the cup prior to the bread, implying that the order is by no means settled (1 Cor. x. 16, 21) ; at the same time there is a general reference to the expected return of Christ (1 Cor. xi. 26).

There seems, therefore, to be confusion in the narratives as to the exact place of the dispensing of the cup. If this last meal were followed by the *Kiddûsh* ceremony, then the cup would come first, since this was the usual order.   A further question, however, has to be discussed, for if the farewell supper became the scene of the *Kiddûsh*, it must have been the *Kiddûsh* for the coming Passover. But the usual interpretation of the available evidence is that Jesus celebrated at the farewell supper the Passover itself.   The Synoptics clearly point to this (Mark xiv. 12 ; Matt. xxvi. 17 ; Luke xxii. 7, 15) ; according to them, the farewell meal was the actual observance of the Passover by Jesus and His friends.   The Fourth Gospel, however, dates the meal on the evening before the Passover itself (xiii. 1 ff., 29, xviii. 28, xix. 14, 31, 42) ; the farewell meal took place with the Passover still in the near future, and Jesus died on the day known as the " Preparation of the Passover," on the evening of which the Passover festival would begin with the eating of the paschal lamb.

We are in the presence of two traditions ; indeed, the Synoptics are not altogether consistent ; Mark (xiv. 12) places the farewell meal on the first day of the unleavened bread, " when they were killing the pass-over," but Matthew, with his closer knowledge of Jewish customs, omits this last detail and agrees with Luke in placing the farewell meal on the day when at 6 p.m. Nisan 14 began, thus making it coincide with the eating of the Passover.   It is precarious to infer inconsistency in the words, " after two days was the Passover and the unleavened bread " (Mark xiv. 1), for this may have been spoken a day prior to the injunction to the disciples to make ready.   Further, while the desire to eat the Passover before He suffered (Luke xxii. 15) may have indicated Jesus' regret thát His wish was not to be fulfilled, it may well be that in the very meal His desire was fulfilled and that the words express His satisfaction that He was able to eat the Passover before He died.

We have to choose between the Synoptics and the Fourth Gospel. Attempts to harmonize bring more confusion, while the Johannine date is to be preferred beyond reasonable doubt. First, if the meal was to be made ready for the first day of unleavened bread, as the Synoptics record, the disciples would scarcely have had time to arrange for it on the same day whereon they were instructed. Second, if the Synoptics are right in regarding the farewell meal as the Passover, the details we expect to see are entirely missing : there is no reference to the roasted paschal lamb, and the bread passed round is ἄρτος instead of ἄζυμα if unleavened bread was passed round. The hymn sung does not necessarily point to the Passover (Mark xiv. 26), for the singing of an *Hallēl* is not peculiar to the Passover celebrations. Third, although the authorities had planned to arrest Jesus prior to the festival (Mark xiv. 2), it seems that, according to the Synoptics, they accomplished their purpose on the day of Passover, an inconceivable proceeding involving such breaches of the law as carrying arms (Mark xiv. 47), buying spices (xvi. 1), the arrival of Simon of Cyrene from the country (xv. 21), buying linen (xv. 46), and, above all, the trial and execution of Jesus on the sacred day. Fourth, Joseph buried the dead body of Jesus at once, because it was Friday afternoon, the hour when the Sabbath began being near (xv. 56).

All these points lead us to decide for the Johannine idea that the farewell meal was not the Passover celebration. It was the social meal prior to the day of Passover, and as the feast drew near, the *Kiddûsh* for the Passover was observed by Jesus and His friends. This hallowing ceremony, known as the Passover *Kiddûsh*, according to the Fourth Gospel, took place on Nisan 14, *i.e.* from 6 p.m. on Thursday to 6 p.m. on Friday. On the

Thursday afternoon Jesus and His friends met for their weekly social meal, and as 6 p.m. approached (*i.e.* the beginning of the new day Nisan 14), they observed the *Kiddûsh* for Passover, and this ceremony is that which has come to be regarded as the first institution of the Eucharist.

The difficulty that Friday was the usual day for the *Kiddûsh* is met by the fact " that in this year the Sabbath day coincided with the first day of the Passover Feast ; on such occasions, according to ancient Jewish law, the Feast superseded the Sabbath." [1]   The usual meal could not take place on the Friday afternoon, for even then the paschal lambs were being slain within the temple precincts ; the Passover was to take place at 6 p.m. that day when normally the Sabbath came in.   Therefore the meal was held on the Thursday afternoon ; at 6 p.m. began the day of Preparation, and the Passover *Kiddûsh* was observed as this came in ; the Day of Preparation really inaugurated the Passover Feast, although it was not reckoned as the first day of Passover in an official sense ; yet since the lambs were sacrificed (Ex. xii. 2-6) on that day, it really began the feast. [2]

Jesus therefore celebrated the Passover *Kiddûsh* during a farewell meal which He had with His disciples. It followed the usual procedure with which they were familiar.   Jesus passed round wine and bread, and connected the symbolism with His own personal mission and intention, in view of His forthcoming death as necessary to what He knew to be His purpose in the Kingdom of God.   But what were the disciples making of all this ?   The " hallowing " of Sabbath or Feast

[1] Oesterley, *op. cit.* p. 175, referring to Pesachim, vi. 1 ff. as authority for the above rule.

[2] Cf. Oesterley, *op. cit.* pp. 158–179 ; M. Goguel, *The Life of Jesus*, pp. 429–451 ; Macgregor, *op. cit.* pp. 33–49, for the whole subject.

was centred in their trust in the God who had chosen Israel ; they were steeped in the lore of the nation's redemption out of Egypt, which the Passover emphasized. Such constituent elements of religious experience formed the experiential basic deposit into which anything new would be received, and either accepted, rejected, or modified for the time being, in accordance with the consistency or otherwise of the new with the ingrained religious consciousness already deeply laid down.

If we take the cup first, as this may well be the order in view of the *Kiddûsh* character of the ceremony,[1] Jesus pronounced the usual blessing upon it.[2] Thereafter He declared that the next time He would drink it would be in the Kingdom of God.   The disciples had no difficulty here ; they were familiar with the idea of the Messianic Kingdom as a banquet, and sayings from prophets, psalmists, and apocalyptists would be in their minds as Jesus thus spoke.[3] Jesus' earlier references to the joys of the coming age as a banquet justify the inference that " the conception of an actual repast for the pious was already an old-established idea,"[4] and the different minds would treat the symbol through the varying eyes of material literalism or spiritual understanding.   In the main, it would be the " sensuous " aspect of the Kingdom that would be prominent ; the next *Kiddûsh* they celebrated with Jesus would be in the literal Messianic Kingdom on the verge of appearing.   And when Jesus

---

[1] Luke xxii. 17 f. ; 1 Cor. x. 16, 21 ; *Did.* ix.

[2] Oesterley, *op. cit.* p. 81, renders this as follows : " Blessed art Thou, O Lord our God, King Eternal, who createst the fruit of the vine.   Blessed art Thou, O Lord our God, King Eternal, who hast chosen us . . . given us . . . Sabbaths for rest . . . this Sabbath day and this feast of unleavened bread. . . ."

[3] Isa. xxv. 6, lv. 1, lxv. 13 ; Ps. xxiii. 5; T.L. xviii. 11 ; En. xxiv. 4, xxv. 4 f.

[4] Dalman, *The Words of Jesus*, p. 111 ; cf. Matt. xxii. 1–14, xxv. 1 ff. ; Luke xiv. 15.

went on to speak of the Kingdom He had appointed that they might eat and drink at His Messianic table (Luke xxii. 29 f.), the disciples had no doubt what this meant for them.

There was, however, the recurrent uneasiness about what Jesus had said of His forthcoming death, and this came once more to the fore as Jesus broke the bread, saying, "This is my body." This piece of profound symbolism pointed to his approaching death as the necessary prelude to the Messianic banquet. His body was to be broken into many fragments. This would be the way in which the eye-witnesses interpreted the symbolism before them,[1] especially when due regard is paid to the eschatological significance of the cup. In the very raising of their hopes of the Kingdom in the cup, the latent cross-purposes with Jesus over His announced death reasserted themselves with the passing round of the bread and the accompanying words, "This is my body." Was it necessary for Jesus to go to such lengths of sacrifice as to suffer death? Yet here was the bread spoken of as if to say, "This stands for my forthcoming sacrifice in my body being broken for you in death."

The sacrificial symbolism was further heightened by the solemn associations of the Passover which Jesus and His friends were duly "hallowing." Were such sacrificial ideas to be connected with Jesus? If so, the very absurdity of the situation would only be the more consciously apparent to the disciples, if His own sacrifice was necessary to the ushering in of the Kingdom.

So far we have viewed the Last Supper in the light of the *Kiddûsh* custom where the cup preceded the bread.

---

[1] The symbolism of Jesus' action is not that of broken fragments coming together into the unity of the loaf, expressive of the unity of the company in fellowship, a conception influenced too much by the *Didache*.

As our records stand, the cup was dispensed also after the bread, and is given a covenantal significance. Nothing would be simpler than to accept the cup in association with a solemn covenant based on the death of Jesus, and yet no element in the Last Supper is more beset with difficulties and uncertainties. So formidable are these as to cause considerable hesitation in accepting this element as authentic. The covenant idea does not appear in connection with the cup that precedes the bread, as in Luke, but this Gospel brings in the covenant cup after the breaking of the bread. Are the two cups of Luke, together with the textual variants here, indicative of the uncertainty which the Church of Luke's age had in respect of the original procedure and significance of the farewell meal ?

If we accept the covenantal significance of the cup, we have to ask what was implied in the words, " this is my blood of the (new) covenant " (Mark xiv. 24). We may set aside the idea of *diathēkē* as meaning here " testament," as if the cup stood for the last bequest of Jesus, the testament which He delivered before His death to " do this in remembrance of me." For the Messianic realism possessing the minds of the eye-witnesses precluded any thought of remembering Jesus when they were to have Him actually at the Messianic banquet. From another angle, the prospective suffering was raising doubts as to whether Jesus was the Messiah after all ; if these doubts triumphed, there would be no incentive to commemorate one who brought such disillusionment. The disciples did not look on the words of Jesus as a testament. The word *diathēkē* would at once arouse echoes of what Moses said in the institution of the covenant associated with his name (Ex. xxiv. 8) ; if Jesus referred to a covenant set up in His blood, it would be a covenant brought about through His

suffering and death. We are not here in the presence
simply of the setting up of mutual conditions of alliance
in a " brotherhood," [1] even if the sharing of the cup
implied a covenant of fellowship in the coming
Kingdom.

If the original idea in a " covenant " is that of a
religious contract between the Deity and His worshippers,
such an aspect passes out of sight as the awareness of
the divine sovereignty emerges ; the " covenant " comes
to centre around the God who deals with men in His
gracious purpose, placing them within a certain relation
to Himself, rather than by means of mutual agreement
to be allies. This attitude of divine grace is well illustrated in Jeremiah's famous covenant passage (xxxi.
31 ff.). Jeremiah's words may well have been in the
mind of Jesus, in view of their essentially spiritual character. Jesus was convinced that through His death men
were to be brought into a new relation with God, in
view of the advent of the Kingdom which that death
was to prelude. The Kingdom was yet to come, yet
God was already in some sense the sovereign ; where
He was not yet King it was in the human heart which
did not fulfil the terms of Jeremiah's covenant, " Know
the Lord." The one spiritual essential to influence the
human heart to acknowledge God was a better knowledge
of God, for if men knew Him truly and experienced Him
as He was, they would enthrone Him in their hearts.
Jesus had this unique knowledge and experience of God ;
He viewed His death as His endeavour to bring to men
this unique knowledge of the Father as He knew Him,
and looked to His death to accomplish in this matter
what His teaching had failed to do. Thus, in the giving
of His body, and in the covenantal reference of His
blood, this new knowledge of God was to be set up for

[1] As Réville thinks, *Les Origines de l'eucharistie*, 1898, pp. 143 ff.

mankind. Jesus may thus have drawn an analogy between His death as inaugurating this new covenant relationship and the ancient covenant set up with its sacrifice.

We have, however, to reckon with the disciples' lack of comprehension as to the significance of Jesus' death. This lack tended to destroy for their minds any " covenant " reference in the cup, since they could see no meaning in Messiah suffering and dying. This empirical probability makes it almost impossible for the eye-witnesses to treat it as a covenant, whatever was in Jesus' own mind on the matter. But there are other serious difficulties. First, it is precisely at this point that our evidence is most confused, as the Lucan variants show. Second, the difficulty caused by the variation in the order of the cup presents an almost insoluble character. If the order of Mark–Matthew–1 Cor. xi. 23–25 be accepted, that is, with the cup following the bread, how are we to account for the order of Luke– 1 Cor. x. 16, 21–*Did*. ix., where the cup precedes the bread ? And if the text of Luke be received as it stands, how account for the two cups ? On the other hand, if we prefer the Luke–1 Cor. x.–*Did*. ix. tradition, we have still to account for the Mark–Matthew–1 Cor. xi. arrangement with its " covenant " cup. The Mark–Matthew tradition may have been influenced by Paul's thought about the Cross as a sacrifice ; the conjunction of the Last Supper with the death of Christ as seen in retrospect has been closely effected in Paul's account of the Supper ; the cup is " the new covenant in my blood," the broken bread points to the sacrificial offering up of Christ. Thus the Pauline Church, and indeed the Church prior to Paul to some extent, reflects the " covenantal " aspect of the Last Supper.

A few tentative suggestions may be offered as to how

the " covenant " cup developed from the original
" eschatological " cup. First, the declaration of Jesus
that He would not drink again of the cup until He drank
it in the Kingdom of God may well have called up
Jeremiah's idea of the new covenant as setting forth
the conditions operative in the new Kingdom. Something may have been said in reference to this covenant
over the " eschatological " cup. Second, the cup that
was passed round and shared was itself an implied
covenant of fellowship, an aspect that came to be
vividly realized as the primitive Church emerged.
Third, Jesus placed His death between the present order
and the new state of life to be brought in with the
Kingdom of God, and thus helped to connect His death
with the new fellowship of the Spirit. This would
suggest the offering up of His blood as " my blood of
the new covenant." Fourth, the passing round of the
bread pointed to Jesus' coming death, and any covenantal
reference that came to be attached to the cup would
inevitably pass to the bread. Such germinal " covenant " ideas are possibly inherent in the whole setting
of the farewell meal.

We may now venture to state our view of the character of the Last Supper. As the Day of Preparation
for the Passover drew near, the *Kiddûsh* celebration
took place. The cup was first dispensed, and was
interpreted in an eschatological sense.[1] Something was
said or implied which formed a subconscious basis for
the later observance of the Supper as the memorial of
the covenant inaugurating the Kingdom of God, and
in this way the eschatological reference of the cup

---

[1] " The eschatological interpretation enables us to reconstruct
more exactly the *milieu* amid which the words of Jesus were spoken
at the Supper, even if it does not exhaust their reference " (J. H.
Srawley, *ERE.* vol. v. p. 542, col. i.).

came to attach to itself germinal ideas of a covenant. This " covenant " character is revealed in the later gospel strata of the Mark–Matthew tradition.   But the reference to the " blood " shed as denoting Christ's death was unnecessary.   In Jewish psychology " body " covered both " flesh " and " blood." The covenant parallelism of the cup would be tautologous since the " body " broken already covered any reference to the shedding of Jesus' blood.   Such " covenant " germs were more likely to attach to the distribution of the bread with the words, " this is My body," including any idea of the shedding of blood.   Therefore the second cup, *i.e.* the " covenant " cup, was unlikely : even if the cup followed the bread it would still be eschatological in character.

Throughout the whole ceremony the reference was to the coming Kingdom of God, and the place of Jesus' death in relation to it.   That death, viewed in retrospect by the primitive Church, came to be interpreted along the lines of divine necessity, and this would lend significance to the covenant aspect, which grew more and more prominent as the Church developed.

If the eschatological character of the Last Supper be accepted, the probability is that Jesus gave no express injunction to " do this in remembrance of Me."   The Mark–Matthew tradition is silent on this, and Luke refers to it only in connection with the bread in that part of his text which is omitted by many good authorities.   Paul is the only straightforward witness to the injunction ; he mentions it in reference to both the bread and the cup, although the cup may have been assimilated to what was required with regard to the bread.   Now Paul claims to have received his tradition from what had gone before him (1 Cor. xi. 23).   It is difficult to discern where tradition ends and Paul's comment or paraphrase enters.[1] We cannot therefore look on Paul's account as conclusive that Jesus commanded the repetition of the rite. Had such an injunction been forthcoming, it is almost inconceivable that the Marcan tradition would have omitted it, for its silence does not at all indicate that the commemoration is implied.[2] Further, the eschatological *milieu* of the Supper tells against any such commemoration, for the next cup the disciples were to share actually with Jesus in the Messianic banquet (Matt. xxvi. 29). For what would be the purpose of an injunction to observe the Supper again and again in remembrance of Jesus when He and His friends were so soon to sit down together at the Messianic banquet itself? The procedure at the Last Supper indicates a series of actions wrought once for all turning on the assurance that the separation of Jesus through death was but temporary, in view of His convincing pledge of His forthcoming triumph. The sharing of the eschatological cup would be thus construed by the disciples.

There were, however, experiential conditions which were to ensure that the rite would be repeated, until it seemed as if Jesus had himself made such a requirement of His friends. The resurrection supervened, and the next *Kiddûsh* celebration took place with the triumphant awareness that Jesus had overcome death. In the joy of such a triumph the solemnities of the Last Supper received new light. The weekly Sabbaths were, as usual, heralded by the ceremony of *Kiddûsh*; the cup was dispensed and the bread blessed, but there was now added the personal and vital association with Jesus

[1] As, for example, in the words, " for as often as ye eat this bread and drink this cup, ye do show the Lord's death till he come," where it is not certain if we have authentic tradition or Paul's own comment on the tradition.

[2] As Gore supposes, *The Holy Spirit and the Church*, p. 55.

in the farewell supper. Thus the weekly *Kiddûsh* was invested with all the wealth of new religious experience centring in the risen Jesus and in the eschatological expectations thereby so vividly heightened. As the disciples passed round the cup and the bread it almost seemed as if Jesus were once again with them, sitting down in the Messianic banquet. In this way the observance of the *Kiddûsh* with the added solemn associations gathering around Jesus, began to develop into an actual observance of that Last Supper itself. Indeed, the very intensity of things may have made it possible for the celebration to become a daily one for the time being, since the Kingdom might be inaugurated any day.

The " breaking of bread " was probably the weekly *Kiddûsh* centring upon the assurance and pledge of the actions of Jesus at the Last Supper. But the newborn joy was also carried into the ordinary meals of the home life, whereat believers would be forcefully reminded at every return of their meals of the significance of the breaking of bread and the sharing of the cup as touching the divine Kingdom to come at any moment. No observance of *Kiddûsh* could henceforth be unrelated to that Last Supper which confirmed their consciousness of being heirs to the Kingdom, in which they and Jesus were to sit down. The Last Supper came gradually to be for them the covenant or the charter of their new status. While the Kingdom was strictly in the future, it became theirs in the present by confident anticipation. The believers felt themselves to be of the family of God, as if the Kingdom had already come upon them. It seemed as if Jesus were present in their "hallowings " showing His wounded hands and side.

Thus the " breaking of bread " began to take on the form of a celebration of Christ's words and actions in the Last Supper, until He should come in the glory of the final consummation. Imperceptibly the observance came to assume the vital authority that it was so commanded by Jesus whom the believers were holding in vivid remembrance until their expectations of His return were realized at last. The basis of it all lay in what the disciples had seen and heard at the Last Supper, and through them the words and actions of Jesus passed into primitive Church observance by way of the *Kiddûsh* celebrations. In remembrance of the Jesus soon to return the believers met joyfully together, and it seemed as if it were none other than Jesus Himself who had enjoined the celebration, so intimately was He related to what they were observing. All this was vividly symbolized in the sharing of the eschatological cup, while the solemn symbolism of the broken bread stood more clearly for the sacrifice of Jesus in His death, now seen to be the divinely appointed way for Messiah. Jesus had been about to give His life for the Kingdom ; in very truth, the believers saw, Jesus was a ransom for many, since through His death He was to inaugurate the new order of things into which many would enter and take their place. And as they broke the bread and awaited His return, they were aware that He was apportioning their places in the new era.

As the gospel was carried further afield and the new Churches came into being, the observance of the Lord's Supper became an integral element in their witness. The dominant original ideas began to fade, and thus the entrance was afforded for ideas and interpretations of the ritual which were foreign to the atmosphere of the Last Supper. These ideas and practices were drawn from the wider pagan world with its magic, its mystery cults, its sacramentarianism, although it is not till the second century that we see these seriously influencing the Christian faith. Within the orbit of the primitive Church, even as this embraced the Gentile Churches, the observance probably retained, for the most part, its primitive character. There is, however, surprisingly scanty reference to the observance in the Acts of the Apostles, or even in Paul's letters. Was the controversy over Peter's withdrawal from the Gentile Christians (Gal. ii. 11 ff.) connected with the observance? If so, Paul's severe criticism turned on the point that Peter had shown that the sacred ordinance was only for Jewish Christians, and that without circumcision there could be no validity attached to the Lord's Supper. We hear of a celebration at Troas in connection with a Christian assembly (Acts xx. 7–12), which is designated as " the breaking of bread." Despite the silence of Acts, however, the summary reference to the " breaking of bread " (Acts ii. 42) indicates that the ceremony was becoming habitual within the primitive Church.

It is possible that we have further information as to the nature of the observance from the *Didache*. The later atmosphere of this writing is undoubted, but there is a primitive Church strain in the eucharistic prayers (*Did.* ix. f.). The cup precedes the bread, and over each the appropriate prayer is uttered.[1] From the prayers it seems that the " cup " was thought of in the eschatological sense ; the reference to " the holy vine of David " recalls a series of concepts which the primitive Church would interpret in an eschatological manner,[2]

[1] The prayer over the cup was, " We give Thee thanks, our Father, for the holy vine of David Thy servant, which Thou hast made known to us through Jesus Thy servant ; to Thee be glory for ever." Over the broken bread the prayer was, " We give Thee thanks, our Father, for the life and knowledge which Thou madest known to us through Jesus Thy servant ; to Thee be glory for ever. As this broken bread was scattered over the hills and having been gathered together became one, so let Thy Church be gathered together from the ends of the earth into Thy kingdom, for Thine is the glory and the power through Jesus Christ for ever."

[2] Such as " let this world pass away," " the Son of David," " Marana tha."

and probably refers to the awaited consummation. Along with the broken bread the cup points to the Messianic banquet ; there is also the thought of sharing in the life of the coming Kingdom, and it is therefore the expression of a fellowship based on a common expectation of salvation consummated through the advent of the divine Kingdom in the power of " Jesus thy Servant." While the broken bread scattered over the hills may be expressive of the common brotherhood of believers who by this time had spread to far distant fields of witness, the underlying idea is still eschatological in the ingathering of the Kingdom and its consummated life of which the bread was the symbol. The *Didache* therefore points to the nature of the observance of the Lord's Supper in the primitive Church. Despite its post-Pauline date, we seem " to discover here some sheltered geological deposit where relics of earlier forms of life are preserved." [1] The conceptions revealed are strikingly more primitive than what we find in Paul. The nature of the parallels between the ideas in the prayers of the *Didache* and the *Kiddûsh* blessings points to the coalescence of the two series in the primitive Church observance of the Lord's Supper.

[1] Macgregor, *op. cit.* p. 148.

CHAPTER XI

THE CHRIST-CONSCIOUSNESS OF THE PRIMITIVE CHURCH

THE roots of the religious experience which caused the primitive Church to emerge lay in the contacts which the eye-witnesses had with the personal Jesus. A vital experience of His creative potency was in being, and this led to the religious upheaval which followed the resurrection appearances. The logic of the final appearance known as the Ascension was that Jesus was now apprehended in His exalted status as the Messiah sitting at the right hand of God, soon to return in the divine Kingdom. This exaltation was at first viewed along the usual crude, literalistic lines, but certain positive factors were already influencing a more spiritual awareness of Jesus.

Once the significance of the death of Jesus was grasped in its connection as the necessary prelude to the advent of the Messianic Kingdom, the more spiritual aspects of the personality and status of Jesus began to emerge. The way of suffering, deliberately chosen and pursued in obedience to the divine will, is at least an intense expression of spiritual vitality which could not fail to be appraised by the earliest believers. Their application of the categories of Israel's traditional Suffering Servant (Isa. liii.) to the suffering Jesus shows the reaction of the primitive Church to this spiritual element. Even the crucifixion as it stood must have had a tremendous emotional effect upon those who loved and revered Jesus, even if it were a stumbling-block to their dim apprehension. The enlightened understanding which came through the resurrection no longer inhibited the subconscious apprehensions of Jesus' significance ; these broke forth and contributed their influence to the growing spiritual perceptions which henceforth were increasingly to find their place in the believers' understanding of Jesus.

Further, the exaltation of Jesus opened up the God-ward significance of Him whom the disciples had known and experienced as Jesus of Nazareth. No one could be conceived to be at the right hand of God's transcendent presence without reflecting that ineffability and spiritual majesty. As a spiritual being Jesus partook of the exalted divine presence, having attained such a status through spiritual qualities evolved through suffering, sacrifice, and obedience to the divine will. The intensely spiritual way in which the Jews conceived God led the believers to postulate a spiritual character similar to the exalted Jesus. Literal expectations still held the field ; at any moment the believers looked for His " sensuous " return to the world. Yet even already there were dynamic spiritual elements present as these emerged to reveal the spiritual character of Jesus ; these were to receive a new emphasis in due course.

This new emphasis emerged with its vital influence as Jesus began to be experienced in His nearness to the believers. Though conceived to be at the right hand of God, He was increasingly felt to be near in His spiritual presence. We are able to discern several hints of the reality and influence of this experiential discovery.

There was, first, the organic connection between Jesus and the eye-witnesses. Such intimate contact cannot be regarded as having ceased when He was conceived to have ascended to heaven. The awareness of His presence with the believers did not evaporate with the Ascension. Even as they were aware of His exaltation, the impelling power of His personality was still in their lives. The mood of personal joyous devotion to Jesus still continued and grew from strength to strength as they remembered His words and ways, His suffering and death, and recounted all these facts to one' another. Jesus was indeed at the very centre of their fellowship.

Further, the sense of personal nearness to Jesus was reinforced in the baptismal experience, which the personal surrender to Jesus, the submission to His influence, and the faith and expectation of salvation evoked. He who underwent baptism became aware that he belonged to Jesus ; the one who administered the rite was aware of being Jesus' deputy as he received the new convert " into the name of the Lord Jesus." Nay, it seemed as if Jesus Himself were actually administering the baptism, and receiving Himself the new devotee into His community of redemption. The celebrations of the Last Supper had Jesus at the centre of the faith therein expressed. This observance was so intimately associated with the personal Jesus that it was not difficult for the eye-witnesses to feel that He was in their midst once more, breaking the bread or dispensing the *Kiddûsh* cup. The cup was His own pledge of the Messianic banquet at which He was soon to sit down with them ; the bread pointed to His death as the prelude to that banquet. Nay, it was as if they were already sitting down with Him in His triumphant return. In very truth Jesus seemed to be in the midst as the believers celebrated the Supper and awaited His footfall on the threshold of the room wherein they were gathered together.

Once more, the awareness of Jesus' nearness and presence with His disciples was encouraged by their experience of the Spirit. The coming of the Spirit was definitely connected with Jesus, who had bestowed the gift upon them (Acts ii. 33). All that Jesus was, in life, in death, in resurrection triumph, in Messianic exaltation, was viewed as the inspiration of the Spirit. In turn, as the Spirit inspired the speech, the healings, the visions, and the varied expression of the primitive community, Jesus would be called vividly to mind. The Spirit was the " earnest " of the presence of Jesus in the midst of the community as well as the pledge of the final consummation of the divine Kingdom.

Perhaps the most potent of the influences which mediated the awareness that Jesus was in the midst of the primitive community lay in His very exaltation at the right hand of God. It was not a matter of being placed in a high position in the heavenly hierarchy ; Jesus was in the place of honour by the side of God. The multiplication of intermediary beings in pre-Christian Judaism seemed to make God very remote from human life, yet the simple faith and piety of the devout made it possible for them to feel that the transcendent God was indeed very near to those who trusted Him. If it were true that no one could look on God's face and live (Ex. xxxiii. 20), or if the remote Deity of the temple cultus permitted the high priest to enter into the ineffable presence only once a year (Ex. xxx. 10), it was also true that there was no escape from His immediate presence (Ps. cxxxix. 7 ff.). If God had His abode in the high and lofty place where no man could enter, it was equally true that He dwelt also in the humble and contrite heart (Isa. lvii. 15). In profound awe Israel regarded it as blasphemy to pronounce the name of God, yet the inner apprehension of the divine presence was the corollary to a faith at once intensely spiritual in its awareness of intimate communion with God Himself, even as it placed Him so far away. The devout worshipper went to the synagogue or temple to

seek God, and moreover, to find Him. Now in so far
as the primitive Church became conscious of the exalted
dignity of Jesus, the believers viewed Him in ineffable
distance, in aloof grandeur at the right hand of the
divine majesty. Yet this very exaltation carried with
it the idea that Jesus was not limited in His approach
to them, nor was their approach to Him restricted.
The characteristic ways of God with His people soon
began to be ascribed to the exalted Jesus. Peter himself
transfers the typically divine quality of grace to Jesus
(Acts xv. 11). Remote as He was, the disciples could
not escape from His immediate presence ; dwelling with
God, He yet abode in their hearts and in the community.

Finally, the transition of the awareness that Jesus
was the exalted Messiah to the consciousness of Him
as present in the midst of the believers was influenced
by the parallel movements in the experience of the
Kingdom and of salvation therein. The Kingdom,
although strictly future, came to be experienced as an
object of present possession as the literal apocalyptic
hope of its consummation faded, the final consummation
being transmuted into expectation of eternal life in the
Kingdom not of this world. Corresponding to this
experiential modification, there was a similar development in the experience of salvation which at first was
primarily eschatological in character. This experience,
in turn, was transmuted into a salvation already
possessed with its ultimate expression in the glory of
eternal life. In the same way the experience which
believers had of Jesus underwent development, since
the Jesus who was the exalted Messiah came to be
experienced as the centre of the Kingdom and of salvation as already in the possession of the believers. The
exalted Jesus came to be the Jesus vividly present in
the " Lo ! I am with you always ! " (Matt. xxviii. 20).

As the apocalyptic hope of His return faded, it was only to give way to the wondrous awareness that Jesus was with His people, that He had been with them from the beginning and had never really left them. The consummation of their experience of Jesus was transmuted from an expectation of Messiah's literal advent into the hope of complete union with Him in the eternal life of the eternal Kingdom not of this world. In this way the eschatological Messiah in exaltation came to be for the believers the Christ of their religious experience, the Messiah who was near to them, the Christ who was in the midst whenever they were gathered together.

It is not suggested that the primitive Church reached out fully to these experiential discoveries, but the religious processes that were to issue at last in the perception of these vital truths were already operative in the religious experience of the primitive Church. Already there was being laid the empirical foundation whereon the later awareness of the mystic being-in-Christ of Paul and of the Fourth Gospel was to rest.

The consciousness of the presence of Jesus also seemed to be a specific quality of a more general sense of the presence of God. What the believers knew of Jesus made them aware of divine activity being present in a vivid and powerful way as it spiritually energized them. The experience of God that went along with apocalyptic expectation was one of the Deity afar off, but who would be ultimately powerful here and now, when the day of the Lord should come. But in so far as what the believers discovered in Jesus, as the object of present religious experience, gave them an experience of God powerful and triumphant in present life, such awareness of present divine energy helped to take the force out of apocalyptic expectation, and with it the hope in the eschatological Christ as the Messiah of apocalyptic consummation. Just so far as the believers experienced the power of God through Jesus, the Christ of present experience came to be the significant fact of their religious life.

We have finally to interpret the minds of the primitive Church believers as to the divine or semi-divine honours their experience of Jesus led them to ascribe to Him, together with the reaction of such ascription upon their own faith and religious experience. Once the identification of Jesus with the exalted Messiah was made, it was inevitable that the categories in which the Jewish mind conceived Messiah's personality and office were applied to Jesus. This does not mean that Jesus was merged into the figure of the suprahuman Messiah, for He had lived among men as Jesus of Nazareth, personally known to the eye-witnesses. Current Messianic expectation, of course, implied the heavenly majesty of Messiah in some of its forms. But a different circle of religious experience is involved in the unique apprehension of a Messiah who had been intimately known as a man, who had given rise to a series of impressions and experiences by the sheer force of His uniqueness and commanding goodness, which were such as to influence the eye-witnesses to apply to Him the highest category save that of actual Deity, and later, to make the tremendous inference that He was exalted to the right hand of God. Thus there would be encouragement to apply to Jesus in exaltation the categories relevant to the suprahuman Messiah, the highest thought-forms available to express the dignity of Jesus as the believers had discovered it in their own experience of Him.

Jesus is the Messiah, the Anointed one, divinely appointed (Acts ii. 36, iv. 27). Even among the Gentile communities the idea of divine appointment in His heavenly status still remained in the use of the title, " Christ," even if the original Messianic significance of the designation was lost.[1] Jesus the Messiah is further known as the " Righteous " one (Acts iii. 14, vii. 52, xxii. 14), the " Elect " one (cf. Luke ix. 35, xxiii. 35),[2] referring to Jesus as chosen by God for Messianic dignity and office, and as the " Son of Man " (Acts vii. 56). If these Messianic ascriptions were affixed to Jesus the probability is that many others were also applied. Of these we may note that Jesus the Messiah is the Judge of the world. He is regarded as the Judge of the quick and the dead (Acts x. 42 ; 1 Pet. iv. 5). According to the gospel tradition, Jesus had appointed the twelve disciples to the office of judging the twelve tribes of Israel, when as the Son of Man He would sit on the throne of His glory, *i.e.* in His capacity as the Messianic Judge (Matt. xix. 28 ; cf. Luke xxii. 30). In the outlook of the primitive Church the function of Jesus as Judge is much emphasized. Peter's speech at Pentecost expounds the theme of impending judgment (Acts ii. 34 f., 38–40). Indeed, it may be that we have here an illustration of the influence of primitive Church reflection upon the growing tradition, and that the presentation of Jesus as Judge is due not to Jesus Himself, but to the application to His person and office of the functions of Messiah as coming to judgment.

[1] " The term Christ, when used alone, is always used distinctly as a Jewish title." " The term Christ, whether used alone or in combination with Jesus, never occurs except in relation to a Jewish environment " (C. Ryder Smith, *Expos. Ti.*, 1907–8, pp. 45 f.). ". . . Change of thought and language came when Christianity passed from Jewish to Gentile life : Jesus came to be interpreted metaphysically rather than historically, so that His self-chosen title was reduced to a surname, and Jesus the Christ became Jesus Christ " (A. T. Cadoux, *op. cit.* p. 158).

[2] Though there is no direct reference to this in Acts, the Lucan references may be a reading back of Messianic titles as applied to Jesus by the primitive Church.

The references of Jesus to judgment are strikingly absent in Mark. His censure on the scribes who are to receive the greater condemnation (xii. 40) is a moral rather than an eschatological judgment, while Jesus has no thought of Himself as the Judge. The Marcan references to " Gehenna " are no more than conventional, and Gehenna plays little part in apocalyptic judgment, being (a) a place of corporal and spiritual punishment in the presence of the righteous (En. xxvii. 2 f., xc. 26 f. ; Ass. Mos. x. 10), or (b) a place of spiritual punishment only (En. xcviii. 3). The " little apocalypse " of Mark (xiii.) has no hint of Jesus as Judge, and apart from the reference to the gathering in of the elect, there is nothing in it that can be construed as judgment (xiii. 27).

On the other hand, both Matthew and Luke emphasize the judgment function of Jesus. Their additions to Mark's account of the Baptist's preaching are eloquent of this ; John's hearers are " a generation of vipers " ironically referred to as fleeing the coming wrath ; not even the sonship of Abraham is any guarantee of salvation, for even now the axe is laid at the root of the tree (Matt. iii. 7–10 ; Luke iii. 7–9) ; further, the coming Messiah is the judge whose fan is in His hand to purge thoroughly the threshing-floor, gathering the wheat into the garner, and burning the chaff in the fire that cannot be quenched (Matt. iii. 12 = Luke iii. 17). Again, the eschatological judgment is seen in the references to the only sign an evil generation shall receive (Matt. xii. 38 f. = Luke xi. 16, 29–32), to the " woes " pronounced over Chorazin and Bethsaida for their failure to repent in view of the coming crisis of the Kingdom (Matt. xi. 21–23 = Luke x. 13–15), or the judgment on the careless slave who fails to await the return of his lord, implying judgment on the heedless generation when Messiah comes un-expectedly to judgment (Matt. xxiv. 43–51 ; Luke xii.

39 f., 42–46). Many will find themselves unexpectedly left outside at the Messianic judgment, when there will be wailing and gnashing of teeth (Matt. viii. 11 f. =Luke xiii. 28 f.), while dire doom awaits the infidelity of the holy city (Matt. xxiii. 37–39 =Luke xiii. 34 f.).

It is remarkable that these eschatological pictures of judgment are absent from Mark. Their cumulative effect is to present us with the Jesus coming to eschatological judgment along conventional lines. They are taken mainly from *Q*, and the sayings of Jesus were recollected in a vivid atmosphere of apocalyptic expectation such as characterized the primitive Church. There is thus a strong possibility that the words of Jesus, as they were gathered up into the gospel tradition, were given an emphatic " judgment " tone in the eschatological sense, in a way they were never originally intended to have. This does not mean that Jesus never referred to issues of judgment, but any such for Him were concerned with the specifically moral and spiritual aspects of conduct and life. There are inner moral elements in apocalyptic judgment, but these are somewhat obscured by the picture series within which they are enclosed. But it is less with the eschatological judgment and more with moral and spiritual issues that Jesus is concerned.

Again, Jesus the Messiah was the Revealer of all things, especially as touching the hidden worlds of righteousness and sin (cf. En. xlvi. 3, xlix. 2, 4). The eye-witnesses recollected that Jesus had warned them that there was nothing hidden that should not be revealed, nothing secret that should not be exposed (Mark iv. 22). In Mark the reference is to the revealing of truth concealed by parables ; so also in Luke (viii. 17) ; but elsewhere in Luke the idea is to the exposing of a man's real nature concealed by hypocrisy (xii. 2). In Matthew (x. 26) the meaning is that the disciples sent out by Jesus are to be the revealers of the great things which in turn Jesus had revealed to them. The religious experience implied in the parables centres round the function of Jesus as the Revealer of the invisible worlds of righteousness and sin, inasmuch as these portray the significant facts of the divine purpose as revealing the divine will, as determinative of the truth of the Kingdom of God. The world of righteousness was the awaited Kingdom where righteousness would prevail, and the righteous be revealed ; the world of sin would emerge from its hiding-place with the Messianic summons to judgment, and the wheat and tares would at last be sorted out (Matt. xiii. 24–30).

Further, Jesus the Messiah was regarded as the quickener of the dead (cf. En. li. 1, lxi. 5). The prevailing idea of resurrection for the primitive Church was that all dead Israelites were to arise,[1] and once more the respective worlds of righteousness and evil are to be revealed, with blessing for the righteous and retribution for evil-doers. Such revealing included the dead at the resurrection, as well as those who were alive at Messiah's advent. Those of the primitive community who had died before the coming of the Kingdom would be raised up.[2]

Again, Jesus the Messiah was looked on as the Vindicator of the righteous, another typical function of Messiah.[3] The righteous are those who are to be saved, and indeed are already being saved by anticipation, to the Kingdom of God. In none other than Jesus the Messiah was salvation to be hoped for (Acts iv. 12) ; He was the Vindicator of His people in the Messianic com-

---

[1] Dan. xii. 2 ; En. i.–xxxvi. (except xxii. 13), xxxvii.–lxx., lxxiii.–xc. ; 2 Macc. vii. 9.

[2] Cf. 1 Cor. xv. 23 ff. ; 1 Thess. iv. 16 ; 2 Thess. ii. 1, reflecting primitive Church ideas.

[3] Cf. En. xxxix. 7, xlviii. 4, 7, li. 5, liii. 6, lxii. 7 f., 14 f.

munity, as He upholds, champions, and rewards their fidelity.

Finally, Jesus the Messiah was invested with pre-existence, an idea derived from apocalyptic. The relevant passages are worth quoting in view of the tendency to account for Jesus' pre-existence from Greek sources. The Book of Enoch refers to the Messiah as pre-existent in three distinctive passages :

" Yea, before the sun and the signs were created,
Before the stars of the heaven were made,
His name was named before the Lords of Spirits " (xlviii. 3).

" And for this reason hath he been chosen and hidden before Him,
Before the creation of the world and for evermore " (xlviii. 6).

" For from the beginning the Son of Man was hidden,
And the Most High preserved Him in the presence of His might,
And revealed him to the elect " (lxii. 7). [1]

The Jesus whom the disciples had known on earth, now exalted to God's right hand, was now regarded as the pre-existent heavenly being familiar to their minds from apocalyptic thought. Paul had yet to make clearer what was involved in such a significant ascription to the person of Jesus, but there is no need to go to the thought of the Græco-Roman world with its ideas of deification to account for such a conception as applied to Jesus. The Jewish environment of the primitive Church provided within itself the needful categories and circle of ideas which made it inevitable that, once Jesus was recognized as the exalted Messiah, the concept of pre-existence would be applied to His person by the primitive Church.

We may now consider the Christ-consciousness of the community which led the believers to designate Jesus as " Lord," the name which became " the common

[1] For translation, see *A. and P.* ii. pp. 216, 228.

appellation of Jesus Christ among His followers." [1] The name was evidently applied at a very early stage (Acts ii. 36, iv. 33 ; cf. Luke xxiv. 34). The Septuagint renders *Yahweh* by " the Lord " (*ho Kurios*), and therefore Greek-speaking Jews who became Christians were hardly likely to transfer the title to Jesus. The strong monotheistic character of their faith would discourage this as an infringement of the sovereign majesty of Yahweh. The ascription must therefore have been made either by Gentile Christians whose monotheism was not so strongly developed, or else Aramaic-speaking Palestinian Jews unfamiliar with the Septuagint began the usage through applying an Aramaic word of dignity to Jesus which did not infringe the divine status of God. The preservation of such a word, " Marana tha," points to the very early ascription of " Lord " to Jesus in the primitive Aramaic-speaking community. It appears in its Græcised form in an epistle of Paul (1 Cor. xvi. 22), and is indicative of the primitive Church usage accepted by the apostle. The *Didache* also has the word (x. 6) in reference to Christ, and thus reveals a primitive Church strain. Therefore the name " Lord " was applied to Jesus at least as early as when the gospel tradition was being put together in its original Aramaic.

The credit for the designation of Jesus as Lord has been given to the Gentile Christians. In the Græco-Roman world *Kurios* was commonly used to indicate respect in addressing a person, not unlike our use of the word " sir," or the complimentary " Mr." Such a usage had its roots in the habit of a person able to command other persons of inferior status such as slaves, *Kurios* being the correlate of *doulos*. The Roman Emperor could receive the exalted designation, *Dominus et Deus*. The devotees of Attis, Osiris, and the like

[1] C. Anderson Scott, *The Fellowship of the Spirit*, p. 58.

designated the mythical hero of his cultus as " Lord." [1]
The supernatural reference of the term is merely
secondary, and Gentile Christians may quite naturally
have applied it to Jesus without divine implications.
It may have been used by them simply to designate
His distinctive position with no thought of placing Him
as God or among the gods.[2] At the same time, the
objects of adoration, the " Lords," are worshipped as if
there were supernatural significance about them, especially in the religious cultus divinities characterized by
Paul as the " lords many " (1 Cor. viii. 5). To such
the name " Lord " was ascribed in adoration, and as
the experience of redemption was central to the devotees
of these cults, the deified hero concerned was thought
of as the redeemer who offered the desired salvation.

There are striking likenesses here to the Christian
attitude to redemption centred in Jesus the " Lord "
who brought salvation to those who believed, *i.e.* to
his devotees. It is therefore not surprising that the
analogies have misled much modern thought into the
supposition that the new faith central in Jesus Christ
adopted one of the names, namely, " Lord," from the
older prevailing mystery cults.[3] Bousset, for example,
thinks that the term came in through the Hellenist-
Christian community of Antioch and elsewhere, reflecting
in idea Jesus the God-man or deified-man of the Hellenistic world of religious experience.[4] But the theory

[1] Cf. " to Epimachus his father and lord " (BGU. 423), " in the
seventh year of Tiberius Claudius Cæsar the Lord " (P. Oxy. 37),
" at the table of the Lord Serapis " (P. Oxy. 523).

[2] We know to-day what " the Lord " means in divine significance, but
this leads no one to mistake the House of Lords for a divine pantheon.

[3] Cf. Deissmann, *Light from the Ancient East*, p. 349, *BC.*, ed. FJ.
and L., vol. i. pp. 410 ff.

[4] *Kurios Christos*, 1913, pp. 111 ff. For a penetrating criticism o
Bousset's standpoint, cf. A. E. J. Rawlinson, *The New Testament
Doctrine of the Christ*, 1926, pp. 92 f., 231 f.

comes to grief on the simple fact that the primitive Church had no need to go to the religious cults of the ancient world for a title significant of supernatural dignity and status. Within the Jewish religious consciousness the earliest believers had pregnant suggestions and categories of exaltation which enabled them to give fitting expression to the Messianic dignity and exalted status of Jesus at the right hand of God, without having to borrow their lofty categories from the table of Serapis. The primitive Church had already to hand in its *milieu* of Messiahship the thought-processes to lead it to designate the dignity of Jesus as deepening insight called forth such designation, and their ideas had the advantage of being native to the soil in which the primitive Church took root.

The probability is that Jesus was regarded as " Lord " as the natural result of His exalted dignity as Messiah, for this carried with it associations of sovereignty not necessarily infringing on the strict monotheism of divine majesty. A. E. J. Rawlinson reminds us that we must look for the earliest ideas of Christ entertained by the primitive community in *Q*, and in the speeches of the earliest chapters in Acts.[1] The word *Kurios* is used some sixteen times in Harnack's reconstruction of *Q*, and of these only three fall to be considered in so far as they may refer to Jesus. (1) Jesus uses a quotation from Deut. vi. 16 to rebut the voice of temptation, but it is not necessary even to contemplate that by " tempt the Lord thy God " Jesus is referring to Himself (Matt. iv. 7 = Luke iv. 12). (2) Jesus once said " not every one that says unto me, Lord, Lord, shall enter into the Kingdom of Heaven " (Matt. vii. 21). With this the saying in Luke should be compared, " Why call ye me Lord, Lord, and do not the things which I say ? "

[1] In *Foundations*, ed. B. H. Streeter, 1913, p. 152.

(vi. 46). Jesus probably used of Himself some honorific title of address where the gospel has the Greek equivalent *Kurios* ; whatever the Aramaic word was [1] it probably indicated the kind of supremacy that called for obedience. Therefore the address, " Lord, Lord," would not be more than a slightly heightened translation of the Aramaic designation. (3) The " Blessed is he that cometh in the name of the Lord " (Matt. xxiii. 39— Luke xiii. 35) is a scriptural quotation (Ps. cxviii. 26) as Jesus refers to His coming in the name of the Lord, *i.e.* God.

As the earliest deposit of the gospel tradition indicates, the use of " Lord " implied at first no more than an honorific title which was probably heightened in the translation into Greek. As soon, however, as Jesus had entered into His state of exalted majesty, " Lord " came to be an acknowledgment of his sovereignty. In making such an affirmation the primitive Church indicated its personal connection with the Messianic sovereign. It was His community by His own right and possession ; He claimed the obedience and entire submission of the believers, and they on their part claimed through Him citizenship of the redeemed in the divine Kingdom. When the new convert had pronounced over him the name " Lord," and confessed, " Jesus is Lord," it signified for him that in being received into the Messianic community he had brought himself under the requirements of submission and obedience to Him to whom the community belonged.

The primitive Church was intensely Christ-conscious. The believers were organically connected through personal contact with Jesus in earthly life, but they

---

[1] Dalman gives *Māri, op. cit.* pp. 324, 328 ; cf. the original word in Dan. ii. 47, iv. 16.

passed into fellowship with the Christ of exaltation. They ascribed to Him the well-known Messianic categories ; they enhanced in their experience of Him their awareness of His heavenly dignity. At the same time they became vitally conscious of His near presence in their midst. Expecting His return at any time, they yet felt His quickening presence close to their hearts. " At the centre of their present joy and expectancy was the thought of Messiah Himself. Marana tha, ' Our Lord, come,' was their keynote ; and as they dwelt on it, their hearts burned within them, fellowship rose to ecstasy, and His presence became so spiritually real, that His returning footsteps often seemed at the very door. The thrill of such hours is felt in the ejaculatory petitions of the *Didache* : ' Let grace come and let this world pass away. Hosanna to the God of David . . . Marana tha.' " [1]

[1] Bartlet and Carlyle, *Christianity in History*, p. 49.

CHAPTER XII

The Conclusion of the Matter

WE have endeavoured to approach the origins of the Christian Church by the empirical method. We might have considered our subject by theological analysis or synthesis of ideas and principles, and, as detached observers, have watched the play and interplay of these religious ideas without reference to the religious experience from which they were evolved. Such an approach would be analogous to that of the "behavourist" who studies the animal or the human being regardless of the inner psychological activity or life experience of the observed subject in conscious or subconscious mental activity. The result would have been to erect an artificial structure of abstractions and concepts, interesting enough to the pursuit and love of analysis, and acquiring strange shapes in any attempted synthesis. If we combine such an approach with the historical method, we obtain a detached, analytic expression of the origins of the Church, but entirely shorn of the "living" element which in the first place made possible Christian history and Christian theology.

A recent illustration of the abstract, analytical approach is afforded by the volumes on *The Beginnings of Christianity* which F. J. Foakes Jackson and Kirsopp Lake have edited.[1] No one would suspect from these thorough researches that there had been any vital

[1] Five volumes, one of which deals with the text of Acts, issued at intervals between 1920–1933, and referred to now and then in our investigation.

phenomenon such as religious experience in the formation of the Church, any more than we could glean from J. B. Watson's Behavourism [1] that man had any mind to be psychologically observed, or from Leuba's study of religion [2] that man, the unit which reveals religious experience, had anything to be religious with.[3] The Behaviourist studies mind by eliminating it; Foakes Jackson and Lake with their learned collaborators have studied Church beginnings by eliminating the vital experiential elements which began what came to be the Christian Church. Their standpoint is that Christianity " appears not a single religion but a complex of many, justified in claiming the name of Christianity by reason of the thread of historic continuity which runs through and connects its component parts. . . . For, like all religions when studied critically, Christianity is a process, not a result." [4] What physiological processes are to the Behaviourists as accounting for the exhibition of phenomena that can strictly be called psychological, so historical processes seem to be for the analytical historian the organic reasons for the display of the religious phenomena which he classifies under the one heading " Christianity."

What is it, however, which gives the start to the historical processes viewed as " Christianity ? " The answer of our discussion is the religious experience of the primitive Church. Here are the ultimate data for the historian or the theologian. If it be objected by the Church historian that he is concerned only with the historical processes at work, we reply that empirical or psychological facts show themselves within the time

[1] *Behaviour*, 1914, *Psychology from the Standpoint of a Behaviourist*, 1919.
[2] *A Psychological Study of Religion*, 1912.
[3] *God or Man*, 1934.
[4] *Op. cit.* vol. i. p. 265.

process. As components in the life of those who experienced the facts, they come within the purview of historical investigation. The neglect of such data causes historical analysis to evaporate the quickening religious facts which in the first instance produced the phenomena and the processes which historical investigation analyses.

If investigation of religious experience goes along with the historical data, we are then saved from inadequate judgments of the beginnings of Christianity such as " a synthesis between Judaism and the Græco-Oriental thought of the Empire." [1] Our investigation has called attention to the religious experience creative of the Christian Church, an experience rooted in the living Jesus who walked on earth, and with whom men came into vital, quickening contact. Why should the Christian Church take its rise around Jesus of Nazareth ? Why did not the Judaism associated with the teaching of John the Baptist as it found its way into Asia Minor (Acts xix. 1–4) where it had its opportunity of reaching a synthesis with Græco-Oriental thought, create such a synthesis as Christianity is supposed to be ? We have, moreover, the fusion of Jewish and Græco-Oriental thought in the philosophy of Philo, whose full knowledge of both sides encouraged him to formulate a synthesis which would claim the allegiance of Jew and Greek, and the noble effort failed. A new philosophy was the result, but no new religion was forthcoming. For all synthetic attempts based on intellectual concepts fail to create religious life. The modern historico-critical method reduces Christianity in its beginnings to a series of ideas sifted out by all the finesse of analysis ; it thereupon discovers by the same analytical processes, many analogous ideas in the wider Græco-Oriental world of

[1] *BC.*, ed. FJ. and L., vol. i. p. 266.

thought and practice ; these parallels are finally synthesized into an amalgam of intellectual concepts which is designated Christianity. Thus the Christian religion is emptied of the very distinctiveness which caused its actual emergence, namely, the power of religious experience inspired by the creative contacts made with the personality of Jesus.

The empirical method we have pursued provides therefore a much-needed corrective to so partial an interpretation of Christian beginnings. To return to Philo who, on the historico-critical principles ought *a priori* to have been the founder of a new religion, we find that an ancient world philosophical synthesis grew out of his teaching, but no religious movement. A new religion emerged around the name of Jesus of Nazareth who inspired the birth of a new community creatively vitalized by religious experience centring in Jesus. Both Philo and Jesus had disciples, but those of Jesus took fire and went forth to preach an experienced gospel received by personal contact with Him.

We may follow the course of the river quite easily in its lower reaches where the stream has become broad and deep, but the story of that river is not told by these expansive aspects, nor by the widening estuary. The upper reaches have to be explored, hidden springs discovered, tiny rivulets followed from their sources, until they join the main stream which pursues its winding way to become a wide and deep stretch of water on which the vessels of all nations may ply to and fro carrying within their hulls the treasures of the earth. It is uncertain and hazardous work to get among the springs in the mountain fastnesses and remoteness, but these are the explanation of the mighty river when viewed from the standpoint of origins.

In terms of religious poetry the Christian Church as a product of religious experience has its springs high among the eternal hills.   Passing from the symbolism of the springs at which we find Jesus Christ and His creative influence to the field of historical reality we discover that " into the stream of passing generations there entered . . . there was seen for about thirty years, Someone who has been ever since the great problem. He was not among those who, while they were here, wrote down words which men may still read.   He wrote nothing.   All we know of what He was, of what He said, is from the memories of His friends.   But what was written in those memories was of such a sort that the world has never since been able to escape from the personal force which grasped it through that reflection." [1] This is why we investigated the various impressions which Jesus made upon those who saw and heard, for it was from those impressions and contacts that the religious experience arose which gave birth to the Christian Church.

We have now to consider the intrinsic worth of the religious experience of the primitive Church.   What was set in motion so long ago still continues among the peoples of the earth.   If salvation is possible to-day in the name of Christ as it was in the primitive Church, there is obviously something of intrinsic value in the experience of a gospel so far-reaching in time and in extent.

The religious experience enshrined in the Old Testament had already tested the ways of God with men. The essence of the divine rule was the revelation of a purpose at once gracious and morally holy.   His power and majesty induce the reaction of awe and wonder in

[1] Edwyn Bevan, *Hellenism and Christianity*, 1921, p. 63.

men, yet He is not aloof from men, but graciously draws them to Him in faith and love.   The moral emphasis worked into Israel's faith by the prophets did not hesitate to set forth suffering as having its potent place within the divine ways with men, whether the suffering be viewed as merited for sin, or as a purifying discipline for the refining of holy character, or in the service of disinterested faith irrespective of prosperity or adversity, or finally as sacrifice, an offering of life for the blessing of many.

These discoveries and affirmations of the best religious experience of Israel passed forthwith into the outlook of the primitive Church, but with all the wealth of added discovery and affirmation bequeathed to the believers through the personality of Jesus. Jesus liberated what in Judaism were limitations and lower associations. The God who was conceived as being inexpressible by images, yet could be localized in the Holy of Holies, was set forth by Jesus to be unconfined to any special place. Through Jesus this liberating of God's accessibility passed finally into the primitive Church. The Jewish limiting of God's gracious contact to one chosen race was doomed to disappear in the creative issue that salvation was for all men. The primitive Church embraced this truth but unwillingly, but the barriers were broken down as the Gentile Churches came into being. Jesus further gave the spiritual death-blow to the limiting view of God which regarded Him as requiring ritual obedience equally with moral, as when circumcision, for instance, is thought to be as necessary to salvation as living a holy life. The ethical emphasis passed into the primitive Church through the apostles' teaching on the new " Way."

The apocalyptic *milieu* in which the new experience was cradled was inevitable in view of the religious environment. But a series of factors tended to relegate eschatological literalism to a secondary place. As the apocalyptic forms and categories, literally conceived, began to fade, the Church, far from fading away with them, became increasingly aware of the greater spiritual truths inherent in these forms. The fading of the temporary and the accidental revealed the inner spiritual and moral glory especially as reinforced by the personality of Jesus.

The later Church doctrine that Jesus died on the cross for the sins of men had its experiential roots in the actual crucifixion and its significance in revealing Jesus suffering and dying that blessing might redound for the many in the coming of the divine Kingdom. The self-surrender to God's will was in its essence an offering for others, a personal sacrifice in death that the way to the Kingdom might be opened up. The sacrifice, of course, is not to be construed as propitiation in the sense that Israel's sin-offerings were viewed as propitiatory to Yahweh. It is the positive oblation which results in redeeming men to the Kingdom. The intrinsic worth of the primitive Church experience here is that it has seized on this fundamental experiential fact in the death of Jesus and bequeathed it to the Church of later ages to develop and interpret it further. Thus the primitive Church laid the foundations for the evangelic experience which future years were to apprehend more fully in the light of deepening insight and knowledge.

The vision of the Kingdom of God was another permanent feature of the new religious experience. The believers were intensely aware of themselves as the community of the Kingdom ; indeed, the community cannot be explained apart from the vision of the Kingdom which reacted on men and formed them into a Messianic fellowship waiting to welcome their exalted Messiah on

His advent. With the decay of the eschatological hope, the Kingdom came to be realized as a present moral and spiritual experience. The Messianic community thus passed over into the Church enjoying the present experience of the Kingdom, of salvation, in the world here and now.

Perhaps the most significant illustration of the intrinsic worth of the primitive Church religious experience lay in its intense consciousness of Christ. Thereby the believers preserved the personal associations that had gathered around Jesus, or at least prevented the transformation of the Jesus of history into a Christ-cult of the Græco-Roman world. If the intrinsic personal connection had been severed, or the original impressions and experiences the eye-witnesses had of Him had been allowed to disappear, the Christian faith might well have degenerated into some mystic cult, and have suffered the eclipse of the cults of the ancient world generally. For these did not last. We know of them only through scattered allusions in ancient literature. But the faith centred in Jesus has lived on through the centuries. The primitive Church, gathering from the enlarging store of profound memories quickened by the new experience in the risen Christ and the Spirit, evolved from its religious experience the evangelic tradition. The unceasing discoveries and affirmations made by the believers aided their appreciation of the various sayings and doings of Jesus as these were put together, and enabled them to sort out the worthiest and the highest, to reject the needless and the unimportant, to reduce unwittingly the legendary to a minimum. For the primitive Church was too near the historic Jesus for legend to have much place in its tradition. Thus out of its Christ-consciousness the primitive Church transferred to the Church of the ages the essential groundwork of the evangelic tradition about Jesus and made possible the growth of the gospels as we have them to-day.

The primitive Church experience was the foundation on which Paul laid his own thought structure. The Church of his age which he so powerfully influenced and built up is organically related to what went before in the primitive Church. Much of what seems to be the original creative activity of Paul is seen to have its roots in what preceded him. When the primitive Church is investigated in its own right and authority, instead of being regarded as a stepping-stone to the Pauline Church, we discover that it is in itself the reason for what follows.

The psychological evaluation of the religious experience of the primitive Church raises several points which bear on the intrinsic worth of that experience.

First, there are the psychologically abnormal elements. These belong to the thought-forms with which the new experience was clothed, and their presence as such is no criterion as to the value of the experience they express. The visionary elements, for instance, belong to the psychology involved, they are raised to the nth degree by the extraordinary stimulus of unique religious exaltation, but the vital religious realities concerned are another matter. We are still left with the causal religious experience which in the first instance gave rise to the abnormal psychology, and the phenomena associated with it. Once more we have to allow for the influence of the apocalyptic inheritance with its wealth of visionary and abnormal elements, its dreams, its trances, its ecstasy, and its vivid pictorial symbolism which provided the *milieu* through which a genuine way of attaining to truth was provided. Further, it is to go beyond the authority of the empirical facts to dismiss the abnormal elements as no more than phenomena to be pathologically accounted for.   Such a conclusion overlooks the religious inheritance and psychology of the believers, and misses the significance of the overwhelming religious energy which had flooded their lives.   It also fails to appreciate the fact that while pathologically conditioned abnormalities produce disintegration of personality, the abnormal experience of the primitive Church believers resulted in the integration of personality.   Even if pathological elements are discernible, they cannot afford any criteria as to the ultimate value of the religious experience which threw up the abnormal phenomena concerned.

Whenever a great religious upheaval occurs there is an abundance of psychical and even physical marvels. Human experience of divine reality as found in the primitive Church was psychologically conditioned by the characteristic racial and religious outlook native to those who received the experience.   The approaches of divine reality would of necessity be through the native ideas, thought-forms, conceptions, and mental categories given to the recipients by their Jewish religious inheritance and environment, and would be apprehended in a manner quite natural to people who unlike more recent generations made no sharp distinction between " natural " and " supernatural," " physical " and " spiritual," " physical " and psychical," " psychical " and " spiritual." Within the psycho-physical manifestations lies the tremendous experience of the spiritual dynamic which Jesus the Christ had mediated of divine reality, and which brought the Church into being.   The abnormal elements are therefore not the significant data in the new experience. The emergence of the primitive Church from a creative religious experience clad often in such elements is the phenomenon of intrinsic worth.

The second point raised by psychological evaluation
is that the religious experience in its inner validity
and truth, the *Ding an sich*, needs to be differentiated
from the thought-forms in which it finds expression or
through which it is interpreted by those who have the
experience. For instance, the eschatological categories
and thought-forms lost their meaning as the Christian
generations succeeded one another. The literal Messiah
exalted at God's right hand, His expected literal descent
in all the panoply of heavenly might, the demons, the
angels and archangels, etc., are all couched in thought-
forms which have long ceased to be permanently intelligible or useful. But their religious and moral content,
enriched by experience of Jesus the Christ, is the abiding
contribution of the primitive Church, handed down to
successive generations. Or again, the thought-forms in
which the Pentecost experience of the Spirit was received,
the windlike noise, the tongues as of fire, the ecstatic
speech, need to be distinguished from the vital religious
content of the experience of the Spirit in the new life
that had come upon the believers. The permanent
element is the inner religious reality which led men to
live a new life hitherto undreamt of ; this life centred
in Jesus the Christ ; the new life had brought its
recipients together in His name into a union with Him
and with themselves, and had fashioned them into the
Church which is His body.

Third, from the standpoint of individual psychology
the religious experience of the primitive Church began
and continued within " the feelings, acts, and experiences
of individual men," [1] moved by the impact of Jesus upon
individual lives, making His impressions and contacts,
and claiming the fullest allegiance. For each convert
there was that personal quickening within the conscious

[1] W. James, *op. cit.* p. 31.

life which made him aware of the power of Jesus. At
the same time we are confronted at the outset with a
growing group experience, a collective religious consciousness of a community relationship to Christ and the
imminent Kingdom. There was the organic union with
Israel as the chosen collective unit of the divine grace
and favour, and the primitive Church never had one
thought that it was any other than belonging to Israel
and sharing its corporate status before God. Again
since man is a social being, the religious experience of
individuals is bound to find expression in a social way.
The findings of anthropological science on this matter
are that the tribal, i.e. the social, expression of religion
precedes the experience of the individual member of
the social unit.[1] On the other hand, W. McDougall,
from the standpoint of social psychology, having stated
the case for a social consciousness over and above that
of the individuals who make up the society, criticizes
it to such effect as to leave no doubt that the theory
is unsubstantiated, and that the social unit need mean
no more than a convenient collective form of reference.[2]
To speak of the group idea in the primitive Church is
probably a useful way of referring to the empirical
discovery that the individual believer was aware of
belonging to the new Messianic community, formed part
of it, shared its privileges, and in the influence of the
larger group found his own experience enriched by the
collective discoveries and affirmations of the corporate
body of believers. In any case, the primitive Church as
a distinct group was more than the sum of the experience
of its individual members, for the sharing of individual
and common discovery and affirmation concerning the
way of Christ heightened the consciousness of all as

[1] Cf. R. R. Marett, *The Threshold of Religion*, 1909, pp. 155-169.
[2] *The Group Mind*, 1927, pp. 30-39.

each inspired the other, and out of the loyalty and
devotion of the many there emerged the self-consciousness
of the Church as the community of salvation.

Fourth, it is necessary to evaluate the religious
experience of the primitive Church in the light of the
recent conclusions reached by the New Psychology.
For example, the herd instinct is regarded as responsible
for the existence of the Church. By applying the principles
of projection and rationalization, the New Psychology
traces the Church's conception of the Divine love to the
need of comfort, which appeals to the great majority
of the depressed masses, and since men feel the need of
a herd leader for humanity God is projected from the
social mind to conserve the values useful to the welfare
of the herd ; this projection, in turn, is regarded as a
supreme supernatural Deity.[1] Or again, Jung, from his
psychological principles, develops the mythical theory
about Jesus. Jesus is the mythical hero of a cult,
gathering up the life expressed in the changes of nature
and the seasons, in the processes of birth and death, in the
activity of the instinct of the psyche ; notwithstanding
the higher aspects which Jung sees in Jesus when He is
compared with other cult heroes, He belongs essentially
to the same category. Jesus is a mythical personification
of the life force or urge for His devotees. Unconscious
processes are symbolized in all that Jesus is claimed to
represent ; all that is seen in Him is the result of the
unconscious processes of those who have thus projected
the workings of their minds upon the shadow figure who
in reality is a personal symbolizing of the *libido*.[2]

From our investigation it will be readily seen that
such interpretations are entirely inadequate. They
reveal an ignorance of history and a lack of awareness

[1] Cf. A. G. Tansley, *The New Psychology*, 1920, p. 159.
[2] Cf. Jung, *Psychological Types*, 1924, pp. 70 f., cf. ch. vii.

of the realities of religious experience. They come to grief on the fact of the historicity of Jesus, which, in face of the sure evidence established by modern scholarship,[1] few critics are willing to deny. Still more do all such attempts overlook the historical discoveries of the primitive Church in its personal contacts with Jesus. The realities of life are ignored in the supposition that the tested and tried affirmations of Christian experience in their higher moral and spiritual values are the products of fantasy and mythical faith. If the historico-critical approach to Christian origins, by its absorption with historical processes, misses the basic facts of the religious experience through failure to think in terms of the empirical as well as in those of the historical, so the purely psychological method, weaving its chain of psychical symbols out of the unconscious mind, by failing to appreciate the historical side of the emergence of the Church, loses its way in a maze of psychological conclusions aloof from historical reality.

If we construe the *libido* from the wider standpoint of Jung, who regards it as the primitive life urge inherent in all living things, we may take the conception of Jesus as symbolizing unconscious processes in the sense that " He is the utterance of that deep-lying life that fills all things, and is the secret of all beauty and movement in the world. Further, if we are prepared to believe that this life in all its manifestations is an utterance of God in the world, or the outgoing of the Divine life and energy into the world . . . we may arrive along this line at a conception of Jesus that has some measure of adequacy." [2] Jung, however, and the New Psychology

---

[1] For a recent criticism of theories of the unhistorical Jesus, cf. M. Goguel, *Jesus of Nazareth*, Eng. Tr., 1926, chs. i.–ii., and *The Life of Jesus*, Eng. Tr., 1933, pp. 61–69.

[2] T. H. Hughes, *The New Psychology and Religious Experience*, 1933, pp. 315 f.

as a whole, would not move along such a line of thought, and indeed, so long as we are in the sphere of the life force on its essentially physical side and the instinctive urges derived from it, we can never explain Jesus nor the primitive Church experience in a way that does justice to the demands of Christian experience. Our life in the world contains more than the specific physical or instinctive aspects, in that there is appreciation of beauty and of truth, to say nothing of a moral conscious-ness quickened by ideals and by the earnest effort of the will to make these ideals real. We have to place Jesus and the primitive Church at least within these higher realms not derived from psychology, and to regard Jesus as the utterance of God's moral and spiritual nature, within the field of history. It is the impact of the moral and spiritual " ultimate " in divine reality, as gathered up to expression in Jesus, with which we are faced in the emergence of the primitive Church. The believers explained their own experience of this " ultimate " by saying that they were filled with the Spirit. They had become aware of the activity of God in them, and that the power of the Spirit was none other than the direct impact of God in all His revelation made through Jesus upon their hearts and lives.

The primitive Church experience is a challenge to the mood of thought engendered chiefly by the New Psychology, with its elimination of the " ultimate " from human experience. Just as sin has become no more than physical and psychological maladaptation, so the forces requisite for human salvation are regarded as lying within man himself, the urges for moral and spiritual progress being found only in the instincts and unconscious powers of the mind. The religious experience which created the Church took its start and derived its sustained inspiration from the vivid awareness of the believers

22

that God had come to their lives in Jesus the Christ as the earnest of their redemption. They found their call in no personification of their instinctive urges and unconscious energies, but in their experience of the divine " ultimate " as expressed in Jesus. Within their experience they had discovered the power of God unto salvation, in the inspiration of which they went forth to proclaim their gospel to all who would hear. In so doing, the primitive Church began the witness of the Christian community as the organized spiritual community of redemption for the world in the grace and love of God as revealed in Jesus.

For it was an experienced gospel with which the primitive Church was concerned as it was set on its agelong course in the world of human life. Combined with the traditional faith and apocalyptic vision of the Jewish religious environment was the experiential recognition and awareness that the Jesus they had known on earth was the risen and exalted Christ at God's right hand. The apocalyptic categories in the primitive Church experience are not original at all in themselves ; what is really original in the primitive gospel " is the centring of it all in a historic personality and the linking it up with the life and mind of the historic Jesus." [1]   In so doing, the believers were animated by their organic relation to the original experiential elements derived from the personality of Jesus. And Jesus Himself, as Deissmann aptly remarks, is " the epoch-making thing." [2]   His personality, animated with His own force of His experience and knowledge of God, passed directly into the primitive Church experience as it took its rise from personal conviction about Jesus as He had been discovered to be in His earthly life and in

[1] Mackinnon, op. cit. p. 31.
[2] The Religion of Jesus and the Faith of Paul, p. 149.

what He had come to be for faith in His exaltation. Such is the unique content of the religious experience of the primitive Church. Little wonder, then, the joyous religious experience, for the first years at least, was for the believers one long feast of Pentecost, a prolonged day of power with the manifold manifestation of the Spirit's presence in signs and wonders, when joy was irrepressible, when unquenchable faith went hand in hand with a tremendous enthusiasm in witness and well-doing, accompanied by a communism of love expressed in self-denying devotion and benevolence, as the dynamic experience of an undimmed faith in Jesus their exalted friend and Messiah carried the believers onward through " the radiant spring morning of the Church." [1] And if the literal apocalyptic hopes did begin to fade, the religious horizons were enlarged in more specifically moral and spiritual directions, for the real dynamic of the Spirit-possessed life had revealed in itself " that the new life had been given to men in Christ Himself and that fellowship with Him was the true fulfilment of the Kingdom of God." [2]

Our investigation of the religious experience of the primitive Church suggests possible modifications in the usual estimate of Church origins.

First, the period we have reviewed ought not to be regarded by ecclesiastical historians as the mere prelude to the larger movement of the Apostolic Age and thereafter. It has the right to be considered in its own distinctive contribution and epoch-making authority. For the discoveries and affirmations of the primitive Church are in themselves the foundations of what the Church came to be in later generations.

[1] To use Mackinnon's phrase, op. cit. p. 33.
[2] E. F. Scott, Beginnings of the Church, p. 108.

Second, the impact of the historical Jesus does not need to be so sharply divided from the actual emergence of the Church as is sometimes supposed. The disciples carried forward into the Church the religious experience created by Jesus in His personal contacts with them. The Crucifixion is the necessary prelude to the exalted status of Jesus, even if it be momentarily a cause of offence to minds unable to reconcile suffering with Messianic dignity. Far from the Cross giving a new turn to events or arresting the work begun by Jesus, it impelled the disciples through to the experiences of His resurrection, and thereby to the founding of the Messianic community. The assumption that the Christian movement was separated in its beginnings from the historical Jesus of Nazareth, in the view of the Cross as a disaster which finally submerged His personality, leaving only His name to indicate a new system or society which He had never contemplated, needs to be revised in view of the organic connection of the primitive Church experience with Jesus, its personal creative originator.

Third, the apocalyptic *milieu* of the primitive Church needs fuller recognition as a dynamic factor in the emergence of the Church than has hitherto been given. We are confronted with no unnoticed religious group struggling for its foothold amidst an unsympathetic environment, but with a community inspired by a vivid awareness of itself as the triumphant community of the new Kingdom soon to be inaugurated. The overwhelming confidence that they were making history, that a great destiny awaited the believers, that even now the Spirit energy of the divine power was already operative among them, such is the essence of the apocalyptic hopes amid which the primitive Church rose to the surface of things. The correlate to this conviction is that even in the very beginnings of the Church there was a community into which men were called to become incorporated through confession of Christ's name and lordship before they could share in the coming blessing of the divine redemption in the Kingdom.

Fourth, in view of the tendency of the historico-critical school, with its method of approach to Church beginnings, to regard the primitive Church as no more than a Jewish sect, and the real Christian movement as a mere amalgam of the discoveries of this sect with the wider world of Græco-Oriental thought, it is necessary to urge with insistence that at no time was the Church a minor Jewish movement. From one standpoint the believers remained faithful to the requirements of their traditional Jewish faith, and to all intents and purposes they were loyal members of the Jewish theocracy. But far wider and deeper differences were implied in their new religious experience. The fact that they were impelled to summon their fellow-Jews to repentance in view of the apostasy in rejecting Jesus the Messiah is significant of a consciousness that they had something vital in religious reality unknown to the Jews. This implied criticism of Judaism as not living up to the best it knew, already set out with such force by Jesus, was destined in time to result in the breakaway from Judaism. The primitive Church was hesitant enough to follow the logic of its experience, but the logic was nevertheless there in vital reality.

Fifth, the tendency in modern scholarship is to lay more stress on the Greek elements in the development of Christianity. This tendency sometimes finds bizarre expression in views which look on historical Christianity as almost entirely due to Gentile influences at work on a bare minimum supplied by Jesus. We have therefore to stress the fact that the cardinal elements of the Christian experience were either already to the fore-

front in the primitive Church, or were implied in the
logic of its experienced gospel, which based its affirmations on the personality of Jesus and the experienced
contacts with Him.   The Christian experience was profoundly modified, of course, as Gentile thought began
to influence it in the course of its expansion in the wider
world during the centuries that followed the Apostolic
Age.   Greek speculation succeeded apocalyptic interpretation and brought considerable modification of the
original substance of the new faith.   This wider influence, however, lay rather in the realms of interpretation
and elucidation of empirical data already given in the
primitive Church experience.   Further, as in the case
of Philo, it was not a question of Jewish Christians
being influenced by Greek thought entirely ; it was
rather that Greeks, or Greek-thinking Gentiles, discover-
ing new spiritual life and power in a Church taking its
start within an intensely Jewish religious environment,
were being profoundly influenced by Jewish thought as
expressed in its purifying by the Church of Jesus Christ.
Thus far, as Christianity spread into the world, it was
Palestine that was doing the influencing rather than
the Greek world.

Sixth, if the problem of the New Testament be " How
did the Jesus of history become the Christ of experience,
with His status as the second person in the Trinity ? "
the study of the primitive Church may be regarded as
making some contribution towards its solution.   We
cannot indeed speak of a primitive Church theology, for
insufficient time had yet elapsed for inward reflection
to discover what was implied in the new relationship to
Jesus the Christ.   But the identification of Jesus with
the exalted heavenly Messiah of Jewish apocalyptic
speculation involved at the outset a remarkable re-
casting of Jewish thought ; the identification was made

on a basis of experience of the personal and the exalted Jesus. It was what the believers had already seen in Him that led them to make so tremendous an inference about Jesus. And their subsequent experience of Him in exaltation carries on what had already been born in them. Thus there is a continuity of experience which was ultimately to have its implied logic thought out as the later Church set Jesus in the most vital relationship to the Eternal Father.

Finally, the so-called gap between Jesus and Paul is seen to have less relevance when the discoveries and affirmations of the primitive Church are thoroughly understood and given their true value. While much has yet to be done before Paul's contribution to Christianity can be accurately estimated,[1] yet there is sufficient ground common to the primitive Church and to the Pauline to warrant the conclusion that Paul was less of an innovator than is generally supposed. Still less can we regard him as the creator of the Church itself. Paul owed much to the Church before him, and we know that he was in closest touch with the Jerusalem Church. Paul was never aware that he was introducing " another gospel " ; he was a convert to the primitive Church which was thus introduced to a thinker and interpreter of the Christian experience devout and original in his outlook. There was bound to be much enrichment of the tradition when Paul brought his own distinctive genius to bear upon the new faith in the light of his own experiential discoveries. But he was convinced in himself that he rested on what had gone before him, and there is every reason to believe that the apostle to the Gentiles was right in his conclusion.

[1] His relation to Rabbinic thought and to Græco-Oriental speculation and religion has yet to be worked out, and as yet the essential data have to be gathered by erudite research in these fields.

The religious experience of the primitive Church is rooted and grounded in Jesus the Christ. Spiritual reality of the highest order was for the first time placed within the reach of men, who, as they received their experiences of His life-creating personality and influence, established the Church on the basis of what they had experienced and were still experiencing in Him. Though not as yet realized, the discoveries were being made which were ultimately to result in the awareness of the divine Sonship of Jesus, and it was only a matter of time before the spiritual logic of the religious experience worked out in the devotion of men of whom it could be said that they had " experienced Christianity as a Divine history of their inner being; believing in Christ, they had obtained access to God ; in the Son they had found the Father. In this innermost, most certain fact of their consciousness, there lay for them the impulse and the necessity to place the person of Christ, the founder of this their new life, in the closest, most vital relation to the Father." [1]

[1] Dorner, *The Person of Christ*, Eng. Tr., div. i. vol. i. p. 47.

APPENDIX I

THE ALLEGED SACRAMENTARIANISM OF PAUL

WITHIN recent years an array of weighty opinion has decided that Paul was a thoroughgoing sacramentarian. " There is little doubt as to the sacramental nature of baptism by the middle of the first century in the circles represented by the Pauline Epistles, and it is indisputable in the second century." [1] Kirsopp Lake is even more decided in an earlier work : " Baptism is for St. Paul and his readers universally and unquestioningly accepted as a " mystery " or sacrament which works *ex opere operato* : and from the unhesitating manner in which St. Paul uses this fact as a basis for argument, as if it were a point on which Christian opinion did not vary, it would seem as though this sacramental teaching is central in the primitive Christianity to which the Roman Empire began to be converted." [2] H. T. Andrews has no doubt that " as far as exegesis is concerned the sacramentarian interpretation of Paulinism has won a decisive victory, and the Symbolical School has been driven off the field." [3] Johannes Weiss thinks that the germs of the later catholic sacramentarianism are already in Paul, although he is cautious against reading too much of this into the epistles : " Nicht, dass der Gedanke des immer wiederholten Opfers Christi hier schon vorhanden wäre, wohl aber ist ein Keim zu dieser katholischen Deutung der heiligen Handlung nicht zu verkennen, zumal da zweifellos Brot und Wein nicht mehr als gewöhnliche Speise empfunden werden, sondern in irgend einer Weise schon Leib und Blut Christi symbolisch darstellen, ja, geradezu verkörpen." [4]

[1] Foakes Jackson and K. Lake in *BC.*, ed. FJ. and L., i. p. 335.
[2] *Earlier Epistles of St. Paul*, 1911, p. 385.
[3] *The Place of the Sacraments in the Teaching of St. Paul*, in P. T. Forsyth's *The Church and the Sacraments*, pp. 154 f.
Urchristentum, p. 508.

One significant fact should be kept clearly before us. It is often assumed that Paul's religious experience and outlook are to be identified with the experience and psychology of the readers of his epistles. If Paul uses a "Mystery" fact as a basis for argument, it does not follow that he accepted it in the "Mystery" sense. He may well have been proceeding from what his Gentile converts were conversant with in order to lead them on to what they did not as yet know or apprehend, namely, that the Christian faith "in Christ" was far beyond the *ex opere operato* of sacramentarianism. The apostle makes contacts in their religious experience, coming alongside them in order to lead them to fuller light and understanding. The "Mystery" which for him denoted union with Christ had this inner religious experience for him in baptism or the observance of the Lord's Supper, but many of his Gentile converts would have no difficulty in reading sacramentarian ideas into such language, just as the disciples read apocalyptic meaning into Jesus' words where no such meaning may have been intended. H. Weinel seems to point the way, when he states that "Dem Apostel, der ohne Riten und Zeremonien das Göttliche in sich erlebt hatte, mussten freilich solche Mysterien ferne liegen. Aber er konnte sich weder dem Zuge der Zeit noch dem Zwang des Gemeindebrauches entziehen, der bereits die Taufe aufgenommen und das Abendmahl in ein Sakrament verwandelt hatte."[1] It was the Gentile environment which began to motive the sacramentarianism that does not really appear, as Schweitzer has stated,[2] until Ignatius (*ad Rom.* vii. 3, *ad Philad.* iv., *ad Eph.* xx.) and Justin Martyr (*Apol.* lxxxvi.), for even the apparent sacramentarianism of the Fourth Gospel (vi. 53–56) has to be understood in the light of the words, "the flesh profiteth nothing : the words that I have spoken unto you are spirit, and are life" (vi. 63). The Christian faith went out amid the peoples of the Græco-Roman world, who brought religious ideas to the interpretation of their new Christian experience, which were not native to the gospel of the Kingdom, but were imported as alien

[1] Paulus, *Zte. Aufl.*, 1915, p. 90.   [2] *Op. cit.* pp. 269 ff.

ideas derived from pagan cults and Mystery Religions, and
as such are of the shell, rather than of the kernel, of the new
faith.

Reitzenstein is the thoroughgoing exponent of the dependence of Paulinism on the Mystery Religions. " Einstweilen
scheint uns aus dem Dunkel der Entwicklungsgeschichte
des Apostels eine Tatsache mit wachsender Bestimmtheit
entgegenzudämmern : er hat ernstlich darum gerungen,
auch den Hellenen Hellene zu werden. Die hellenistische
religiöse Literatur muss er gelesen haben ; ihre Sprache redet
er, in ihre Gedanken hat er sich hineinversetzt, wohl weil
die gleiche Gedankenwelt ihn schon früher berührt hat. Jetzt
schlossen sich diese Gedanken mit innerer Notwendigkeit an
die neue, über alles Judentum hinausgehende Lebenserfahrung.
So gewannen sie für ihn . . . lebendige Kraft." [1] The re-
mainder of Reitzenstein's book is devoted to various studies
bearing on the Mysteries, and they are mainly linguistic in
character, but it is noteworthy that the literature of which
the author makes copious use to explain Paul's thought
comes from a much later age, and thus he tends to read back
into earlier times the ideas and religious experience of a later
age. A step further, and the primitive Church is included
within the orbit of the Mystery Religions with their sacramentarian ideas, and we have Bousset who makes not only
Paul but also the primitive Church communities borrow
largely from the Mysteries.[2]

H. A. A. Kennedy reveals an opposite tendency to that
of Reitzenstein. After an exhaustive study of the terminology
of the Mysteries he concludes that " the evidence we have
adduced from the Old Testament makes it wholly superfluous
to seek for the explanation of any of these terms in Hellenistic Mystery Religion. What we do learn from the parallels
is the ability of his (Paul's) readers to catch the meaning of
the more or less technical terminology, due not merely to
a course of instruction in the Old Testament, but to their
acquaintance with a religious vocabulary already current

[1] *Die Hellenistischen Mysterienreligionen*, Zte. Aufl., 1920, p. 66.
[2] *Kurios Christos.*

among the Mystery Associations." [1] Such a verdict, however, goes too far in the Jewish direction, and does not allow for the new contacts with the pagan environment. Paul may have known where he stood with his technical Pharisaic training, but it is psychologically improbable that the Greek-speaking converts from the Gentile cities should bring to their new faith the presuppositions and ideas derived from Judaism ; the " God-fearers " were not at home in the Jewish outlook even though they accepted the Jewish doctrine of God.

A more mediating position is put forward by Deissmann,[2] who makes the fullest allowance for the Judaic elements in Paul's experience, yet gives due recognition to the Hellenistic influences ; he therefore inclines to give less credit to the operation of ideas from the Mystery Religions. S. Angus details the faith and practice of the Mysteries, and, while drawing attention to many parallels between Christianity and these, he rightly refuses to draw hazardous inferences which imply dependence. Indeed, he is more concerned, and rightly so, with placing the Christian Faith and the Mysteries in contrast with each other.[3]

APPENDIX II

RABBINIC PARALLELS AND THE GOSPELS

THE researches of Strack-Billerbeck (*Das Evangelium nach Matthäus erläutert aus Talmud, u.s.w.*, 1922, and *Das Evangelium nach Markus, Lukas und Johannes und die Apostelgeschichte erläutert aus Talmud, u.s.w.*, 1924), George Foot Moore (*Judaism*, 1927), Israel Abrahams (*Studies in Pharisaism and the Gospels*, Series I., 1917. Series II., 1924), and C. G. Montefiore (*Rabbinic Literature and Gospel Teachings*, 1930) have shed a flood of light on New

---

[1] *St. Paul and the Mystery Religions*, 1913 p. 198.
[2] *St. Paul*, chs. iv.–vii.
[3] *The Mystery Religions and Christianity*, 1925.

Testament interpretation by reason of the numerous parallels
found in the Talmud to the Gospel sayings, all of which are
set forth with cumulative completeness by these writers.
All these new facts are a valuable corrective to the former
tendency to overdraw Judaism in unfavourable terms when
compared with the Christian Faith.

At the same time, the tendency now is to go too far the
other way. " The conviction that Jesus was Himself native
to the outlook of Jewry has become so general that the
problem nowadays is rather how so typical a Judaism ever
developed into a distinct and world-wide religion. He was
Himself a child of the synagogue who absorbed and appreciated the best of contemporary Rabbinism ; He fastened
upon aspects of religion which are not indeed original to
Him but in Him were freed from less elevated ideals ; He
focused the sublime teaching of Isaiah and Micah, the
doctrines of the Shecinah and the Bath Qôl into a single
system ; His purpose was not to destroy the law but to
fulfil it, and His mission only contemplated the lost sheep of
the house of Israel. Such is the familiar argument."[1]   A
typical view illustrative of this is seen in Branscomb, " The
work and teaching of Jesus comes out of the main stream of
Jewish development," with the added feature that He
intensified the ethical demands of Judaism and freed it from
peculiar ethnic characteristics.[2]

The idealization of Judaism in the later Rabbinic outlook
should be given its fullest weight. In a lengthy review of
G. F. Moore's *Judaism*, Dobschütz writes : " Es mag sein,
dass die früheren Darstellungen, indem sie viele unbedeutende
Einzelheiten in den Vordergrund stellten, Zerrbilder des
Judentums geboten haben und dass wir bei Moore eine
richtige Korrektur finden. Aber ich kann nicht umhin, den
Eindrück, den ich gewonnen habe, dahin zu formulieren,
dass Moore nun nach der anderen Seite hin einseitig wird und
ein Idealbild zeichnet, das auch nicht zutrifft."[3] Moore
reveals a subtle tendency to take Rabbinic Judaism in its

[1] C. E. Raven, *Jesus and the Gospel of Love*, 1931 p. 245.
[2] *Jesus and the Law of Moses*, 1930, pp. 270 f.
[3] In *TS und K.*, 1929, i. p. 131.

higher moods as indicative of the religious quality of the Rabbinic literature as a whole. For example, he gives full weight to Midrashim as the higher exegesis of Scripture, but where a subject appears with its limitations in religious and ethical outlook such as the chastisement divinely sent to women dying in childbirth for neglecting three obligations exclusive to them, or children dying for the sins of their parents through divine retribution, he turns the edge of the inevitable ethical criticism by stating that " most of the opinions recorded are mere midrash, which is not to be taken more seriously than it was meant." [1] But why are these not to be taken as seriously authoritative an expression of Rabbinic teaching as the noble passages such as on the Father in Heaven ? Here the Rabbinic idealization glosses over the more fantastic and absurd elements in the Rabbinic literature, and the whole taken together should be the true characterization of Judaism. " It seems characteristic of the Rabbinical tradition that it should put together . . . the ridiculous and the sublime without seeing the incongruity," [2] and in any true estimate of the religion portrayed the higher and the lower features should be taken together. Rabbinism seems to have perpetuated in harder measure the same mixture in the old faith of Israel in placing primitive ritual survivals and high moral requirements on the same level of divine revelation.

The use of parallels, further, carries with it certain handicaps. All the Rabbinic parallels to the Gospels are much later than the Gospels. They prove nothing in the way of dependence, for Rabbinism may well have been influenced by the growing faith of Christianity. Further, if the Rabbis taught very much what Jesus did, and Jesus be a typical Rabbi, how was it that the new faith which broke away from the national restrictions and became a gospel of world salvation centred around Jesus, and not around Hillel or Shammai ? Again, if Jesus were a product of embryonic Rabbinism, why did He leave out so much that Rabbinism considered

[1] *Op. cit.* vol. ii. p. 249.
[2] Headlam, *Life and Teaching of Jesus*, 1923, p. 82.

essential ? The Rabbis are tested not only by what Jesus may be supposed to have taught on parallel lines to their doctrine, but by what He omitted to teach. If Jesus drew on the Rabbis for so much of His teaching as enunciated in the Sermon on the Mount, why did He leave so much out from what was afterwards gathered up in the Talmud ? Finally, the contact of Rabbinism with the Christian faith as this went out into the ancient world, may have led the former to read back into the Law and the Traditions some of the distinctive religious experience and outlook of the Christian faith, much after the manner of Philo, who, confronted by the intellectual challenge of Hellenism to the traditional Jewish religion, read back into the patriarchs and Moses many tenets of Greek wisdom and made Moses the true founder of Greek philosophy.[1]

APPENDIX III

The Resurrection Appearances : Jerusalem or Galilee ?

THE Marcan-Matthæan tradition assigns the appearances to Galilee whither the disciples proceeded by the instruction of the women, and where they were to behold the risen Jesus (Mark xvi. 7 ; Matt. xxviii. 10). Mark's narrative breaks off at the point where the women are told to inform the disciples that they were to go to Galilee, but Matthew states that the eleven disciples went there and saw the risen Jesus who gave them command to make disciples of all the Gentiles (xxviii. 16–20). The Johannine Appendix gives a resurrection scene in which Peter figures very prominently, and thus witnesses to the Galilean tradition (xxi.).

On the other hand, the Lucan-Johannine series reveals the disciples remaining in Jerusalem in obedience to a command of Jesus (Luke xxiv. 49 ; Acts i. 4, 12), there to await the promised gift of the Spirit (Acts i. 8). The appearances

[1] Cf. W. Fairweather, *Jesus and the Greeks*, 1924, pp. 174–179.

are all in Jerusalem or in the immediate vicinity. Matthew, indeed, gives an appearance of Jesus to the women returning from the tomb, but this instruction is absent from Lucan-Johannine tradition, which presents the disciples themselves as examining the empty tomb (Matt. xxviii. 9 f. ; Luke xxiv. 12 ; John xx. 4 ff.). The women are reminded by the angel that Jesus had told His disciples when in Galilee that He would rise again (Luke xxiv. 6 f.).

These divergent traditions seem irreconcilable, and the acceptance of the one would logically imply the rejection of the other. The difficulty is not overcome by the suggestion, that, given the resurrected Jesus, there would be no geographical limits to His appearances. But there are geographical limits imposed on the disciples, who are still bound to earth as human beings. As the narratives stand, there are two sets of conflicting commands and experiences, and no clue is given as to their solution. If our discussion on the experience of the disciples during the period between the Cross and the Resurrection has validity (pp. 122–25), we have the additional factor of religious experience as a point in favour of the Jerusalem tradition.

This is not to admit that Jesus never spoke of His intention to go to Galilee after rising from the dead (Mark xiv. 28). The truth of such an intention receives from the nonfulfilment of the prophecy an unintentional support, that is, when the force of the words, " I will go before you," is seen in the light of the expectation of the divine Kingdom. J. Weiss takes this phrase to mean, "ich setze mich an eure Spitze und führe euch nach Galiläa," which, taken with "there ye shall see me " means in a Messianic sense, "nachdem ich mich hier in Jerusalem nach meiner Auferstehung mit euch vereinigt habe, führe ich euch in die Heimat ; dort wird dann das kommen, worauf wir warten-das Reich Gottes." [1] But there was no fulfilment in Galilee of the advent of the Kingdom. A new Messianic community arose in Jerusalem probably because the solution of the experiential conflict between the death and the resurrection

[1] *Urchristentum*, p. 12.

of Jesus occurred in the very locality where the conflict
had been intensified to its climax in the Cross, namely, in
Jerusalem ; the Resurrection experiences coincided with the
solution of the experiential conflict at Jerusalem (pp. 124 f.).

How, then, did the Galilean tradition arise ? The words
about the scattering of the sheep and the flight of the
disciples (Mark xiv. 27 f.) were followed by an intimation that
after Jesus was risen from the dead He would go forward to
Galilee, and there the disciples would see Him. But the
Galilean expectation was not fulfilled. There is no evidence
that the disciples fled away from Jerusalem in the momentary
panic of Jesus' arrest (p. 125). They were more likely
to hover near the scene in view of the strange hold Jesus
still had upon them (pp. 122 ff.). The disciples were not in
a fit state of mind to remember intimations of Jesus, and
thus there would be no impulsive influence to urge them into
Galilee. Besides, were they not all disillusioned in their
Messianic hopes by the death of Jesus ?

At all events, Mark has accepted the fact that such an
intimation was given, and is content to note that the disciples
may or even ought to have gone to Galilee, causing the angel
at the tomb to instruct the women to tell the disciples to go
there. Matthew has this tradition in a more developed
form, since the command now comes through the risen
Jesus Himself to the women, bidding the disciples to go to
Galilee, where they should see Him ; in obedience the
disciples assemble in Galilee and receive His farewell instructions. The Johannine Appendix has developed the
tradition a little more by following up with the story of an
appearance while the disciples were back at their own trade
of fishing. The Galilean appearances seem therefore to be
due to the product of later reflection working on certain
remembered intimations of Jesus of something He had said
about going to Galilee and bringing in the Kingdom.

APPENDIX IV

THE TEACHING OF JESUS ON THE HOLY SPIRIT

THE only direct references to any teaching Jesus gave on the Spirit are :

(1) Mark xii. 36 (cf. Matt. xxii. 43). This is no more than an expression of the familiar idea that Scripture was written through the Spirit's inspiration (pp. 69, 186).

(2) Mark xiii. 11. Jesus promises His disciples that the Spirit would speak in them when they were handed over for trial. This promise should not be dismissed along with Mark xiii. as the mere intrusion of apocalyptic into the authentic gospel tradition, and therefore to be regarded only with reserve. Nor is the reference necessarily due to the reflection of later experience.[1] While it is true that the saying " undoubtedly agrees with the experience of Christian confessors and martyrs," [2] the extraordinary crisis at hand which Jesus had in mind demanded extraordinary qualities, and the Spirit was regarded as the source of the inspiration for the abnormal moment. It would be not merely a voice in the disciples speaking what they should say ; it would be the Spirit actually speaking, using their vocal organs, so that the words they actually uttered in the hour of crisis would reveal that it was not they, but the Spirit that was actually speaking (pp. 192, 199). It is possible that Jesus is here drawing on his own experience, and we have seen reason for ascribing all that Jesus said and did to the activity of the Spirit within him (pp. 152-54). The sudden mobilization of personality in suitable reply at the critical moment of trial is naturally accounted for by the Spirit's indwelling ; a precogitated reply in defence may savour of self-regard, but the abnormal conditions would demand purely " God-regard " in the simplicity of the Spirit's control. When face to face with enemies in the name of Christ there is possible a marked

[1] E. F. Scott, *The Spirit in the New Testament*, 1923, p. 73.

[2] H. W. Robinson, *The Christian Experience of the Holy Spirit*, p. 130.

accession of the Spirit, thus affording another instance of the
experience summed up in the words, " Where two or three are
gathered together in My name, there am I in the midst "
(Matt. xviii. 20).

(3) Matt. x. 20 (cf. Luke xii. 12). The same series of
empirical ideas is discerned in the promise of Jesus that the
Spirit would speak in the disciples as they went out on their
preaching tour, but this may be no more than an echo of
Mark xiii. 11 above, which in the growth of gospel tradition
has found its way into this story.

(4) Luke xi. 13. Jesus states that the Heavenly Father
will give the Holy Spirit to them that ask Him ; the
parallel saying in Matt. vii. 11 has " good gifts " for " Holy
Spirit," and since Jesus has already spoken of the custom of
fathers to give good gifts, rather than evil, to their children,
it would seem as if the Matthæan form of the saying is the
authentic one. The Western Text (D Lat(vt.) Orig. Amb.)
has " good gift " in Luke xi. but this may be no more than a
scribal harmonization in view of Matt. vii. since the reference
to the " Holy Spirit " would not likely be understood. Yet
the Lucan " Holy Spirit " may be in contrast to " evil
things " which ordinary fathers give to their children :
" if ye then, being evil, give good gifts unto your children,
how much more will your heavenly Father give the Holy
Spirit . . . ! " i.e. instead of the corresponding thing in
evil, an evil spirit ? There was much similarity between the
two forms of spirit-experience (pp. 198–200). In this case
the Holy Spirit is the gift of God to His children.[1]

(5) Matt. xii. 28. Jesus declares that the power in Him
which enables Him to cast out the demons is the Spirit of
God, but the Lucan parallel replaces " Spirit " by " the
finger of God " (xi. 20). Luke's version is probably the
right one, inasmuch that if " Spirit " had stood in Q he
could hardly have avoided using it in view of his frequent
use of the word, while in Matthew the word " Spirit " may
have entered to prepare the way for the teaching about
forgiveness and the Spirit in Matt. xii. 31 f.[2] And yet there

[1] A. T. Cadoux, The Parables of Jesus, 1931, pp. 76 f.
[2] Cf. A. H. McNeile, op. cit. ad. loc., and E. F. Scott op. cit. p. 74.

is something to be said in favour of " Spirit " as being the
original rendering, for the question was as to what sort of
Spirit it was by which Jesus cast out demons (pp. 93 f.).
The idea of the Spirit of God was undoubtedly there, and
from the standpoint of the eye-witnesses there would be no
question as to the underlying activity in casting out demons,
namely, the presence of the Spirit.   There is thus an intimate
connection between the Spirit of God and the activity of
Jesus.   This empirical truth is further reinforced by

(6) Mark iii. 28–30, a statement of Jesus that there is
no forgiveness for the blasphemy against the Holy Spirit.
The Spirit is contrasted with Jesus Himself.   Whatever be
the precise theological meaning of the words, the point for
us is that the eye-witnesses have laid hold of the vital fact
that " the power behind His (sc. Jesus') miracles is that of
the Spirit." [1] The casting out of the demons heralded
the Kingdom, and the Spirit was the power behind this as
behind all the activity of Jesus (pp. 69, 152 ff.).

(7) In addition to the statements of Jesus we have the
story of the descent of the Spirit at His baptism (Mark i. 10),
and the Spirit as the unseen energy which drives Him into
the wilderness (ver. 12).   The knowledge of both these
experiences of Jesus which the disciples had, must in the
first place have come from Jesus Himself, and they would
view such experiences, as indeed Jesus did, as resulting from
the activity of the Spirit of God.

(8) Among the fragments which we have of the Gospel
to the Hebrews there are two agrapha which purport to be
sayings of Jesus.   " And if any accept the Gospel according
to the Hebrews, where the Saviour Himself saith, ' Even
now did my mother the Holy Spirit take me by one of
mine hairs, and carried me away unto the great mountain
Thabor ' " [2]: " if any one receive that saying, ' Even now my
mother the Holy Spirit took me and carried me up unto
the great mountain Thabor.' " [3]   The real interest of these

---

[1] E. F. Scott, *op. cit.* p. 76.
[2] Quoted in Orig. on John ii. 12.
[3] *Ibid.* " On Jeremiah," homily xv. 4.

passages is the reference to the Spirit as " mother," but this is due to the fact that the Hebrew for " Spirit " (*ruach*) is feminine. The reference is presumably to the Temptation of Jesus (Matt. iv. 1 ff. ; Luke iv. 1 ff.), and embodies a quasi-physical operation to the Spirit. There is no ground, however, for supposing that the words go back to Jesus.

APPENDIX V

" THE TWELVE " AND THE APOSTLES

" THE Twelve " is the designation given to a body of personal disciples of Jesus. Mark and Luke expressly state that they were appointed to such a position, while Matthew implies the same fact (Mark iii. 14 ; Luke vi. 13 ; Matt. x. 1). In the Synoptics " The Twelve " are rarely referred to as " apostles " ; Mark twice does so (iii. 14, vi. 30) ; but in the former reference the phrase " whom also he named apostles " is a later addition to the text, being absent from the Old Latin and the Old Syriac, but retained in Aleph BC*. Swete is so impressed with the textual authority as to accept the phrase, but he is not quite sure about it, since he says, " the name was not perhaps given at the time." [1] More likely we have here a Western non-interpolation from Luke.[2] Now Luke makes far more frequent use of " apostles," both in his gospel and in Acts. On the other hand, Mark refers many times to " The Twelve " without using " apostles " to describe them (iv. 10, vi. 7, ix. 35, x. 32, xi. 11, xiv. 10, 17, 20, 43), while Matthew has the more natural word " disciples " in some of these instances.

" The Twelve " seem to be special attendants and messengers of Jesus (pp. 106 ff.) ; the mission on which they are sent is to preach the Kingdom of God and to cast out demons (Mark iii. 14 f.). Nowhere in Mark are " The Twelve " looked on as the basis of a new organization. Their function as " messengers " is seen even in Luke with

---

[1] *The Gospel of St. Mark*, 3rd edn. 1920 *ad. loc.*
[2] Cf. *BC.*, ed. FJ. and L., vol. v. p. 37.

358 EXPERIENCE OF THE PRIMITIVE CHURCH

his more formal designation of them as " apostles " (xi. 49),
but Matthew follows the Marcan impression here (x. 7).

On the whole, the message of the preachers was eschatological in character ; even where Jesus was not thinking in
apocalyptic, they would tend to view it from such a standpoint in their capacity as assessors at the divine judgment
when the Kingdom was come (Matt. xix. 28 ; Luke xxii. 30 ;
cf. pp. 208 f.).

The eschatological hope, however, did not mature. The
Messianic community emerged at last into the Church with
its experience of the Kingdom as actually present in the
world (pp. 246–8). Organization began to receive a powerful
stimulus, and " The Twelve " came to be viewed as a sort
of apostolic collegium, a closed corporation, viewed not
eschatologically, but officially by the organized Church.
Luke reveals this later approach, especially in the Acts. The
concluding charge of Jesus is to " The Eleven Apostles "
(Acts i. 2, 13), while Luke submits as one of his qualifications
for the authenticity of his chronicle the fact that his record
is based on the duly authoritative witness of " The Apostles "
(Acts i. 2 f.). They had personal experience of the resurrection, of what Jesus had said and done during His life, but
these qualifications were held by many more than " The
Eleven " (pp. 106 f. 122 f.). Even women could be apostles
on this basis (Luke viii. 1 ff.). The election of Matthias seems
designed to fill up the vacancy in the collegium caused by
the death of Judas, but no more was really empirically
implied than the desire to complete the number of twelve
in view of the imminent Kingdom, so that the number of
eschatological assessors may be complete (Acts i. 15 ff. ;
cf. pp. 207–9). The collegium appears in " the teaching of
the Apostles " (Acts ii. 42), and the words which follow,
" and the fellowship," lead some commentators to explain
the fellowship as " the fellowship of the Apostles "(pp. 222 f.).
The Eleven Apostles and Peter are the interpreters of the
Pentecost phenomena (Acts ii. 14 ff.), and to them the
quickened hearers apply as to what they ought to do to be
saved (Acts ii. 37).

But Luke betrays the fact that there were other apostles beside " The Twelve." There is Barnabas (Acts iv. 36, xiv. 14), and Paul has no doubt that he is just as much an apostle as any of " The Twelve " (Rom. i. 5, xi. 13 ; 1 Cor. iv. 9, ix. 1 f., xv. 9 f. ; 2 Cor. xii. 12 ; Gal. i. 17, etc.). Paul never seems to have heard of " The Twelve " as understood in any official sense as a collegium ; at least he quotes the phrase once only (1 Cor. xv. 5), and here is referring to primitive tradition. There is further the discrepancy in the names which appear in the various lists (Mark iii. 16–19 ; Matt. x. 2–4 ; Luke vi. 14–16). Had " The Twelve " been so important a body in the primitive Church, the names would have been better preserved ; there would be less uncertainty about who were " The Twelve " in the first place. Further, the position of James the Lord's brother as president of the Council of Jerusalem suggests that he, although not an official apostle, nor even numbered among " The Twelve," took precedence of every one, apostle or non-apostle, collegium or non-collegium. Paul's list of resurrection appearances (1 Cor. xv. 3 ff.) mentions an appearance to " The Twelve," and afterwards " to all the Apostles," suggesting that " The Twelve " still retained their status of personal attendants of Jesus, while " the Apostles " were a more general class.

Despite the conflicting presentations of " The Twelve " and " the Apostles," there is no need to conclude with J. Weiss[1] that there is no historic evidence for the appointment of " The Twelve." The facts seem to be that Jesus originally selected a few disciples as His personal attendants and messengers, and made the specific number up to twelve in view of His message of the Kingdom, which they were sent out to announce. There may well have been other disciples similarly engaged ; indeed, we hear of seventy being sent out (Luke x. 1 ff.). But why was the appointment of " The Twelve " connected with the mission of heralding the Kingdom ? The answer lies in the eschatological character of their function and number. The number was more important than the office.

On the other hand, Luke, reflecting the later Church

[1] *Op. cit.* p. 34.

theory, has set forth " The Twelve " as an official collegium, and the words " the Apostles " have been narrowed down to be almost synonymous with " The Twelve " as the governors and administrators of the Church. In view of this later theory why was the story of the appointment of " The Twelve " by Jesus, and with such differing functions from those ascribed by Luke in Acts, invented ? Their inconsistency with the later standpoint suggests at least that if invented, the story would have been related with an eye to the later theory. On the contrary, the narration of the appointment of " The Twelve " by Jesus stands out in its simple naïveté, as is illustrated by the subsequent efforts to bring it more into line with the later idea (Mark iii. 14).

The facts also suggest that " The Twelve " were not a closed corporation governing the Church as the early chapters in Acts hint. Such governing body as there is consisted of a wider group with James at the head, and he was not one of " The Twelve," nor is there any hint that he was ever included with " The Twelve." [1] How is it that the original leadership of Peter on whom was conferred " the keys of the Kingdom of Heaven " (Matt. xvi. 19) passed over to a man who was not of the collegium ? The question is insoluble because Acts tells us nothing about it, but it points to the fluidity of the apostles' authority rather than to the existence of any apostolic college. Even the believers at large appoint " the Seven " (Acts vi. 2 ff.) ; here once more the textual variants (the MS. B reads " let us choose," i.e. the apostles are the appointing body) reveal the later ideas influencing the earlier traditions. But serious doubts are entertained about the Western Text at this point,[2] and the ordinary text reveals a less ordered and consistent state of things in the primitive Church than the harder conception of an apostolic collegium in existence would allow.

[1] Cf. Acts xv. 13 and " elders " in xv. 6.
[2] J. H. Ropes in BC., ed. FJ. and L., vol. iii. 1926 p. 59.

APPENDIX VI

WHO WERE THE HELLENISTS?

IN Acts vi. 1 the Hellenistic section of the primitive Church obtrudes itself for the first time, and somewhat unexpectedly. Who were the *Hellēnistai*? A large body of opinion regards them as " Hellenistic Jews who were largely represented in Jerusalem at this time, and even proselytes, who were also numerous in the city." [1] On the other hand, the view that these Hellenists are definitely Gentiles has found recent expression by H. J. Cadbury,[2] but there is nothing in his analysis of the etymology of the word and its appearance in post-Nicene writers which really precludes the view that *Hellēnistēs* may well be a Greek-speaking Jew, the word reasonably denoting " any one who practises Greek ways—whether a Greek himself or a foreigner." [3]

There are three instances of the word in Acts :

(1) In vi. 1 the almost certain reference is to Hellenistic Jews, including Gentile proselytes to Judaism, and God-fearers who would not take the final step of circumcision. The author of Acts is very careful throughout his work in matters involving language : he is careful to tell us that Paul did not understand the vernacular of Lycaonia (xiv. 11) ; we are reminded that Paul was not to be confused with an Egyptian unable to speak Greek (xxi. 37), and that Paul addressed the crowd before the castle of Antonia in Aramaic (xxii. 2). Further, it seems hardly historical to assume the presence of specific Gentiles so numerous as to cause a dissension in the Jerusalem Church. There were Gentiles among the members, but they were well within Judaistic influence ; even the publicans and sinners were all on the Jewish fringe, and these elements would be present. " The Seven " were

[1] A. C. McGiffert, *op. cit.* p. 76, supported by Bartlet, *Apostolic Age*, p. 28 ; J. Weiss, *op. cit.* p. 119, " griechisch redenden Juden " ; H. J. Holtzmann, *Apostelgeschichte* on vi. 1, Hort, *op. cit.* pp. 50, 206.
[2] In *BC.*, ed. FJ. and L., vol. v. pp. 68 ff.
[3] *Ibid.* p. 60.

probably Hellenistic Jews, one being a proselyte (Nicolaus, vi. 5), but the presence among them of a God-fearer is not precluded. The Greek names of " The Seven " cause no difficulty, since Jews under Greek influences, and still more proselytes and God-fearers, had such names.

(2) In Acts ix. 29 the converted Paul disputes with Hellenists in Jerusalem, and the subject of disputation, Jesus the Christ, points to the Greek-speaking Jews or proselytes as being indicated here, for Jesus as yet meant nothing to the larger world of the Gentiles. Professor Cadbury seems too ready to read the Lucan theory of the Church's universal mission from its inception into the references when he says that " there is no reason why the author may not be supposed to have introduced here a prompt fulfilment of the prediction made at Paul's conversion that he would be a missionary to the Gentiles." [1] Why, then, did not Luke show this desire as he narrates Paul's missionary journeys where the apostle to the Gentiles is shown as beginning with the Jews of the Diaspora, and finding these obdurate, turns to the Gentiles (Acts xiii. 5, 14, xiv. 1 ; cf. xiii. 44–46) ?

(3) In Acts xi. 19 f. we get the first preaching to the Gentiles by converts from Cyprus and Cyrene, the *Hellēnistai* being the object of their message, in contrast with those who were limiting their preaching to Jews only. Here the connotation of the term is the Gentiles as such. A variant reading *Hellēnas* (AD Aleph) points to what was probably the original reading, *i.e.* Greeks.[2]

---

[1] *Op. cit.* p. 70.

[2] Cf. F. H. A. Scrivener, *A Plain Introduction to the Criticism of the New Testament*, 4th edn. 1894, vol. ii. pp. 370 f., and see discussion on the text here by J. H. Ropes, *BC.*, ed. FJ. and L., vol. iii. *ad. loc.*

APPENDIX VII

Jesus and Apocalyptic

SINCE the famous discussion of Schweitzer [1] there has been much debate as to how far Jesus viewed His mission in terms of apocalyptic thought, and it cannot be said that as yet the problem is satisfactorily solved. The discussions usually reveal either the tendency to give the apocalyptic influence its fullest vogue, with the distinctive ethic of Jesus being reduced to a mere *interimsethik*,[2] or else the apocalyptic is explained away in the interests of the ethic.[3]

The pressure of the apocalyptic facts has made it difficult to deny the influence of apocalyptic thought-forms in the outlook of Jesus ; on psychological grounds we expect that, if He were truly a human being as well as divine, He would be found thinking in terms of the divine purpose as His contemporaries did ; the originality of Jesus lay not in that He overrode the apocalyptic thought-forms and conceptions, but in the unique moral and religious content with which He enriched the religious experience lying at the heart of apocalyptic when viewed as a product of fervent faith in the divine righteousness and goodness. One instance of Jesus' uniqueness here lies in the way He applied the significance of suffering to His consciousness of being Messiah. The nearest His contemporaries could reach to this was the Danielic triumph of the saints in the Kingdom after their sufferings ; even if the connotation of the disputed phrase, " Son of Man " means no more than this,[4] Jesus at the very minimum could be regarded as sharing Himself in the sufferings of the saints as the prelude to the Messianic triumph ; but when, as Messiah, He said that suffering and death were for Him the necessary way to Messianic triumph, He filled

[1] *The Quest of the Historical Jesus*, 1910, Eng. Tr. chs. xv.–xx.
[2] Schweitzer is typical of this outlook.
[3] C. W. Emmet in the *Expositor*, vol. viii. 4.
[4] T. W. Manson, *op. cit.* pp. 210, 227 ff.

out both ethically and spiritually the Messianic idea by combining with it the idea of redemptive suffering as the way of the divine will.

We have to allow in the Gospels for what Dobschütz defines as illustrations of " alteration by intrusion of eschatology " (Matt. vii. 21, xiii. 24–30, 47–50 ; Mark xiii.), and " eschatological utterances of Jesus being transfigured into historical predictions " (as Matt. xxiii. 37–39, and Luke's forecast of the Fall of Jerusalem, xxi. 20) [1] Such modifications, intrusions, and alterations would find one source in the tendency of the disciples to construe what Jesus said in terms of literal apocalyptic, and another in the eschatological outlook of the primitive Church with its influence on the Gospel tradition.   But when allowance has been made for these extraneous influences, we are faced with unquestioned apocalyptic elements in the outlook of Jesus.   The Kingdom of God, the category of Messiah, the expectation of the coming crisis, are all integral to the eschatological " Weltanschauung " of Jesus.   It is not sufficient to regard these essential ideas as purely prophetic, for they received their development from the process of reinterpreting unfulfilled prophecy, which is the essence of the psychology of apocalyptic. Jesus inevitably characterized much of what He had to say by the use of eschatological thought-forms, otherwise He would never have been intelligible to His hearers.   Where Jesus transcended the categories He met with a lack of response, or even with latent opposition.

[1] *The Eschatology of the Gospels*, pp. 80–90, 91–94.

INDEX OF BIBLICAL, APOCRYPHAL, AND APOCALYPTIC REFERENCES

(a) THE OLD TESTAMENT

(c) THE PSEUDEPIGRAPHA.

(d) THE NEW TESTAMENT.

INDEX OF SUBJECTS AND AUTHORS

Death of Jesus (Messiah), foundation laid for later Church doctrine, 329.
— — — and the Last Supper, 295.
— — —, viewed in the light of Suffering Servant, 255 f., 306.
— — —, necessary prelude to advent of the Kingdom, 329.
— — —, influence on the New Community, 306 f.
— — —, redemptive significance of, 29, 257.
Deissmann, A., 25 n., 195, 281, 319 n., 338, 348.
Demons, 47, 65–67.
— and the Kingdom, 66.
— and the Primitive Church, 163, 201 f.
—, power of Jesus over the, 77, 83, 93, 94, 201.
— recognize the "numinous" quality of Jesus, 93 f., 201.
Demon-possession and the Kingdom, 94.
— —, its character, 93 f.
— —, psychology of, 200 ff.
— — and Spirit-possession, similar symptoms for both, 197–200.
— —, connecting links with experience of the Spirit, 202 f.
— —, dividing elements, 203 f.
— — and Spirit-possession, vital differences between, 204 ff.
— —, the Spirit's place in cure of, 201–2.
— —, numinous quality of, 83, 94, 197 ff., 199, 202.
Diaspora, 259.
Dibelius, M., 13 n., 85 n.
Didache, The, 41, 238, 242, 275, 318, 322.
— —, eucharistic prayers, 41, 304.
— —, witness to the Last Supper and its observance, 295, 298, 304 f.
Disciples, call of, 107 f.
—, The, a term for the Primitive Church, 212 f.

Disciples, The Twelve (see under "Twelve").
—, women, 123, 136.
— mainly Galileans, 107 f.
—, an inner circle, 106 f., 112.
—, militant Messianic elements among, 108.
—, Gentile and semi-Gentile elements, 87–90.
—, modification in their attitude to the Law, 109 f.
—, outlook steeped in apocalyptic, 55 f., 114, 363 f.
—, Jesus recognised as Messiah by, 110 f.
— do not recognize what sort of Messiah Jesus is, 116 f.
—, "minus" elements in their experience, 113 f.
— have the "sensuous" idea of the Kingdom, 115 f.
— at latent cross-purposes with Jesus, 12.
— fail to discern the significance of the suffering idea in Messiahship, 116 f.
— fail to recognize the real significance of Jesus, 120 f.
— desert Jesus at the Crucifixion, 118, 120.
—, creative power of Jesus in subconscious mind of, 123.
—, their inner conflict or "complex" solved by their Resurrection experience, 124 f., 135 ff.
—, eye-witnesses to the Resurrection, 127 ff.
—, their psychology, 129, 150.
— formed into a Messianic Community, 150, 154.
— understand the death of Jesus, 138, 252, 255 ff.
—, their influence in the growth of gospel tradition, 15 f., 16–21, 22, 90.
—, their power over demons, 201 f.
—, their possession by the Spirit, 146, 150, 201 f., Chapter VII. passim.
Dobschütz, E., 349, 364.
Dorner, I. A., 344 n.
Dougall, L. and Emmet, W. C., 51 n.
Dunkerley, R., 41 n.